# DICTIONARY

## OF ISLAMIC WORDS & EXPRESSIONS

DARUSSALAM

# DARUSSALAM

YOUR AUTHENTIC SOURCE OF KNOWLEDGE


## HEAD OFFICE

Prince Abdul Aziz
Bin Jalawi street.
P.O.Box: 22743,
Riyadh 11416
K.S.A.
Tel: 00966 -1- 4033962
00966 -1- 4043432
Fax: 00966 -1- 4021659
E-mail:
info@darussalam.com
darussalam@awalnet.net.sa
Website:
www.darussalamksa.com

## K.S.A. Darussalam Showrooms:

- **Riyadh**
  Olaya branch:
  Tel: 00966-1-4614483
  Fax: 4644945
  Malaz branch:
  Tel: 00966-1-4735220
  Fax: 4735221
  Suwaydi branch:
  Tel 00966-1-4286641
  Suwailam branch:
  Tel & Fax:
  00966-1-2860422
- **Jeddah**
  Tel: 00966-2-6879254
  Fax: 6336270
- **Madinah**
  Tel: 00966-04-8234446,
  8230038 Fax: 04-8151121
- **Al-Khobar**
  Tel: 00966-3-8692900
  Fax:00966-3-8691551
- **Khamis Mushayt**
  Tel & Fax: 00966-072207055
- **Yanbu Al-Bahr**
  Tel: 0500887341
  Fax: 8691551
- **Al-Buraida**
  Tel: 0503417156
  Fax: 00966-06-3696124

# DICTIONARY
## OF ISLAMIC WORDS & EXPRESSIONS

ROMANIZED
ARABIC-ENGLISH

Prof. Mahmoud Ismail Saleh

3rd EDITION
1432 A.H./ 2011

DARUSSALAM
YOUR AUTHENTIC SOURCE OF KNOWLEDGE
Riyadh • Jeddah • Al-Khobar • Sharjah
Lahore • London • Houston • New York

بسم الله الرحمن الرحيم

*In the Name of Allah,*

*the Most Gracious, the Most Merciful*



*King Fahd National Library Cataloging-in-Publication Data*

**Saleh, Mahmoud Ismail**

Dictionary of Islamic words & expressions./Mahmoud Ismail saleh ..Riyadh , 2011

365 p : 21cm

**ISBN:978-603-500-117-5**

1-Islam - Dictionaries 2- Islam - Dictionaries English I.Title

210.3 DC 1432/5055

**L.D. no. 1432 / 5055**

**ISBN: 978-603-500-117-5**

# CONTENTS

# Introduction

It is a well known fact that any reasonable understanding of Islam requires some knowledge of the language of the Qur'an, Arabic, due to the following reasons:

1. The two main sources of Islamic teachings, the Qur'an and the Sunnah, are in Arabic. There have been many attempts to render the meanings of these into other languages through translation. However, no translation can really convey the whole meaning of the original text, especially of religious or literary nature. For no two languages in the world have exact equivalents for their lexicons, even if they belong to the same family of languages. Naturally, the gap increases with the distance between the relevant languages in history and culture; the greater the difference (such as between Arabic and English) the wider the gap, and it is hard even for the cleverest of translators to close it. Besides, many Qur'anic verses and words have more than one meaning, which a

translator has to choose from; thus, the translation is by nature restricted and incomplete in such cases. Examples abound even in one "surah" (chapter) of the Qur'an, the first one, where we find words like, "al-Hamd", "ar-raHmaan, ar-raHiim" that are rich with meanings and implications which have only been partially conveyed in the various translations.

2. The bulk of references on various Islamic subjects have been written in Arabic. For even scholars living in non-Arabic speaking lands have most often made their valuable contributions in Arabic. There are tens of thousands of books on Islamic issues and topics, including Qur'anic exegesis, theology, jurisprudence, principles of Qur'anic exegesis, *tajweed* (rules of correct recitation of the Qur'an), principles of *hadeeth* (prophetic traditions) authentication, principles of Islamic jurisprudence etc. Very little of these references have been translated into other languages.

3. There are many key terms and expressions, such as *"raHmaan, Salaah, zakaah, 'umrah, 'ishaa', tajwiid, laa Hawla walaa quwwata illaa bi-llaah"* which are not easy to translate into other languages.

Since the majority of the followers of Islam are not native speakers of Arabic, and many of them may not have the chance to learn it properly, translation has been resorted to, however incomplete it may be. But even good translators always find it difficult to translate the special terms from Arabic. A cursory look at the translation of various Islamic works would reveal the discrepancies between the Arabic text and its translation, on one hand, and the different renderings of the same Arabic terms by different translators or even by the same translator at different times.

Attempts have been made by Muslim scholars to compile glossaries and dictionaries of Islamic terms to help both translators and readers of Arabic texts. But we find that despite the efforts made in these works, none of them is fully satisfactory for some reason or another, including the background of the author and his/her area of interest and the arrangement of the entries.

It is with the objective of filling some of the gaps or shortcomings in these attempts that this Dictionary of Islamic Words and Expressions has been prepared.

The present dictionary has the following characteristics:

4. It is written with the speaker of English in mind, though speakers of Arabic will find it useful as well. A knowledge of Arabic is not required. Therefore, the entries have been arranged according to their romanized pronunciation. This is accompanied by the word or expression in Arabic script, followed by an explanation or commentary.

5. The words and phrases have been selected on the basis of their special technical senses and/or their frequency in the Islamic religious writings. Often, general meanings and senses are ignored in the Dictionary.

6. An index of the words or expressions in Arabic script, according to the rules of Arabic alphabetical system, is given at the end of the dictionary for the benefit of Arab users of the Dictionary.

7. The comments or definitions are given in a brief and simple manner. Wherever appropriate, references to relevant verses of the Holy Qur'an are made. The reader will find more information there.

## Method of Using:

8. The Dictionary, as mentioned earlier, is arranged according to the romanized script and English alphabetical system. (A transliteration table is given below.) Therefore, Arabic words that have small and capital letters (e.g., "h, H or s, S") are grouped together, though these symbols represent different Arabic letters and sounds.

9. A special mention should be made of the case of the words that include ( ' and ' – hamzah and 'ayn) consonants, such as "'adab" and " 'iddah " These are arranged according to the vowels that follow them, since they are not letters of the English alphabet.

10. In the transliteration, a distinction is made between (-iyy) as in "nabiyy" ('prophet') and (-ii) as "fii" ('in'). This makes the word easier to spot when it occurs in combinations, such as "nabiyy-uun" ('prophets') or "nabiyy-uk" ('your prophet')...etc.

11. The taa' marbuuTah (feminine marker in nouns) is usually written (h), which is the pause form. But in cases where it is normally pronounced for liaison purposes, as in "zakaat al-fiTr" it is written (t).

12. The definite article (al-) is assimilated to the consonants that follow them, such as "al-Salaah" (which is transliterated "aS-Salaah" according to its pronunciation in Arabic). This makes the word easier to read by non-native speakers of Arabic.

13. Normally, nouns are given in their singular forms, but if the plural form is frequently used or it is heard more often than its singular form, then the word is given in the plural form too.

14. Arabic nouns that have irregular plural forms (and a few others) are normally followed by their plural form or singular forms (if the entry word is in the plural form) in parentheses (with pl. meaning plural and sg. meaning singular). Examples: "khuluq (pl. akhlaaq)" and "naSaaraa (sg. naSraaniyy)". This makes it easier for the reader to recognize them when they are encountered in both their singular and plural forms.
15. Verbs, which are normally given in their basic past tense forms, are accompanied by the present tense forms between parentheses, because the reader would most often see them in these two forms.
16. Wherever appropriate, cross-reference is made to other entries in the Dictionary, which is indicated by putting the Arabic word between double quotes.
17. Double quotes are used for Arabic words in quotations and for cross-reference purposes. A word in double quotes is found in its place in the Dictionary. The reader may refer to it if he so wishes. Single quotes, on the other hand, are used to give the English meaning of the Arabic words and expressions in the comment/ definition part.

I sincerely hope that this Dictionary will be of some help to the readers of Islamic works and the seekers of knowledge about Islam and its lofty teachings.

Mahmoud Ismail Saleh, Ph.,
Professor of Applied Linguistics
Riyadh, Rabi' I, 1432 A.H./ February, 2011.

# Transliteration Table

For practical reasons, the following system of transliteration of Arabic letters has been adopted.

| Arabic Letter | Name | Transliteration |
|---|---|---|
| ا | 'alif | aa (if a vowel) |
| ء | Hamza | ' |
| ب | Baa | b |
| ت | Taa | t |
| ث | Thaa | th |
| ج | Jiim | j |
| ح | Haa | H |
| خ | Khaa | kh |
| د | Daal | d |
| ذ | Dhal | dh |
| ر | Raa | r |
| ز | Zaay | z |

| | | |
|---|---|---|
| س | Siin | s |
| ش | Shin | sh |
| ص | Saad | S |
| ض | Daad | D |
| ط | Taa | T |
| ظ | Zaa | Z |
| ع | ‘ayn | ‘ |
| غ | Ghayn | gh |
| ف | Faa | f |
| ق | Qaaf | q |
| ك | Kaaf | k |
| ل | Laam | l |
| م | Miim | m |
| ن | Nuun | n |
| ه | Haa | h |
| و | Waaw | w or uu (for the vowel) |
| ي | Yaa | y or ii ( for the vowel ) |
| ـَ | fatHa | a ( short vowel as in ago ) |
| ـُ | Damma | u ( short vowel as in put ) |

# Aa

**'aabid (pl. 'ubbaad) عابد (عباد)**

Worshipper, devotee
A person devoted to worshipping Allah.

**'aabiq آبق**

Runaway slave

A slave who runs away from his master for no legitimate reason.

**'aad عاد**

People of 'Ad
A people of the Arabian Peninsula to whom Allah sent the Prophet "huud" (Hood). It is said that they lived in the Yemen area. (See, e.g., the Qur'an, 11: 50-60).

**'aadaab (sg. 'adab) (آداب - أدب)**

Manners, rules of conduct
Good morals and manners are mentioned by the Prophet (PBUH) as criteria of superiority of a believer over others. A Muslim is supposed to observe the laws of Islam in every aspect of his life, including the daily conduct of affairs (be that social, economic, political...).

**'aadam آدم**

Adam
The first human being created by Allah. His mate was Eve. (See the Qur'an, 2: 30-38 for references to his creation, sin, repentance...)

**عادل aadil'**

just, fair

**(al – 'aakhir) الآخر**

The Last

A Divine Attribute of Allah. The One after Whom no one and nothing exists, because He is the Only Everlasting Being.

**الآخرة (al-'aakhirah)**

The Hereafter

Belief in life in the Hereafter (in the physical and spiritual senses) is one of the six corner-stones of "'iimaan" (faith) in Islam.

**'aakil ar-riba آكل الربا**

Devourer of usury
Anyone who lends people money with interest / usury is guilty of devouring it, which means he purchases his food with money earned in that manner.

Aa

## 'aalam al-barzakh عالم البرزخ

Intermediate state

See **"barzakh"**.

## 'aal' imraan آل عمران

Family of Imran

In Chapter 3 of the Qur'an, this refers to the family of Maryam (Mary), the mother of 'iisaa (Jesus) (PBUH).

## 'aal al-bayt آل البيت

family of the Prophet (PBUH)

Literally, the members of the household. The term is used to refer to the wives of the Prophet (PBUH), his offspring and Muslim uncles and cousins, who were forbidden to accept "sadaqah".

## 'aal muHammad آل محمد

family of Muhammad

See 'aal al-bayt.

## 'aalaa (yuulii) (آلى يُولي)

To decide or make 'iilaa'

See 'iilaa' for the special sense of deciding to desert one's wife in bed.

## 'aalam al-ghayb عالم الغيب

The unseen world

Literally, 'the world of the unseen,' including the future and the Hereafter, which is known only to Allah.

## 'aalam ash-shahaadah عالم الشّهادة

The visible world

The present material world, as opposed to the Hereafter or the future, for example, which are not visible or known to us. The opposite of "'aalam al-ghayb " (the unseen world).

## 'aalim (pl. 'ulamaa') عالِم (علماء)

scholar

In Islamic texts, the term usually refers to a scholar specializing in religious fields of knowledge.

## 'aam al-bu'uuth عام البعوث

Year of Deputations

The ninth year of the Hijrah is called the Year of Deputations, because deputations came from all over Arabia to the Prophet (PBUH) at Medina to declare their conversion to Islam and to learn about it.

## 'aam al-fiil عام الفيل

Year of the Elephant

The year 570 AD, when the Abyssinian viceroy in Yemen decided to invade Mecca and destroy the Ka'bah with an army that had elephants, but they were all miraculously destroyed. (See the Qur'an, 105). It was in this year that the Prophet Muhammad (PBUH) was born.

## 'aamana (yu'min) (آمن يؤمن)

To believe

When the verb is used in an unqualified manner in the Qur'an it refers to believing in Allah.

## aamiin آمين

Amen

May God answer the prayer! The expression said at the end of the recitation of the Opening Chapter of the Qur'an, which ends with the prayer, "Guide us to the Straight Path, the Path of those who gained Your Favour, not those who deserved Your wrath, nor those who have gone astray." (the Qur'an, 1: 6-7). It is often heard after hearing all types of supplication.

## 'aaqib (al-) العاقِب

The Last

The reference is to Prophet Muhammad (PBUH) being the last Prophet and Messenger of Allah.

## 'aaqilah عاقِلة

Blood money payers

Relatives, such as ancestors or descendants who are responsible (with the murderer) for paying the blood money to the family of the murdered victim.

## 'aaqil 1 عاقل

Wise

## 'aaqil 2 عاقل

Sane

Legally, this means someone who is of sound mind; therefore, he is responsible for his actions.

## 'aariyyah عارِيّة

Loaned object

Something borrowed from someone. Naturally, it should be returned intact as much as possible.

## 'aamil (pl. 'ummaal) عامل (عمّال)

Governor

In classical use, the governor appointed by the caliph to rule a certain area in his name.

## 'aaS(in) (pl. 'uSaah) عاص (عصاة)

Sinner, rebellious

The term means 'sinner' if he is rebellious against Divine commands; otherwise, it means a persistently disobedient person.

Aa

## 'aashuuraa' عاشوراء

Tenth of Muharram

The tenth day of the first month of Islamic calendar. It is sunnah to fast this day, with one day before or after it. On this day also al-Husayn (grandson of the Prophet {PBUH}) was martyred at Karbalaa' in Iraq.

## 'aataa (yu'tii) az-zakaah آتى (يؤتي) الزكاة

give alms, pay the poor dues

Paying "az-zakaah" (poor dues) is one of the five pillars of Islam. It is paid on savings, commodities, live stock as well as agricultural produce.

## 'aayah 1 (pl. 'aayaat) آية 1 (آيات)

Sign

In the Qur'an we are told that all types of creation are signs from Allah for man to ponder upon, hence reach the conclusion of His greatness.

## 'aayah 2 (pl.'aayaat) آية2 (آيات)

Verse

A verse from the Qur'an (part of a "suurah" (chapter).

## 'aayah 3 (pl.'aayaat) آية3 (آيات)

Proof, evidence

## 'aayat al-kursiy آية الكرسي

Verse of the Throne

This refers to verse 256 of Chapter 2 of the Holy Qur'an. It consists of ten sentences about Allah, giving twenty of His Attributes and five of His Names. The Prophet (PBUH) strongly recommended reciting it after regular "Salaah" as well as before going to bed, as a source of protection for a Muslim from Satan and other evils.

## aazar آزر

Terah

Prophet Abraham's father. (See the Qur'an 6:74).

## abaaHa (yubiiH) أباح (يبيح)

To permit or make lawful

## أبد abad

Forever

This is usually contrasted with "'azal" (time immemorial). It refers to time that has no end.

## 'abd 1 (pl. 'abiid) عبد 1 (عبيد)

male slave, bondsman

A slave was a man captured in a just war or the son of a bondswoman.

## 'abd 2 (pl. 'ibaad) (عبد 2 عباد)

Servant, worshipper

In the context of man's relationship to Allah, the word is usually translated 'servant'.

## 'ablagha (yubligh) أبلغ (يبلّغ)

To convey

To convey a message.

## 'abraar (sg. barr(un) أبرار (بر)

righteous people

## 'abTala (yubTil) أبطل (يبطل)

To invalidate

To make something or some action invalid, such as laughing which makes "Salaah" (prayer) invalid.

## 'adaa' 1 أداء

performance

Performing a religious rite, such as formal prayers and pilgrimage to Mecca.

## 'adaa' 2 أداء

Payment

Paying back a loan or debt.

## 'adaalah عدالة

Justice, integrity

In the science of hadeeth, the term means the integrity (of the narrator).

## adab (pl. aadaab) (أدب آداب)

Rule of behaviour / etiquette

See " 'aadaab."

## addaa (yu'addii) أدّى (يؤدي)

to do

In the case of" Salaah" (formal prayer) this means 'to perform' while for "zakaah" it means paying it.

## addaba (yu'addib)(أدب يؤدب)

To teach manners

To teach or inculcate good manners. Prophet Muhammad is reported to have saidأدبني ربي فأحسن : تاديبي ("My Lord has inculcated in me the best of manners.")

## 'adhaab عذاب

Punishment, torture

## 'adhaab al-qabr عذاب القَبر

Torture of the grave

The torture sinners and unbelievers suffer in their graves, starting with the punishment upon giving the wrong answers to the questions put by "munkar wa nakiir."

## 'adhaan أذان

Call to prayer

The call to any of the five daily prayers.

## 'adhdhana (yu'adhdhin) أذن (يؤذن)

To call to prayer

To say the" 'adhaan" loudly for people to know it is time for "Salaah".

## 'adhkaar (sg. dhikr) أذكار (ذكر)

Verbal prayers, invocations

Any prayers in which one glorifies, praises or seeks Allah's forgiveness.

## 'ad'iyah ma'thuurah أدعية مأثورة

Traditional prayers

Often this refers to the prayers that are reported in the traditions of the Prophet Muhammad (PBUH).

## 'aDl عضل

Prevention from marriage

Preventing a woman from marriage by various means either by the guardian or a former husband.

## (al--'adl ) العدل

The Ever Just

A Divine Attribute of Allah. The One Who is never unfair in His decisions.

## 'adl عدل

Justice, fair dealing

The Qur'an teaches Muslims to be just in dealing even with enemies (5: 2 and 8) and that they be fair even if it is against relatives (the Qur'an, 6: 152.)

## 'adl (pl. 'uduul) عدل (عدول)

Man of integrity

As an adjective, the term is used in the science of hadeeth in describing narrators, and in describing witnesses too, to mean a person of integrity, Allah-fearing and honest.

## 'afaaDa(yufiiD)min arafaat
## أفاض (يفيض) من عرفات

To move from 'Arafah

To flow or move away from 'Arafah /'Arafaat at the end of the ninth day (after sunset) of the month of pilgrimage.

## 'afiif عفيف

Chaste, dignified

The term covers both chastity and self-respect, in the sense that a person does not commit illicit sexual intercourses and does not debase himself in any way.

## 'aflaHa (yfliHu)
## أفلح (يفلح)

To be successful, to prosper

This word expresses the meaning of success in its most comprehensive sense, both in this world and the Hereafter. (See the Qur'an, 23: 1 and 9: 9).

## 'afTara (yufTir)
## أفطر (يفطر)

To break one's fast

To have breakfast or to break one's fast by eating or drinking, for example.

## العفو (--afuww (al'

The Supreme Pardoner

A Dinvine Attribute of Allah. The One Who not only forgives but also erases all sins from the records of His servants. This Attribute is best manifested in the Qur'anic verse, where all "sinners" are called "not to despair of Allah's mercy". See verse 53 of Chapter 39 of the Qur'an.)

## 'afw 1 عفو

Forgiveness, pardon

## 'afw 2 عفو

Unneeded things

The word in this special sense is found one in the Qur'an, with reference to charity. (See the Qur'an, 2:219.)

## 'aHaadiith (sg. Hadiith)
## أحاديث (حديث)

prophetic traditions

For a definition see" Hadiith".

## 'aHbaas (sg. Hubs)
## حُبُس (حبيس)

Endowments

See "Hubus".

## 'ahd (pl. 'uhuud)
## عهد (عهود)

Covenant, solemn promise

## 'aHdatha 1 (yuHdith)
## أحدث 1 (يحدث)

to make "Hadath"

To do something that causes ritual impurity, such as passing wind or urinating.

## 'aHdatha 2 (yuHdith) (أحدث 2 (يحدث

to innovate

To do something in the religion that was not taught or observed by the Prophet (PBUH). (See "bid'ah".)

## 'aHkaam (sg. Hukm) (أحكام (حكم

rulings

There are degrees and types of rulings in Islam, according to which every act is judged: obligatory(farD/ waajib), strongly recommended (sunnah), plausible (mustaHabb), not recommended/ implausible (makruuh), forbidden (Haraam).

## 'ahl al'ahwaa' أهل الأهواء

libertines

People who follow their whims in their words and actions.

## 'ahl adh-dhimmah أهل الذمة

protégés of the Islamic State

Christians and Jews who live in peace in an Islamic State and pay the "jizyah" (protection money or head tax).

## 'ahl al-bayt أهل البيت

Household of Muhammad

Members of the household of the Prophet Muhammad (PBUH). See "'aal al-bayt."

## 'ahl al-fatrah أهل الفترة

interval the of People

People who lived in a period during which no particular messenger from Allah was sent to them.

## 'ahl al-kabaa'ir أهل الكبائر

Major sinners

People who commit major sins. (See "kabiirah (pl. kabaa'ir)".

## 'ahl al-kahf أهل الكهف

people of the cave

The young people referred to in the Qur'an 18:9-22. They miraculously spent about 300 years asleep in the cave where they had sought refuge earlier.

## 'ahl al-kitaab أهل الكتاب

People of the Book

This refers to Jews and/or Christians. It means the people with (originally) revealed scriptures.

Aa

## ahl al-qiblah أهل القبلة

Muslims (people of the qiblah)

The people who pray towards the Ka'bah.

## 'ahl ar-ra'y أهل الرأي

Men of opinion

Scholars ,like Abu Hanifah, who give weight to analogy and logical deductions as a source of Islamic law. They are contrasted with "'ahl an-naql" or conservatives who insist on textual evidence (Qur'an and hadeeth).

## 'aHmad أحمد

most praise worthy

This is one of the names of the Prophet Muhammad (PBUH)). His coming was foretold by Jesus (PBUH) by this name. (See the Qur'an, 61: 6).

## 'ahsana-llaahu 'azaa'akum أحسن الله عزاءكم

Sincere condolences!

One form of prayer said to a bereaved person, asking Allah to console him.

## 'aHSana (yuHSinu) أحصن (يحصن)

to be chaste

To protect oneself from illicit sexual relations. (See "muHSan / muHSanah.("

## 'a'immat al-Hadiith أئمة الحديث

leading scholars of hadeeth

Scholars who are upright, have strong memory and are well versed in matters of the text and science of prophetic traditions. (See Hadiith.)

## 'ajal (pl. 'aajaal) أجل (آجال)

Appointed time

This term applies to any appointed time. It is sometimes used to refer to the end of one's life (death).

## 'ajnabiyy (pl. 'ajaanib) أجنبي (أجانب)

stranger

The term refers to someone who is not "maHram" to a female person. Therefore, he should not be alone with her.

## 'ajr (pl. 'ujuur) أجر (أجور)

Wage, reward

In its general sense the word means wage or payment made for service rendered. But in the spiritual sense it refers to reward from Allah.

## 'ajr (al--) wath-thawaab
## الأجر و الثواب

Reward and compensation

Rewards and compensations given by Allah to a Muslim for any good deed, including refraining from a sinful act.

## 'akh min ar-raDaa'(ah)
## أخ من الرضاع / الرضاعة

foster-brother

We may also hear "'akh bir-raDaa'". A male person who shared the suckling of milk with another person of a different mother and father.

## 'akhlaaq (sg. khuluq)
## أخلاق (خلق)

morals, moral values

Good conduct is an essential part of the religion. The Prophet Muhammad (PBUH) is reported to have said, "I have been sent only to perfect good morals and conduct." Moral values in Islam are objectively determined by the Qur'an and the teachings of the Prophet (PBUH).

## 'akhlafa (yukhlif)
## أخلف (يخلف)

to forswear, break a promise

Breaking a promise is considered by the Prophet (PBUH) one of the four signs of a "munaafiq" (hypocrite).

## أكل الربا akl ar-ribaa'

devouring usury

See "'aakil ar-ribaa".

## 'alaamaat an-nubuwwah
## علامات النبوة

signs of prophethood

Signs that prove that someone is a true Prophet of God.

## 'alaamaat as-saa'ah
## علامات الساعة

signs of the Hour

Signs of the approach of the Day of Judgment, one of the greatest being the sun's rising from the West.

## 'alayhi uS-Salaau was-salaam
## عليه الصلاة و السلم

Peace and blessings be upon him

An expression usually said upon the mention of the Prophet Muhammad (PBUH) or his name, out of reverence. Sometimes, it is shortened to "'alayhi as-salaam" (Peace be upon him – PBUH).

## 'alayhis-salaam
## عليه السلام

Peace be upon him

An expression a Muslim says upon the mention of any Prophet of Allah or hearing reference to him. It is often abbreviated as (PBUH).

## 'aliim (al--) العليم

The Omniscient

A Divine Attribute of Allah. The One Who knows everything, past, present or future, open or secret.

## 'aliyy (al--) العلي

The Ever-Exalted

A Divine Attribute of Allah. The One Who is Exalted above everyone and everything.

## Allaah الله

Allah/ God

In Arabic there are two words for 'god' in English: "ilaah" which means any deity and "allaah" which means the One and Only God. Therefore, some Muslim writers insist on using the Allah when reference is made to God (in the capital G sense). Naturally, this does not mean that a Muslim worships a special God Who is different from the God of all peoples and creatures. On the contrary, the third verse of Chapter I of the Qur'an clearly says: "Lord and Cherisher of the worlds/ universes". In another verse, Muslims are instructed to tell the People of the Book (Christians and Jews): "We believe in that which has been revealed to us and revealed to you; our God and your God is One, and unto Him we surrender." (the Qur'an 29:46). In fact, all speakers of Arabic, including Jews and Christians, use the word Allah to refer to God.

The Prophet of Islam, Muhammad (PBUH) has said that Allah (God) has ninety-nine names (or attributes), called "al-asmaa' al-Husnaa ('the Most Beautiful Names'). For examples of these names, see the Qur'an, 2: 256 ("Verse of the Throne"; 6: 101-103; 59: 22-24. However, the most concise description of the concept of Allah (God) can be seen in the following: "Like Him there nothing; He is the All-hearing, the All-seeing" (the Qur'an, 42:11) and the Chapter of Purity of Faith (112). This translates as: "Say [O Muhammad]: 'Allah (God) is One. God is the Self-Sufficient Master Whom all creation needs. He did not give birth to any, nor was He born. And there is none equal or comparable unto Him."

It is clear that the Islamic conception of Allah (God) emphasizes absolute uniqueness and perfection.

Aa

## 'allaahu 'akbar الله أكبر

Allah is Greater / the Greatest

This expression means both greater in the comparative form and greatest, in the superlative form. It is said to remind one that no one is greater than Allah; therefore, we should not fear any but Him.

## 'allaahumma اللهم

O Allah / Allah! (God)

Usually, this expression is used in supplications, such as " allaahumma - ghfirlii " ( O Allah, forgive me!).

## 'amaan (al--) الأمان

security

A pledge given to someone (especially from the enemy camp) for his/ her safety and security.

## 'amal (pl. 'a'maal) عمل (أعمال)

Deed

Anything one does. It includes even thoughts and words said by a person. (See below.)

## 'amal al-jawaariH (pl. 'a'maal al-jawaariH) عمل (أعمال) الجوارح

physical deed

The reference is to the actions one takes. Literally, the expression means the deed(s) of the parts of the body.

## 'amal al-lisaan (pl. 'a'maal al-lisaan) عمل (أعمال) اللسان

Words and utterances

The things one says. Literally, it means deed(s) of the tongue.

## 'amal al-qalb (pl. a'maal al-quluub) عمل القلب (أعمال القلوب)

mental act

Thinking, including intentions, is considered a type of deed for which one may be rewarded or punished. Literally, the term means 'deed of the heart'.

## 'amaanah 1 أمانة

Honesty, trustworthiness

An important quality of a good believer who should be honest and trustworthy.

## 'amaanah 2 (pl.'amaanaat) أمانة 2 (أمانات)

Trust, responsibility

Something one is entrusted with to keep and preserve, which could be material or moral / religious. (See, for example, the Qur'an, Chapter 2: 283; Chapter 4: 58; Chapter 33: 72).

## 'amah (pl. imaa')

### أمة (إماء)

slave girl, bondswoman

## 'amat allaah أمة الله

female person, servant of Allah

Literally, it means the slave girl or bondswoman of Allah. It is the feminine counterpart of "'abdullah" (the slave/ servant of Allah).

## 'amiir al-mu'miniin

### أمير المؤمنين

prince / leader of the faithful

This was the term coined by Caliph Umar ibn al-Khattab, the second Righteous Caliph, to refer to himself and other caliphs (successors to the Prophet Muhammad (PBUH)).

## 'amma (ya'umm) (أم يؤم)

To lead

To lead worshippers in a congregational prayer.

## 'amr (pl. 'awaamir) (أمرأوامر)

Order, command, decree

This noun is derived from the verb "amara" which means to command or order.

## 'amr bil-ma'ruuf

### أمر بالمعروف

enjoining what is right

This means both teaching and enjoining what is good and right. The complementary act to this is "nahy'anal-munkar" (forbidding/ stopping what is evil and wrong).

## 'amwaal (sg. maal)

### أموال (مال)

wealth, possessions, property

Literally, "maal" means money. But it is often used to mean anything that a person possesses.

## 'anbiyaa' (nabiyy)

### أنبياء (نبي)

prophets

See "nabiyy."

## 'anSaar (sg. 'anSaariyy)

### أنصار (أنصاري)

supporters

See" anSaariyy".

## (anSaar' .pl) anSaariyy'

### أنصاري (أنصار)

Supporter

One of the residents of Medina who welcomed the Prophet Muhammad) PBUH (and his immigrant companions .The term is contrasted with" muhaajir" ('immigrant' to Medina).

## 'aqaa'id (sg. 'aqiidah)

### عقائد (عقيدة)

Articles of faith, theology

The general meaning of the word is 'beliefs' or 'articles of faith', but

Aa

it is also used short for "'ilm al-'aqaa'id" (the study of beliefs or articles of faith), hence theology.

**'aqaama (yuqiim) aS-Salaah 1 أقام (يقيم) الصلاة 1**

To perform the "salaah", announce readiness for it

To perform the regular formal prayer.

**'aqaama (yuqiim) aS-Salaah 2 أقام (يقيم) الصلاة 2**

It is also used to mean saying the "'iqaamah", announcing the readiness for worship.

**'aqd al-qiraan عقد القران**

joining in wedlock, marriage

Performing a marriage ceremony. It could also mean marriage.

**'aqd an-nikaaH عقد النكاح**

joining in wedlock, marriage

Performing a marriage ceremony. It could also mean marriage.

**'aqiidah (pl. 'aqaa'id) عقيدة**

faith, belief, creed

Something that one has a firm belief in; it is often used to refer to the religion.

**'aqiiqah عقيقة**

'aqeeqah

Celebrating the birth of a new baby, usually by slaughtering a sheep and distributing its meat or making a meal with it for a group of people.

**'aql 1 عقل 1**

Sanity

In legal terms, this refers to the ability to reason and think.

**'aql 2 (pl. 'uquul) عقل 2 (عقول)**

Mind, reason

The capacity that enables one to think.

**'aqsama (yuqsim) أقسم (يقسم)**

To take an oath, swear by Allah

Even when the word "billaah" is not said, this verb usually means swearing to Allah, meaning 'Allah is my witness to something'. In Islam one should not swear by anyone or anything other than Allah.

**'aqTa'a (yuqTi') أقطع (يُقطع)**

To grant land

In Islam history this means to grant a piece of land, usually by a Muslim ruler.

## araak أراك

Araak tree

A tree from which misiwaak, a fragrant stick used by many Muslims as a natural tooth brush since the days of Prophet Muhammad (PBUH).

## 'arafah / 'arafaat عرفة / عرفات

plain of 'Arafah

The plain near Makkah where pilgrims spend the ninth day of the month of pilgrimage. Stay in 'Arafah is one of the major rites, without which pilgrimage is considered null.

## 'araja (ya'ruj)(عرج يعرج)

To ascend

To go up to heaven.

(See the Qur'an, 70: 3.) From this verb we have the word "al-mi'raaj" ("The Ascension".)

## 'arHaam (sg. raHim)

## أرحام (رحم)

Wombs, blood relatives

In religious texts, the second meaning is probably more frequently intended.

## 'arkaan al-iimaan

## أركان الايمان

Pillars of faith

There are six pillars or corner-stones of faith in Islam: belief in God, the angels, the revealed scriptures, God's messengers, the Hereafter (including physical resurrection and life after death) and predestination. Five of these are mentioned in the Qur'an (2:177).

## 'arkaan al-islaam

## أركان الإسلام

pillars of Islam

There are five pillars or corner-stones of Islam, mentioned by the Prophet Muhammad (PBUH): testifying that there is no deity except Allah and that Muhammad is His messenger, performing the five daily prayers, paying the poor dues, fasting Ramadan and pilgrimage to Makkah (for those who can afford it).

## 'arraaf

## عرّاف

Soothsayer

A person who claims to know the unseen and the future. It is forbidden for a Muslim to resort to such people for consultation, because only God the Almighty knows these things.

## 'arsh (pl. 'uruush)

## عرش (عروش)

Throne

The word is found in the Qur'an (27: 23 and 38).

### 'aSaa (ya'Sii) (عصى يعصي)

To disobey, to sin

The noun commonly heard is "ma'Siyah" ('sin').

### عصبة aSabah'

paternal male relatives, agnates

Some writers have defined this term as "male relatives on the father's side who take the remaining estate, if any, after the heirs with fixed shares have received their shares."

### عصبية aSabiyyah'

Partisanship

Unfair partisanship and prejudice are forbidden by Islam, because a Muslim should be fair and just even to enemies.

### 'asbaaT (sg. sibT) أسباط (سبط)

Grandsons, Israelite tribes

In the Qur'an, the word is used in both senses: children of Prophet Jacob (Qur'an 2:136) Israelite tribes (7: 160). In Islamic writings, we also have the expression "sibT rasuuli-llaah" referring to a grandson of the Prophet (PBUH): al-Hasan or al-Husain.

### 'aSHaab al-aykah أصحاب الأيكة

People of the Thicket

The reference is to the people of Prophet Shu'ayb. (See, e.g., the Qur'an, 15:78; 26:176-190.)

### أصحاب الفيل aSHaab al-fiil'

People of the elephant

The army led by the Abyssinian king Abrahah to destroy the Ka'abah in 570 G.E. (See reference in the Qur'an, Chapter 105.)

### 'aSHaab al-jannah أصحاب الجنة

People of Paradise

Reference is usually to the believers. (See the Qur'an, 59:20.)

### 'aSHaab al-kahf أصحاب الكهف

people of the cave

See "'ahl al-kahf."

### 'aSHaab an-naar أصحاب النار

people of Hell

Reference is usually to disbelievers. (See the Qur'an, 59:20.)

### 'aSHaab rasuuli-llaah أصحاب رسول الله

companions of Allah's Messenger

Muslims who met the Prophet Muhammad (PBUH) are technically known as his companions. They are the best generation of Islam, and a good Muslim should show them due respect and reverence.

## 'aSHaab ash-shimaal

## أصحاب الشمال

the disbelievers

The term is probably based on the fact that disbelievers will receive their records of deeds in their left hands on the Day of Judgment. (See the Qur'an, 56: 41-56).

## 'aSHaab aS-Suffah

## أصحاب الصّفّة

people of the suffah

See" ahl aS-Suffah."

## aSHaab as-sunan

## أصحاب السنن

Compilers of the sunnah

Compilers of the Prophetic traditions (Hadiiths) on Islamic jurisprudence.

## 'asharah (al--) al-mubashsharuun

## العشرة المبَشّرون

the Ten Promised Paradise

The ten companions of Prophet Muhammad (PBUH) who were given the tidings of being among the dwellers of Paradise in the Hereafter.

## 'aSHaab al-yamiin

## أصحاب اليمين

The believers

The term is probably based on the fact that believers will receive their records of deeds in their right hands on the Day of Judgment. (See the Qur'an, 56: 27-38.)

## 'ashhur (al--) al-Hurum

## الأشهر الحرم

The sacred months

The four months of "Rajab, Dhul Qi'dah, Dhul-Hijjah" and "MuHarram."

## 'ashhur al-Hajj أشهر الحج

Months of pilgrimage

The months of" Shawwaal, Dhul-Qi'dah" and the first ten days of "Dhul-Hijjah" are known as the months of pilgrimage.

## 'ashraka (yushrik)

## أشرك يشرك

To ascribe partners

To worship others besides Allah (God), or ascribe Divine attributes to them. It also includes the claim that we need intermediaries between us and God.

## 'asiib (عسيب عُسُب)

Palm branch

A palm branch stripped of its leaves. The Arabs sometimes used to write on it.

## 'askara (yuskir)

## أسكر (يسكر)

To intoxicate

Aa

To negatively affect one's capacity of discrimination and thinking.

## 'asmaa' allaah al-Husnaa أسماء الله الحسنى

Most Beautiful Names of Allah

These are the ninety-nine names or Divine Attributes of Allah, such as "ar-raHmaan, al-ghafuur" (The Gracious, the Most Forgiving). Often we find the word attribute used instead of name in this context.

## 'aSl ('uSuul) 1(أصل (أصول

principle

Principles or foundations upon which other issues ("furuu'") are based.

## 'aSl ('uSuul) 2 (أصل (أصول

lineage

For a person, his father and grand fathers.

## 'asmaa' ar-rijaal أسماء الرجال

Biographical dictionary

A special type of Islamic writing where the names of people of special interest (e.g., "Hadiith" narrators) are listed along with biographical information on each.

## 'aSr (al--) العصر

later afternoon

The time when the shadow of an object is twice its length.

## 'astaghfiru-llaah أستغفر الله

I ask Allah for forgiveness

This is the shortest form of "istighfaar", which is a highly recommended act of worship and remembrance of Allah. (For some of the blessings of istighfaar, see the Qur'an, 71:10-12.)

## 'athar (al--) الأثر

Traditions

Sometimes, this word is used to refer to unverified traditions of the Prophet (PBUH) or sayings of his companions.

## 'a'uudhu bi-llaah أعوذ بالله

I seek refuge with Allah

This is short for the expression, "a'uudhu bi-llaahi min-shshayTaan-irrajiim" ('I seek refuge in Allah from Satan the accursed one'), which a Muslim is required to say before reciting the Qur'an. (See the Qur'an, 16:89) or whenever we have evil thoughts (See the Qur'an, 8:200). We may hear this expression in exclamations to express denial of wrong doing.

## awaamir wa nawaahii أوامر ونواهي

Injunctions and prohibitions

Teachings of the religion regarding what to do (is required) or not to do (isforbidden).

## 'awHaa (yuuHii)
## أوحى (يوحي)

To reveal, inspire

Usually, this refers to Allah when He sends a message to a messenger of His. Very often, this is done through Archangel Gabriel. In other cases, the word may mean to prompt someone, for example, to do something.

## awliyaa' (sg. waliyy)
## أولياء (ولي)

Saints, guardians, protégés…

See the different meanings of "waliyy."

## 'awraat (sg. 'awrah)
## عورات (عورة)

In the plural the word is sometimes used to mean deficiencies or weaknesses hidden by a person from others.

## 'awrah (pl. 'awraat)
## عورة (عورات)

private part

The term normally means the part of the body that should not be seen by others; hence have to be covered in public. For a male, the minimum is the area between the navel and the knees. For an adult female, the whole body with the exception of the face and hands should be covered in the presence of strangers.

## awsuq (sg. wisq)(أوسُق (وِسق

wisqs

A unit of dry measure. See wisq.

## aws (al--) الأوس

The Aws tribe

One of the two major tribes that lived in Medina at the time of the Prophet Muhammad (PBUH). The other being "al-khazraj."

## (yuuSii) awSaa
## أوصى (يوصي)

To bequeath

According to Islamic law ,shares of legal heirs) e.g ,.children, parents ,spouse (…are not subject to the will ,but are specified by the Qur'an .(11-12 :4) One of the purposes of the will is the allocation of not more than one third of the legacy for others ,if one so desires ,such as for charity or endowments.

## (awtara) yuutir(أوتر (يوتر

To pray witr

To pray an odd number of "rak'ahs", usually one. It is

sunnah for a Muslim to make his last prayer in the night a witr.

**awwaab أوّاب**

Oft-returning , oft-repenting

A person who always repents and seeks Allah's forgiveness.

**awwal (al--) الأول**

The First

A Divine Attribute of Allah. The One before Whom no one and nothing ever existed.

**awwala (yu'awwilu) أول (يؤول)**

to interpret.

**a'yaan (sg. 'ayn) أعيان**

objects

Concrete objects of any nature.

**aymaan (sg. yamiin) أيمان (يمين)**

Oaths

**'ayn al-yaqiin عين اليقين**

absolute certainty

The level of certainty that one reaches when he sees signs that confirm his belief in the truth of something.

**ayyaam al-biiD أيام البيض**

Days of luminous nights

The middle days of the lunar month, which are 'luminous' due to the full moon. Specifically, they refer to the 13th -15th, which a Muslim is recommended to fast.

**ayyaam an-naHr أيام النحر**

Sacrifice days

The days on which a Muslim (pilgrim or not) may slaughter his sacrifice, starting with the Feast of Sacrifice ('iid al aDHaa) and the next 3 days.

**ayyaam at-tashriiq أيام التشريق**

Tashreeq days

One of the meanings of "tashreeq" is 'meat drying', since pilgrims probably used to slaughter their sacrifices and dry the extra meat for use later. These are the 11th -13th days of Dhul-Hijjah (month of pilgrimage).

**ayyim (pl. ayaamaa) أيم (أيامى)**

Single (male or female)

Another common meaning for this word is 'widow / widower'. (See the Qur'an, 24: 32 for the first meaning).

**ayyuub أيوب**

Job

One of the prophets mentioned in the Qur'an. He is usually cited for his exemplary patience and endurance of difficulties. (See the Qur'an, 38: 41-44).

## azal أزل

Time immemorial

This is usually contrasted with "'abad" (forever or eternal). It refers to time that has no beginning.

## 'aziimah (pl. 'azaa'im) عزيمة (عزائم)

Spell, incantation

Linguistically, the word means will or determination. As a term it means a spell or incantation.

## 'aZiim (al--) العظيم

The Ever-Magnificent

A Divine Attribute of Allah. The One Who is Great and ever glorified by others.

## 'aziiz (al--) العزيز

The Ever-Mighty

A Divine Attribute of Allah. The One Who is Most Powerful and High.

## azlaam (sg. zalam) أزلام (زلم)

lot arrows

Arrow like pieces of wood that were used by Arabs for casting lots, especially in gambling. (See the Qur'an 5:3.)

## 'azl 1 عزل

Stripping from authority

Removing a person from a position of authority, such as governorship or position of a judge.

## 'azl 2 عزل

Coitus interruptus

The deliberate withdrawal of the penis from the vagina before ejaculation. In the hadeeth we find reference to this practice by early Muslims, who were not forbidden from doing it.

## azlaam أزلام

idols

Objects worshipped by pagans.

## 'aZZama allaahu ajrakum عظم الله أجركم

May Allah multiply your reward!

An expression normally said to a relation of a deceased person to show condolences.

# Bb

## baaghii (pl. bughaat)

### (باغي) بغاة

Rebel
Someone who revolts against a legitimate ruler.

## baa'in

### بائن

بائن baa'in
Finally divorced
A woman who is divorced for the third and final time. She may not go back to her former husband except after the fulfillment of certain conditions. See "Talaaq baa'in."

## Baa'ith (al--)

### الباعث

The Resurrector
A Divine Attribute meaning the One Who resurrects the dead. (See the Qur'an 2: 56.) The word also means the One Who sends messengers and things. (See the Qur'an, 16: 36.)

## Baaqii (al--)

### الباقي

The Everlasting
A Divine Attribute meaning the One Who survives everybody and everything.

## Baari' (al--)

### البارىء

The Initiator of Creation
A Divine Attribute meaning the One Who has initiates the creation of everyone and everything. The term should be compared to the Attribute "al-khaaliq" which means 'the Creator' and "al-MuSawwir" ('the Shaper' of created beings). See, for example, the Qur'an, 59: 24).

## BaaSiT (al--)

### الباسط

The Expander or Generous Provider
A Divine Attribute meaning the One Who expands everything or Who is very generous in His favours and provisioning.(For the first meaning, see the Qur'an, 30: 48; the second meaning is found in verses like 26 in Chapter 13.)

## Ba'atha1 (yab'athu)

### (بعث) يبعث1

to resurrect ,bring back to life
See" al-ba'th."

## Ba'atha2 (yab'athu)

### (بعث) يبعث 2

To send
To send a message or messenger.

## baaTil 1 باطل

invalid

As an adjective the word means invalid ,as opposed to" SaHiiH" (valid, correct).

## baaTil 2

## باطل 2

falsehood

In this sense the term is contrasted
with "Haqq" (truth) (See the Qur'an, 8:8).

## baaTin (al--)

## الباطن

The Hidden

A Divine Attribute meaning the One Who cannot be seen by anyone.

## Badii' (al--)

## البديع

The Originator

A Divine Attribute meaning the Originator of all creations. (See, the Qur'an 2: 117 and 6: 101.)

## badr بَدر

Badr

A location south of Mecca where the first major battle in Islamic history took place (See ghazwat badr .)

## balaagh بلاغ

Declaration

It could also mean conveying a message.

## balagha (yablugh)

## بلغ (يبلغ)

to become of age.

## ballagha (yuballigh) ar-risaalah

## بلغ (يبلغ) الرسالة

To convey the message

## baghiyy (pl. baghaayaa)

## بغي (بغايا)

prostitute

Naturally, Islam forbids any sexual relations outside marriage. Clear punishments have been stated in Islamic law for prostitution.

## baghy بغي

Transgression, infringement

Doing injustice to others or simply transgressing.

## baqii' (al--) البقيع

Medina Cemetery

The cemetery of Medina, to the East of the Prophet's mosque. It is sometimes referred to as "jannat al-baqii'" or "baqii' al-gharqad". The cemetery has been in use since the days of the Prophet Muhammad (PBUH), and in it are buried his foster mother, some of his wives, children and companions.

Bb

## baraa' (al--) البراء

Disavowal

The term is found in the context of a Muslim's relationship with disbelievers. It is contrasted with "al-walaa'" (loyalty) which a Muslim should show to other Muslims.

## baraa'ah براءة

Innocence, freedom from

In the Qur'an this word is found at the beginning of Chapter 9 to mean freedom from obligation.

## barakah بركة

Blessing

Often, the term is used to refer to plentifulness.

## barru(n) (pl. 'abraar) بر (أبرار)

Righteous

## barzakh برزخ

Barrier, interval between lives

In Islamic theology, the term refers to the interval between death and resurrection, or between life in this world and life in the Hereafter.

## bashiir بشير

Bringer of glad tidings

One of the tasks of the Prophet was to bring glad tidings to the believers; hence he is described as "bashiir" in the Qur'an. This term is contrasted with "nadhiir" (warner).

## baSiir (al--) البصير

The All-Seeing

A Divine Attribute of Allah. The One Whose Sight encompasses everything.

## baSiirah (pl. baSaa'ir) بصيرة (بصائر)

Insight

The capacity to gain an accurate and good intuitive understanding of affairs.

## ba'th (al--) البعث

The Resurrection

Resurrecting the dead. Often we read the term "yawm al-ba'th" to refer to the Day of Resurrection (Judgment).

## batuul (al--) البتول

The pious and chaste one

This term is often used to refer to Maryam / Mary (mother of the Prophet Jesus).

## bayaan at-tabdiil بيان التبديل

statement of abrogation

Indicating that a certain ruling has

been abrogated by the legislator (e.g., Prophet Muhammad (PBUH)).

## bay' al-gharar (al-jahaalah) بيع الغرر (الجهالة)

Deceitful sale

The sale of something that looks good, but actually bad.

## bay' as-salam بيع السلم

Postponed delivery sale

A sale agreement in which the seller promises to deliver the goods at a later date.

## bay' mu'ajjal بيع مؤجل

Deferred sale

A transaction in which the delivery of the purchased goods is made at a later date.

## bay'ah بيعة

oath of allegiance, pledge

Giving an oath of allegiance to someone. The verb is baaya'a (yubaayi')

## bay'at ar-riDwaan بيعة الرضوان

Pledge of (Divine) Pleasure

This refers to the pledge Muslims gave to the Prophet Muhammad (PBUH) at Hudaybiyah, near Makkah to fight the disbelieving Makkans if asked to. We find reference to this in the Qur'an (48: 10 and 18).

## bay'at al-'aqabah al-'uulaa بيعة العقبة الأولى

First 'Aqabah Pledge

The pledge made by twelve people from Yathrib (Medina) to the Prophet Muhammad (PBUH) at a place near Makkah to accept the teachings of Islam. The Prophet (PBUH) sent with them the first Muslim missionary, Mus'ab ibn 'umayr.

## bay'at al-'aqabah ath-thaaniyah بيعة العقبة الثانية

Second 'Aqabah Pledge

The pledge made by seventy-three Yathribite people, including two women, to the Prophet Muhammad (PBUH), at a place near Makkah, to defend him as they would their own selves and families if he migrated to their town, Yathrib (Medina).

## baynuunah kubraa بينونة كبرى

Major / absolute finality

The divorce after which a woman may not go back to her former

husband, unless she marries another man, consummates her marriage, then gets separated by divorce or death of the second husband. A new marriage contract is required.

## Baynuunah Sughraa

### بينونة صغرى

Minor / relative finality

The case in which a divorced woman may not return to her former husband except with a new marriage contract.

## bayt (al--) al-'atiiq

### البيت العتيق

The Old House

The word "al-bayt" is often used to mean the House; i.e., the House of Allah (al-Ka'bah) in Makkah. Sometimes, it is modified by the word 'atiiq which means 'the ancient' or al-Haraam 'the sacred'.

## bayt (al--) al-Haraam

### البيت الحرام

The Sacred House

The Sacred Ka'bah. The mosque around it is known as "al-masjid al-Haraam" (the Sacred Mosque).

## bayt (al--) al-ma'muur

### البيت المعمور

Oft-frequented House

According to Islamic tradition, this is a house in the seventh Heaven around which thousands of angels circumambulate. It is believed to be parallel/ perpendicular to the Ka'bah on Earth.

## bayt (pl. buyuut) allaah بيت (بيوت) الله

House of Allah/ God

Any mosque or house of worship.

## bayt al-maal بيت المال

Public treasury

This is short for "bayt maal al-muslimiin", which means the Muslim public treasury from which the Muslim government spends.

## bayt al-maqdis بيت المقدس

Jerusalem

Before instructions were given to the Prophet (PBUH) to face the Ka'bah in his prayers, he used to face Jerusalem; hence, it is called the first of the two "qiblahs". The mosque in Jerusalem, known as "al-masjid al-aqSaa" (the furthest mosque), is one of the three mosques in the world that are worthy for a Muslim to make a special journey to. Today, people use the word 'al-Quds' for the city.

## bayt an-nubuwwah بيت النبوة

Household of the Prophet

## bayt aT-Taa'ah بيت الطاعة

Husband's residence

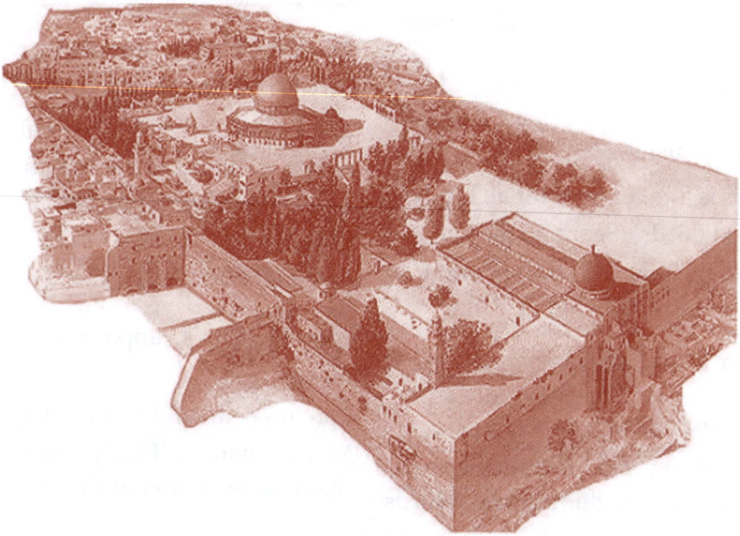

In modern legal terms, the residence where the court decides a wife should stay with her husband.

Bb

## bayyinah (pl. bayyinaat) بينة (بينات)

clear evidence

## bid'ah (pl. bida') بدعة (بِدَع)

Innovation ,heresy

A worship type act not sanctioned by the religion.

## bint labuun بنت لبون

Three year old she-camel

Terms like this one and" bint makhaaD" are found in the discussion of "zakaat" on camels.

## bint makhaaD بنت مخاض

she-camel in 2nd year

A term usually found in the context of discussion of "zakaat" on camels.

## birr (al--) البر

Righteousness

This is a cover term for all kinds of good deeds. (See, e.g., the Qur'an, 2:177.) It is sometimes used to mean taqwaa ('God fearing).

## birr al-waalidayn بر الوالدين

Dutifulness to parents

Observing one's duty towards his parents, including kind words and behaviour and obedience to them, except in violation of Divine commandments. (See the Qur'an, 17:23 and 31:14-15.)

## bishaarah بشارة

Good tidings

In the Qur'an the word "bashiir" is found, referring to Prophet Muhammad (PBUH), to mean a bringer of glad tidings to the believers.

## bismillaah بسم الله

In the Name of Allah

It is "sunnah" to begin any activity by saying this expression.

## bismi-llaahi-rraHmaani-rraHim بسم الله الرحمن الرحيم

In the Name of Allah, the Beneficent, the Merciful

This is the full form of "basmalah", which is found at the beginning of all Qur'anic "suuraas" except Chapter 9.

## bi'that an-nabiyy بعثة النبي

The Prophet's appointment as messenger

The time at which the Prophet Muhammad (PBUH) received the first revelation of the Qur'an,

brought to him by Archangel Gabriel while he was in retreat at the Cave of Hiraa' in Makkah (around the year 609 G). He was forty years old.

## buhtaan

## بهتان

Slander, wrongful accusation

The word is used to refer to a serious slander or false accusation.

## buluugh بلوغ

Puberty

Reaching the age of physical maturation. For males, the growth of pubic hair and ejaculation (of semen). For girls, this means starting menstruating. (The word originally means 'reaching').

## buraaq (al--) البراق

Buraq

A winged horse like animal which carried Prophet Muhammad (PBUH) during the israa' journey.

## burhaan برهان

Decisive proof

Providing evidence to prove a certain point or demonstrate its validity.

## buTlaan بطلان

Invalidation, invalidity

An example is the invalidation of the prayer if one talks or laughs while praying.

# Dd

## daabbatu-l-arD دابة الأرض

The Reptile of Earth

The name of a monster that will appear in the final days of this world. Its rise is one of the clear signs of the approach of Doomsday.

دابة

## daa'iyah (pl. du'aah) داعية (دعاة)

preacher of Islam

Someone who preaches or calls to Islam, especially among non-Muslims. But it could also mean a person who preaches religion to Muslims as well.

## Daallu(n) (pl. Daalluun) ضال (ضالون)

astray, in error

Someone is termed "Daall" if he lost his way or went astray. In Chapter 1 of the Qur'an, "al-Daalliin" has been interpreted by some to refer to Christians.

## Daamin 1 ضامن

guarantor, liable person

A person who guarantees a borrower, for example, or someone who is liable for indemnities.

## Daamin 2 ضامن

Guarantor

The person who takes the responsibility of making sure that the guaranteed person will do what is required of him.

## daaniq (pl. dawaaniq) دانق (دوانق)

Daniq

A small fraction of a "dirham" (1/6 dirham). Metaphorically, it is used to mean an insignificant amount of money (like penny in 'penniless').

## daar (ad--) al-'aakhirah الدار الآخرة

Abode of the Hereafter

The term could also refer to the life Hereafter.

## daar al-'ahd دار العهد

Abode of treaty

Non-Muslim territories that have a peace treaty with the Islamic State.

## daar al-baqaa' / al-khuluud

## دار البقاء / الخلود

Abode of Eternity

The reference here is to the Hereafter, as opposed to this world where life is temporary.

## daar al-fanaa' دار الفناء

Vanishing world

This world where life is temporary, as opposed to life in the Hereafter which is eternal.

## daar al-ghuruur دار الغرور

Abode of delusion

This world where things are ephemeral and may not be real. Man is constantly being exposed to delusions and temptations.

## daar al-Harb دار الحرب

Abode of war

Hostile territories, under un-Islamic rule.

## daar al-hijrah دار الهجرة

Adobe of migration

The town of al-Madinah al-Munawwarah (Medina) to which the Prophet (PBUH) migrated from Makkah after thirteen years of preaching and frustration.

## daar al-islaam دار الإسلام

Abode of Islam

Territories under Islamic rule and sovereignty.

## daar al-ibtilaa' دار الابتلاء

Abode of tests and tribulations

The reference is to life in this world, where one is being constantly tested with favours and afflictions by Allah. A true believer will show gratitude for the favours and patience and acceptance in the face of afflictions.

## daar al-khilaafah دار الخلافة

The seat of caliphate

The seat of the ruling caliph, capital of the state.

## daar al-khuld دار الخلد

Abode of eternal life

The life Hereafter is so called because life there has no end.(See the Qur'an, 41: 28.)

## daar al-kufr دار الكفر

Abode of disbelievers

Territories that are under the control of Non-Muslims.

## daar an-na'iim al-muqiim

## دار النعيم المقيم

Abode of eternal pleasure

The reference is to Paradise where a believer enjoys unlimited types of pleasure endlessly.

## daar as-salaam دار السلام

Abode of peace

The reference is to Paradise. But the term has been used by Muslims to name some places, taking the expression in its literal sense.

## Daarr (aD--)الضار

The Harm Inflictor

A Divine Attribute of Allah. The One Who inflicts harm if He so wishes, and nothing may befall people against His Will.

## daawuud داود

David

The Prophet David who fought Goliath and killed him. He was also a king of the Israelites. (For examples of his story, see the Qur'an, 38: 17-26: 251).

## da'aa 1(yad'uu) (يدعو) 1 دعا

To pray, supplicate

Often, the verb in this sense is followed by the word Allah.

## da'aa 2(yad'uu) (يدعو) 2 دعا

To call, invite

As a religious term, to invite people to Islam or to God's way.

## dafn دفن

Burial

Burying a deceased person.

## dahriyy دهري

Atheist

A follower of material atheism who denies the existence of God.

## dahriyyah (ad--) الدهرية

Atheism

The philosophy that denies the existence of God, believing only in material beings.

## dajjaal (ad--) الدجال

The false messiah

He is called "al-masiiH ad-dajjaal". According to Prophetic traditions, the false messiah will appear near the end of time. He will perform some unusual feats that help him gather many followers and lead many astray.

## Dalaalah ضلالة

Aberration, going astray

See "Dalaal."

## Dalaal ضلال

Aberration ,going astray

Not following the right path set by the religion.

## dalaalat an-naSS

## دلالة النص

Inferred meaning

Whatever is understood from the Qur'an or teachings of the Prophet (PBUH).

## daliil 1 (pl. adillah)

## دليل1 (أدلة)

Proof ,evidence

Something that proves the truth of a claim.

## daliil 2(pl. adillaa')

## دليل2 (أدلاء)

Guide

A person who guides people in doing something.

## Dalla (yaDill)

## ضل (يضل)

To go astray

To follow a path other than the one set for people by God.

## Damaan ضمان

Security ,guarantee

## damm fidyah دم فدية

Expiation blood

An animal offering made in expiation for a sin or a religious error ,such as missing some pilgrimage rite ,or doing something a pilgrim should not do.

## dam an-nifaas دم النفاس

Lochia

Blood discharge after child birth, which is considered as impure as menstruation .A Muslim woman should not pray ,fast nor touch the Qur'an until the bleeding completely stops ,and she bathes.

## Dara'a( yaDra )'ila-llaah

## ضرع (يضرع) إلى الله

Fervently pray to Allah

Pray with utmost humility and submission to Allah.

## Darar(pl .aDraar)

## ضَرَر (أضرار)

Harm ,damage

As a religion of peace ,Islam makes it mandatory upon its followers not to cause harm to others.

## DariiH( pl .aDriHah)

## ضريح (أضرحة)

Tomb, Grave

Usually, the term refers to tombs of special people, like famous pious men ("'awliyaa' SaliHiin" ('saints'), as opposed to "qabr" ('general tomb').

Dd

Dd

## Darrah( pl .Daraa'ir)

## ضرّة (ضرائر)

Co-wife

Other wife of a man with more than one wife.

## Daruuraat( aD--) tubiiH al-maHZuuraat

## الضّرورات تُبِيح المحظورات

Necessity knows no laws

Necessity makes illegal things legal .For example ,if one is literally dying of hunger he may eat forbidden food to protect his life.

## Daruurah( pl .Daruurat)

## ضَرُورة (ضرورات)

Necessity

Normally ,absolute necessity) such as a matter of life or death ,(which in Islam may make forbidden things ,such as eating carcasses, permissible.

## Daruuraat(aD--)al-khams

## الضّرورات الخمس

The five essentials

The five basic necessary things for a human being :life ,religion, mind ,honour ,possessions .We can say that these represent the minimum human rights .One of the main purposes of Islamic law is to protect these rights.

## da'wah دعوة

Call ,invitation

Calling people to God or to Islam, or any religion.

## da'wah(pl.da'awaat/ ad'iyah)

## دعوة ( دعوات / داعية )

Supplication ,prayer

Verbal prayers addressed to Allah.

## da'wah( pl .da'waat)

## دعوة (دعوات)

Invitation

An invitation to a meal or a ceremony.

## da'wah' ilaa Allah

## دعوة إلى الله

Call to Allah,

propagation of Islam

Calling people to the way chosen for them by their Creator ;i.e. propagation of Islam and its teachings.

## dawaraan دوران

Interdependence

In the Science of Principles ,the mutual relationship between underlying cause and a ruling:

if one is lacking the other will be invalid.

## dayn( pl .duyuun)
## دين (ديون)

Debt

Money borrowed from someone or owed to him for some reason or another.

## dayyaan(ad--)
## الدّيّـان

The Judge

The One Who judges people's actions and rewards or punishes them.

## dhaakir ذاكِر

Rememberer of Allah

A person who remembers Allah by glorifying Him and reciting "dhikr" and the Qur'an etc. The feminine is "dhaakirah".

## dhaat (adh--) الذّات

Entity, person

We often find this term along with or contrasted with "Sifaat" (attributes) with reference to Allah. It means "adhdhaat al-ilaahiyyah" (' the Divine Entity.')

## dhaat al-bayn ذات البين

Between people

Often, we find this term in expressions like "iSlaaH dhaat al-bayn" (making peace between two people in conflict).

## dhaat al-laah ذات الله

Allah's Entity

The term refers to Allah's Entity, as opposed to His Attributes ("Sifaat").

## dhaat an-niTaaqayn
## ذات النطاقين

Double belted

The female with two belts.
The reference is Asmaa'daughter of Abu Bakr (RA). It refers to the incident in which she tore her waist belt into two halves, using one to tie a food bag she prepared for the Prophet (PBUH) and her father on the night of their departure of Mecca for Medina.

## dhabH ذبح

Slaugheter

## dhabiiH (adh--)
## الذبيح

Sacrifice

The word actually means 'the slaughtered one'. It is used to refer to Ishmael son of Prophet Abraham. The allusion is to their story in which Abraham was about to sacrifice his son Ishmael

Dd

in obedience to Allah's command. (See the Qur'an 37:100-109.)

## dhabiiHah (pl. dhabaa'iH)

## ذبيحة (ذبائح)

Slaughtered animal

## dhanb (pl. dhunuuh)

## ذنب (ذنوب)

Sin

Anything that violates the teachings of the religion.

## dharii'ah (pl. dharaa'i')

## ذريعة (ذرائع)

Pretext

Originally, it means medium or means to something. Technically, it refers to an excuse for doing something. (See "sadd adh-dharaa'i'.)

## dhawuu al-qurbaa

## ذوو القربى

Relatives, kinsfolk

People related to a person.

## dhawuu al-arHaam (sg. dhuu ar-raHim)

## ذوو الأرحام (ذو الرّحم)

Relatives, kinsfolk

## dhikr (pl. adhkaar)

## ذكر (أذكار)

Remembrance (of Allah)

Any form of verbal prayers in which Allah's name is mentioned, including recitation of the Qur'an, is considered "dhikr" or "dhikru -llaah" (mentioning / remembering Allah).

## dhimmiyy (pl. ahl adh-dhimmah )

## ذمّي (أهل الذّمّة)

Protected citizen

A Christian or Jewish citizen of an Islamic State.

## dhiraa' (pl. 'adhru / 'adhri'ah)

## ذِراع (أذرع / أذرِعَة)

Cubit

The length of the forearm.

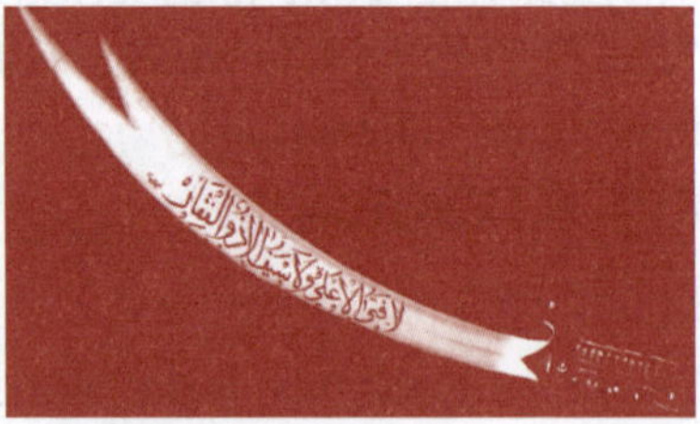

## dhuu al-fiqaar ذو الفقار

Zul-fiqaar

The name of the sword of the Prophet Muhammad (PBUH). Some say it is the name of the sword of Ali ibn Abi Taleb (RAA), the Prophet's cousin and son-in-law

## dhuu al-Hijjah ذو الحجة

Dhul-Hijjah

The twelfth month of the Islamic calendar, known as the month of pilgrimage.

## dhuu al-Hulayfah ذو الحُليفة

Dhul-Hulayfah

A location a few miles south of Medina on the way to Mecca where pilgrims from Medina, and those who pass through it, start wearing their iHraam.

## dhuu al-jalaal wa al-ikraam ذو الجلال و الإكرام

The Majestic and Generous

A Divine Attribute of Allah.The Lord of Majesty and Generosity. Some people have translated this attribute as 'the Mighty and Glorious'.

## dhuu al-kifl ذو الكفل

Dhul-Kifl

A prophet of the Arabs whose story, we are told, is like that of Ezekiel. A brief mention of his name is given in the Qur'an (38: 48).

## dhuu an-nuun ذو النون

Jonah, Jonas

Literally, this means 'of the whale'. It is a nickname given to the Prophet "yuunus" (Jonas) because of his story with the whale that swallowed him, then threw him ashore.(See his story in the Qur'an, 37: 139-148; 21: 78-88).

## dhuu an-nuurayn ذو النورين

Man of two lights

This is used to refer to the third righteous caliph "'uthmaan ibn 'affaan" since he married two daughters of the Prophet Muhammad (PBUH), successively.

## dhuu al-qarnayn ذو القرنين

Zul-Qarnayn

The name of a man of God about whom we read a short story in the Qur'an (Chapter 18: 83-98). Some scholars have identified him with Alexander the Great.

Dd

## dhuu al-qi'dah ذو القعدة

Zul-Qi'dah

The eleventh month of the Islamic calendar.

## dhuu raHim (pl. dhawuu raHim)

## ذو رحم (ذوو رحم)

Relative

A kinsman or blood relation3.

## diinaar( pl .danaaniir)

## دينار (دنانير)

Dinar

A golden coin used by Muslims throughout history. At the present time, it is a currency name used in some Arab countries (Bahrain, Iraq, Jordan, Kuwait, Tunisia).

## diin( pl .adyaan)

## دين (أديان)

Religion

Religious way of life or teachings.

## diiwaan( pl .dawaawiin)

## ديوان (دواوين)

Record ,department

Literally, it means official record. The term was used in Islamic history to mean, among others, something like a government 'Department' or 'Ministry' . For example "diiwaan al-jund' was the government department responsible for "jund' (soldiers, their records and salaries).

## dirham(daraahim)

## درهم (دراهم)

Dirham

A silver coin used by Muslims for many centuries. The word comes from Greek drachma. In terms of weight it is said to be 1/12 of an "uuqiyyah" (ounce). Nowadays, there are some Arab countries that use the word for their currencies (UAE and Morocco).

## diyah( pl .diyaat)

## دية (ديات)

Blood money

Money paid by the killer to the family of a person killed, intentionally or by mistake.

## du'aa( 'pl .ad'iyah)

## دعاء (أدعية)

Supplication ,verbal prayer,

Praying to Allah.

## du'aa 'al-istiftaaH
## دعاء الاستفتاح

Opening prayer

The prayer said after making the first" takbiirah" in formal prayers. It is followed by "suurat al-faatiHah" (the Opening Chapter of the Qur'an).

## du'aa' al-qunuut
## دعاء القنوت

Supplication of submissiveness

Usually, this refers to the supplications one says in "Salaat al-witr", the last prayer one performs at night.

## dubur aS-Salaah دُبر الصّلاة

After the prayer

Some say it means at the end of the prayer, before finishing it. Supplications are recommended at this time, since this is one of those occasions when supplications are more apt to be answered by God.

## dunyaa 1 دنيا

This world

Life in this world, as opposed to the Hereafter.

## dunyaa 2 دنيا

Worldly affairs

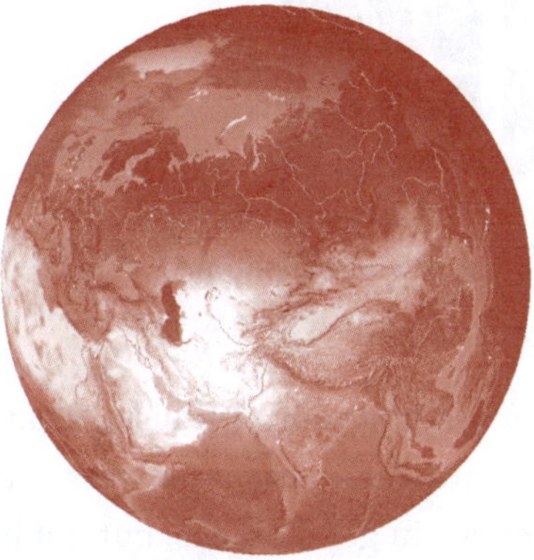

Affairs related to worldly and material matters, as opposed to "diin" (religion and spiritual affairs).

## dunyawiyy 1 دنيوي

Secular

Related to worldly affairs.

## dunyawiyy 2 دنيوي

Worldly, secular

Something that belongs to life in the present world, as opposed to "'ukhrawiyy". It is also used to contrast with "diiniyy" (religious).

## duruuz (sg. darziyy)درزي

Duruze

A cult known for secrecy of beliefs and practices .The followers of this cult are found in Lebanon and Syria.

# Ff

## fa'l Hasan فأل حسن

Good omen

As a religion of optimism, Islam encourages its followers to believe in good omens, but not be detracted by bad ones.

## faaHishah الفاحشة

Fornication, adultery

Often the word comes with the verb "irtakaba" (to commit) to mean commit illicit sexual act.

## faaHishah (pl. fawaHish) فاحشة (فواحش)

Shameful or vile deed

## faajir (pl. fujjaar) فاجر (فجّار)

Libertine, immoral

A licentious person who does not respect any rule of morality or decency.

## faaruuq (al--) الفاروق

The prudent

A nickname given to 'Umar ibn al-Khattab (RAA) the second righteous caliph. The word actually means someone who discriminates good from evil or right from wrong.

## faasid فاسد

Invalid

Not acceptable, due to unfulfillment of some prerequisites.

## faasiq فاسق

Sinner, untrustworthy

A corrupt person whose testimony may not be accepted in an Islamic court of law. (An example of the use of this word is found in the Qur'an, 49: 6.)

## faata (yafuut) فات (يفوت)

To be missed

In Arabic to say that one missed something, we would say X was missed by him. So "faatatnii Salaat al-'aSr" means "I missed the afternoon prayer.'

## faatiHah (al--) الفاتحة

The Opening Chapter

See "fatiahat al-kitaab."

## faatiHat al-kitaab فاتحة الكتاب

The Opening Chapter

Literally ,the Opener of the Book, meaning the first chapter of the Qur'an.Oftencalled" al-faatiHah." It is the most frequently recited chapter of the Qur'an ,since one has to recite it at least 17 times a day ,in the five daily prayers .It is often recited by Muslims on many occasions ,such as closing a deal/ an agreement ,like marriage.

## faaTimiyyuun(al--)

## الفاطميّون

The Fatimites

An Islamic dynasty that claims to be descendants of Fatimah (daughter of the Prophet (PBUH).

## faDiilah( pl .faDaa'il)

## فضيلة (فضائل)

Virtue

A good quality.

## faDl 1 فضل 1

Distinction ,preference

In the well known Farewell Speech of the Prophet) PBUH,( he said" :laa faDl li'arabiyyin 'alaa' ajamiyyin' illaa bittaqwaa". '(There is no distinction or preference for an Arab over a non-Arab except through piety and God-fearing.)'

## faDl 2(pl. 'afDaal)

## فضل2 (أفضال)

Favour ,blessing

A common expression in which we hear this word is" haadhaa min faDli Rabbii" ('This is a favour bestowed upon me by my Lord, which was said by Prophet Solomon – the Qur'an, 27:40). It is often said to express gratitude to Allah for a certain blessing from Him.

## faDl 3(pl. fuDuul) فضل3 (فضول)

Surplus, excess

Beyond one's needs.

## faHshaa' فحشاء

Abomination, shameful deeds

For an example of the use of the word in this sense, see the Qur'an, 16: 90.

## fajr (al--)الفجر

Dawn

The time of the appearance of the first true light in the east, usually about an hour and a half before sunrise in normal zones.

## fajr (al--) al-kaadhib

## الفجر الكاذب

False dawn

The appearance of some light in the east before dawn. It does not spread like the real dawn.

## fajr (al--) aS-Saadiq
## الفجر الصّادق

Real dawn

The true break of daylight.

## fakku raqabah
## فكّ رقبة

Manumission, freeing a slave

Setting a slave free is considered one of the very highly recommended acts of devotion. Sometimes, it is a "kaffaarah" (expiation) for some sins. (See the Qur'an, 90:13.)

## falaaH فلاح

Success, prosperity

The most frequent use of this word is in the 'adhaan (call to prayer) in the expression: "Hayyi 'ala al-falaaH," meaning 'Hurry to success' (in this world and the Hereafter). Prosperity here refers especially to the spiritual aspect.

## faqiih (fuqahaa')
## فقيه (فقهاء)

Jurist

A scholar that specializes in the study of Islamic law.

## faqqaha (yufaqqih)
## فقه (يفقه)

To teach

To teach someone or give him the ability to understand, especially religious matters. Naturally, the doer in the second instance is God.

## far' al-insaan
## فرع الإنسان

Descendant

A son or daughter or a descendant of them. This is opposite to "aSl" (predecessor).

## far' (science of principles)
## فرع (علم الأصول)

Offshoot

In the Science of Principles, something based on another ;e.g,. the ruling against beer on the basis of prohibition of wine.

## faraa'iD (sg. fariiDah)
## فرائض (فريضة)

inheritance shares

See "farD (pl. faraa'iD)".

Ff

## faraj فرج

Relief

A common expression in which we find this word is "'inna faraja-llaahi qariib" (Surely, relief from Allah is coming soon).

## farD1 فرض

Mandatory ,obligatory

Required by the religion.

## farD 2 (pl. furuuD)
## فرض 2

Obligatory act / deed

Something a Muslim should do or observe ,such as the five daily prayers and the fast of Ramadan.

## farD 3 (pl. faraa'iD)
## فرض 3 (فرائض)

Inheritance share

Obligatory share of inheritance. The distribution of the inheritance has been specified in the Qur'an, and should not be subject to a will) .See the Qur'an(.11-13 :4 , There is a science in Islam for this, called'" ilm al-faraa'iD" (science of inheritance shares).

## farD 'ayn فرض عين

Individual obligation

An act that has to be done by every Muslim, such as praying five times a day.

## farD kifaayah
## فرض كفاية

Community obligation

Something that the whole community is responsible for. If some members do it, that would suffice. If none does it then the whole community is at fault and has sinned. An example is funeral prayer; someone has to do it.

## fariiDah 1
## فريضة 1

Mandatory, obligatory

Required by the religion.

## fariiDah 2 (pl. furuuD)
## فريضة 2 (فروض)

Obligatory act

See "farD (pl. furuuD)".

## farj (pl. furuuj)
## فرج (فروج)

Genitalia

Sex organ of a man or a woman, though it is normally used for females in common usage.

## farraja allaahu kurbatan
## فرّج الله كربة...

May Allah relieve X of his / her difficulties

This prayer is often said when we hear of someone being in a difficult state. (See "faraj").

Ff

## farsakh (pl. farasikh)

## فرسخ (فراسخ)

Farsakh

A linear measurement which is roughly equivalent to 5544 meters.

## fasaad فساد

Corruption

Doing bad things.

## fasaad al'-amal

## فساد العمل

Invalidity of a deed

See "fasada (yafsud)".

## fasada (yufsud)

## فسد (يفسد)

To be corrupt or invalid

To become bad for a person or invalid for things or actions.

## fasakha (yafsakh)

## فسخ (يفسخ)

To cancel ,annul

## faskh فسخ

Cancellation ,annulment

Cancelling a contract) including that of marriage (or considering it void.

## faskh al'-aqd

## فسخ العقد

Cancelling a contract/

an agreement

Cancelling an agreement or considering a contract null and void.

## fatana 1 (yaftin)

## فتن 1 (يفتن)

To tempt

To tempt one to do something wrong.

## fatana 2 (yaftin)

## فتن 2 (يفتن)

To test or try with affliction

This sense is found only in the context of Allah testing believers with afflictions. (See the Qur'an, 29: 2).

## fatana 3 (yaftin)

## فتن 3 (يفتن)

Persecute

To persecute someone (by burning, e.g.) because of his religious beliefs. (See the Qur'an, 85:10).

## fatH khaybar

## فتح خيبر

Conquest of Khaybar

Victorious entry of the citadel of Khaybar, north of Medina, by the Prophet Muhammad (PBUH) and his companions.

## fatH makkah فتح مكّة

Capture of Makkah

Victorious entry to Makkah by the Prophet Muhammad (PBUH) and his companions in the eighth year of Hijrah.

## fattaaH (al--)الفتاح

The Supreme Opener

A Divine Attribute of Allah. The One Who opens the doors of His treasures, mercy and victory for His servants. The word could also mean 'the Supreme Judge'. (See the Qur'an, 34: 26.)

## faTuur فطور

Breakfast

In Ramadan ,the meal one takes after sunset.

## fatwaa فتوى

Legal opinion

The opinion given by a religious scholar on an issue.

## fawaat ar-rak'ah

## فوات الرّكعة

Missing a rak'ah

In congregational worship, a person has missed a "rak'ah", and has to do it after the imam finishes the "Salaah" if he joined the group after the imam has raised his head from the bowing position. (See "rak'ah").

## fawwaDa (yufawwiD) 'amrahu

## فوّض (يفوّض) أمره

To confide one's cause to

Very often we hear the expression: "fawwaDa 'amrahu ilal-laah" to mean that someone has entrusted his cause to Allah or left the matter in Allah's hands. (See the Qur'an, 40: 44.)

## fay' فَيء

Gains from enemy, Spoils, booty,

Things won from the enemy of Muslims without a fight, as opposed to "ghaniimah" and "'anfaal".

## fidyah 1 فدية

Ransom

Money paid to liberate a war captive.

Ff

Ff

## fidyah 2 فدية

Expiation ,atonemtent

See "kaffaarah". (See the Qur'an, 2: 184 & 196.)

## fii sabiili- llaah في سبيل الله

For the cause of Allah (God)

Literally, this means in the way of Allah. Usually the expression means anything done for the sake of Allah, more specifically "al-jihaad".

## fil-manshaTi wal-makrah في المنشط و المكره

Under all conditions

We find this expression in examples such as remembering Allah or duties towards Him under all conditions .This means that one does not forget God whether he is happy or miserable .It is also found in the context of obeying a Muslim ruler in matters that are consistent with the teachings of Islam.

## fiqh فقه

Islamic jurisprudence

Fiqh or'" ilm al-fiqh" covers teachings regarding all areas of life related to worship and transactions. The word originally means 'understanding'.

## firaash (pl. furush) فراش (فرش)

Conjugal bed

The word is used sometimes to refer to the owner of conjugal bed, the husband. For example, in the hadeeth the illegitimate child legally belongs to the husband of the mother ("al-walad li-lfiraash…").

## fir'awn فرعون

Pharoah

In the Qur'an, reference is made to the Pharaoh who had encounters with the Prophet Moses. He is considered a typical example of tyranny and disbelief. (See, e.g., the Qur'an, 10: 83.)

## firdaws فردوس

Paradise

In Islamic teachings, this is a special place in "jannah" ('the Garden') or paradise in English. (See the Qur'an, 18: 107 & 23:11.)

## firinj (al--) / al-firinjah
## الفرنج / الفرنجة

Franks

In Islamic history, this term was used to refer to Europeans.

## firqah (pl. firaq)
## فِرقة (فِرَق)

Sect

A group of people who share a sub-set of beliefs and practices of a certain religion.

## fis-saraa'i waD-Darra'
## في السّراء و الضّراء

Under all conditions

We find this expression in examples such as remembering Allah or duties towards Him under all conditions. This means that one does not forget the remembrance of God whether he is happy or miserable.

## fisq فسق

Sinfulness, moral depravity

Doing forbidden things.

## fiTaam فِطام

Weaning

Stopping breast-feeding of a baby, normally at the age of two.

## fitan (sg. Fitnah)
## فتن (فتنة)

Trials, temptations, tribulations

See "fitnah" 1-4.

## fitnah 1 فتنة

Religious persecution

The term is found in the Qur'an in this sense, among other senses. (See, e.g., 2: 192 and 193).

## fitnah 2 فتنة

Allurement, temptation

Temptation or a source of temptation that may distract a believer from his duties or might lead one to sin. (See the Qur'an, 8: 28).

## fitnah 3 (pl. fitan)
## فتنة 3 (فتن)

Affliction, test

A good or bad thing that happens to a person, which is normally considered a test of a Muslim's faith. (See the Qur'an, 21: 35).

## fitnah 4 (pl. fitan)
## فتنة 4 (فتن)

Dissention, sedition

(See the Qur'an, 9: 47 and 48).

## fiTrah فطرة

natural disposition, nature

This term is found in a Prophetic "Hadiith" which says every human being is born according to his natural disposition as a Muslim. His parents make him a Jew, a Christian or a Magian.

### fujuur فجور

Immorality, depravation



This term could also mean transgression.

### furqaan (al--) الفرقان

The Criterion

One of the attributes or names of the Qur'an, being the Criterion by which people's actions and things are to be judged. (See the Qur'an 25: 1.)

### furuu' (far') 1

### فروع (فرع) 1

Branches

The word is used in both its physical and metaphorical senses. As a term, it is often contrasted with "'uSuul" (principles, foundations), which means issues that are based on those principles.

### furuu' (sg. far') 2

### فروع (فرع)2

Descendants

Sons, daughters and sons' descendants. Sometimes we have 'uSuul wa furuu' meaning ascendants and descendants of a person.

### fusuuq فسوق

Wickedness, lewdness

See the Qur'an,2: 197 & 49: 7.

### futuuH (aat) (sg. fatH)

### فتوح (فتح)

Islamic conquests

This term is used in Islamic history to refer to the various battles in which Muslims conquered non-Muslim lands.

# Gg

## ghaafil (pl. ghaafiluun) غافل (غافلون)

Unaware, heedless

Generally, someone who is unaware of things around him / her. But it is often used to refer to someone who neglects his duties towards his Creator and/or does not remember God. (See "ghaflah" and the Qur'an, 7: 205.)

## ghaalaa (yughaalii) غالي (يغالي)

To exaggerate

To be excessive in something, be it a belief or an act.(See "ghuluww".)

## ghaar Hiraa' غار حراء

Cave of Hiraa'

The cave in "jabal an-nuur" (Mount of Light) where the Prophet Muhammad (PBUH) used to retreat, before Islam, for contemplation.

## ghaar thawr غار ثور

Cave of Thawr

The cave in which the Prophet (PBUH) hid during his migration

from Makkah to Medina with his friend Abu Bakr. (See the Qur'an, 9: 40).

## ghaarim (pl. ghaarimuun) غارم (غارمون)

Person in debt

Person in debt, whether because of borrowing or because he has to pay blood money, for example. Such a person deserves to receive alms and charity.

## ghaaz(in) (pl, ghuzaah) غاز (غزاة)

Fighter for the Cause of Allah

A participant in a holy war against the enemies of Islam in a land of the believers.

## Ghabn غبن

Fraud

Fraud or deception in a transaction, such as selling something deficient, without the buyer's consent. The buyer is called "maghbuun".

## ghaDD al-baSar

## غض البصر

Lowering the gaze

Not gazing improperly at somebody. Believers are required to lower their gaze especially in the presence of the opposite sex, out of modesty. (See the Qur'an, 24: 30-31).



## ghadr غدر

Betrayal, treachery

An example, is killing someone from behind or without warning or betraying someone who trusts you.

## ghalbat aZ-Zann

## غلبة الظن

Higher probability

Indications are stronger in favour of some opinion or ruling.

## ghaffaar (al--) الغفار

The Most Forgiving

A Divine Attribute of Allah. The One Whose forgiveness has no limits.

## ghaflah غفلة

Inattention, oblivion

Inadvertent negligence, or a state of forgetting about Allah and that He is watching us.

## ghafuur (al--) الغفور

The Ever-Forgiving

A Divine Attribute of Allah. The One Who keeps forgiving the repenting sinners, and Whose forgiveness knows no limits.

## ghaniimah (pl. ghanaa'im) غنيمة (غنائم)

Spoils of war

What is won from the enemy in a legitimate war.

## gharuur (al--) غرور

Satan the Deceiver

Al-gharuur is used in the Qur'an to refer to the most deceitful being, Satan, because he entices people, especially through false promises, to commit sins and do wrong things. (See the Qur'an, 31: 33.)

## ghaniyy (al--) الغني

The Self-Sufficient

A Divine Attribute of Allah. The One Who has no need for anyone or anything. (See the Qur'an, 6: 133.)

## ghargharat al-mawt

## غرغرة الموت

Gargle of death

The time when the soul departs the body. At this time repentance from sins or disbelief is not accepted from anyone.

## ghaSb غصب

Illegal seizure

To take something, often a piece of property, by force.

## ghayb (pl. ghuyuub) غيب (غيوب)

Unseen thing

Something that we cannot see, be it in the past, present or future, but especially the future.

## ghaybat al-'imaam غيبة الإمام

Occultation of the imam

The Shi'ite belief of the temporary disappearance of the twelfth imam, al-Mahdiy, to appear in the later days.

## ghayrah غَيرة

Jealousy

A feeling of envy of others who have something we do not have. It is also used to mean a sense of vigilance or feeling of protection of one's female relatives.

## ghayZ غيظ

Rage

Uncontrolled temper or extreme annoyance of something / someone.

## ghazwah غزوة

Battle, campaign

The term normally refers to a campaign or battle which was under the leadership of the Prophet Muhammad (PBUH). This is contrasted with "sariyyah" (expedition) where someone else leads.

## ghazwat al-aHzaab غزوة الأحزاب

Battle of the Clans/confederates

This was one of the most dangerous battles in early Islamic history, which took place in the fifth year after the Hijra. A reference is given in the Qur'an to this Battle in the Chapter that has the name "al-aHzaab" (33: 9-25). It is also known as "ghazwat al-khandaq".

## ghazwat badr غزوة بدر

The Battle of Badr

The first battle in Islamic history between the Prophet (PBUH) and the Muslims (about 300) against the polytheists of Makkah (more than 1000), and the Muslims came out victorious, with many leaders of Quraish killed or captivated. The Battle started on the 17th of Ramadan, second year of Hijrah.

## ghazwat banii an-naDiir

## غزوة بني النّضير

Campaign against Banii an-NaDiir

The campaign against the Jewish tribe at Medina who conspired with the pagans against the Prophet (PBUH) and the Muslims, violating a treaty to the opposite effect. They were expelled from Medina.



## ghazwat banni qaynuqaa'

## غزوة بني قينقاع

Campaign against Banii Qaynuqaa'

Banuu Qaynuqaa' was the last Jewish tribe to be expelled from Medina because of their constant harassment of the Muslims and their violation of the peaceful coexistence agreement with the Prophet of Islam. They settled in a place on the Northern borders of Arabia.

## ghazawat banii qurayZah

## غزوة بني قريظة

Campaign against
Banii Qurayzah

The campaign against the Jewish tribe that had agreed to defend Medina with the Muslims against outsiders, but when the city was besieged and the Muslims were busy fighting, this tribe decided to side with the enemy against their former allies. Upon the withdrawal of the "aHzaab" (clans) they were punished in the way that was decided by the judge they chose themselves. The campaign took place in the 5th year after Hijrah. (See the Qur'an, 33: 9-26-7.)

## ghazwat Hunayn

## غزوة حُنَين

Battle of Hunayn

The Battle that took place at Hunayn (near Makkah) between the Muslims led by the Prophet (PBUH) and the polytheists in the eighth year of Hijrah. For the first time, the Muslim army was larger than that of their enemy, but they were ambushed and routed in the beginning. But they were victorious in the end. (See the Qur'an, 9: 25-26).

## ghazwat al-khandaq

## غزوة الخندق

Battle of the Trench

The Battle that took place in the fifth year of Hijrah. It is called so because for the first time in Arab history a trench was dug by the

Muslims, at the suggestion of Salman al-Farisi, to protect Medina from the attackof the polytheists. It is also called the Battle of the Clans, because the Quraish of Makkah managed to bring many clans with them to fight the Muslims. See ghazwat al-aHzaab.

## ghazwat khaybar

غزوة خيبر

Campaign of Khaybar

The campaign that took place against Khaybar, the stronghold of Jewish tribes in North Arabia, which had become 'a hornet's nest' of the enemies of Islam. The forts of Khaybar were reduced one by one in the seventh year of the Hijrah.

## ghazwat mu'tah

غزوة مؤتة

The Expedition of Mu'tah

The Expedition sent by the Prophet (PBUH) to the North West of Arabia in the eighth year of Hijrah, to fight Byzantines who had killed the Muslim emissary to their governor. This is probably the only campaign given the name of "ghazwah" which was not carried out under the direct command of the Prophet Muhammad (PBUH).

## ghazwat tabuuk

غزوة تبوك

The Tabouk Campaign

The Campaign that was made during the summer of the ninth year of Hijrah to the southern borders of the Syrian Region under the leadership of the Prophet (PBUH). It ended peacefully, because the enemy forces did not show up.

## ghiibah

غيبة

Backbiting

Saying something bad about a Muslim in his absence, even
if it is true. This is forbidden by the Qur'an. (See 49: 12). It is a greater sin if what is said is false, because then it becomes an act of aggression.

## ghinaa an-nafs

غنى النفس

Contentment

Literally, richness of the self, meaning self independence or sufficiency.

Gg

## ghishsh ar-ra'iyyah
## غش الرعية

Betrayal of subjects

A ruler's insincere or deceptive dealing with the people under his rule.

## ghufraan غفران

Forgivness

Similar in meaning to "maghfirah".

## ghulaah

## غلاة

Extremists

People who believe in or call to extreme views especially in religious matters.

## ghuluul غلول

Stealing from spoils

Taking anything from the spoils of war before they are officially distributed by the person in charge. It is considered a great crime. (See the Qur'an, 3:151).

## ghuluww غلو

Extremism, excessiveness

Extremism and excessiveness even in religious matters is frowned upon by Islam, which is a religion of moderation. Prophet Muhammad (PBUH) is reported to have said: "It was ghuluww that caused the destruction of people before you."

## ghunnah غنة

Nasalization

The production of a sound with the air escaping through the nose, as we do when we pronounce the /n/ and /m/. Normally, the vowel that precedes these nasal consonants is nasalized. Compare, e.g., the pronunciation of the vowel /a/ in 'at' and 'ant'.

## ghuruur غرور

Vanity

In common usage the word means vanity and conceit. But in the Qur'an it is often used to mean deception and false promises. (See the Qur'an, 4: 120).

## ghusl غسل

Washing the body

Washing the whole body, including the head. This is required in the case of a major ritual impurity ("Hadath akbar"), such as after sexual intercourse or menstruation, for one to be able to pray.

# Hh

## Haa'iD حائض

Menstruating female

A menstruating female is not supposed to pray, fast or touch the Qur'an. She may, however, recite it from memory. Sexual intercourse is also forbidden during menstruation.

## haabiil هابيل

Abel

The good son of Adam who was killed by his brother Cain (See the Qur'an, 5: 31).

## haadii (al--) الهادي

The Supreme Guide

A Divine Attribute of Allah. The Only and True Provider of guidance.

## HaaDinah حاضنة

Nursemaid

A woman who breastfeeds somebody else's baby. (See "murDi'ah").

## HaafiZ حافظ

Memorizer, protector

The literal meaning of the word is 'protector/ keeper', but in Islamic writings, the word is often used to refer to someone who has memorized the whole Qur'an and/or many Hadiiths.

## HaafiZ al-qur'aan حافظ القرآن

Memorizer of the Qur'an

This term is used in the Muslim World to refer to a person who has memorized the Qur'an and can recite it from memory. Sometimes, we hear the word HaafiZ alone to refer to such a person.

## HaafiZ li-farjih حافظ لفرجه

Chaste

Literally, it means someone who protects his genital (from sinful acts), which is a characteristic of a good believer (the Qur'an, 23:5).

## HaafiZ li-Huduudi-llah حافظ لحدود الله

Observant of Allah's limits

A God fearing person who obeys His commands.

## haajar هاجر

Hager

The second wife of the Prophet Abraham (PBUH) and mother of the Prophet Ishmael. She is the one who accompanied the Prophet "Ibraahiim" (Abraham) to Mecca and was, with her son Ismaa'iil (Ishmael), the first settlers there. Her walking between "Safa and Marwah" in frantic search for water for her baby son is commemorated in the ritual of "sa'y."

## Haajj (pl. Hujjaaj) حاج (حجاج)

Pilgrim

A pilgrim to Mecca.

## Haala (yaHuul) al-Hawl حال (يحول) الحول

One year passed

In the payment of alms ,we always see the stipulation of the passage of one full lunar year 354) days.(

## Haamil حامل

Pregnant

Unlike other women ,the waiting period'") iddah") for a divorced pregnant woman is childbirth. Only then may she remarry. Pregnancy may be a legitimate excuse for breaking the fast of Ramadan.

## Haamil (pl. Hamalah) al-qur'aan حامل (حملة) القرآن

Memorizer of the Qur'an

A person who knows the Qur'an by heart. This expression is less frequently used than "HaafiZ".

## Haanith حانث

Oath breaker, perjurer

Someone who does not fulfill what he / she has sworn to Allah to do.

## haaruun هارون

Aaron

The brother of the Prophet Moses. He was sent by Allah along with Moses to Pharoah at the request of Moses, who said that Aaron was more articulate than him. (See the Qur'an, e.g. 28: 34-35).

## haaruut wa maaruut هاروت و ماروت

Haroot and Maroot

Names of two angels in Babylon who are associated with magic. (See the Qur'an, 2: 102.)

## haashimiyy هاشمي

Hashemite

A member of the Hashemite tribe of the Prophet Muhammad (PBUH) or a descendant of that tribe.

## hadaa (yahdii) هدى (يهدي)

To guide

To show someone the right way.

## HaDaanah حضانة

Child custody

Taking care of a child: upbringing, feeding, clothing…

## HaDar (al--)الحضر

Sojourn, residence

Residing in a certain place or staying for a long period, as opposed to a person on travel ("safar"). This is important with regards to rulings related to "Salaah" and "Sawm" (prayer and fasting), such as shortening the formal prayers and breaking the fast.

## Hadath akbar حدث أكبر

Major ritual impurity

Major ritual impurity means that a Muslim should have a shower or wash the whole body, including the head, before he / she can pray or touch the Qur'an. This type of impurity may be caused by having sex, ejaculation, wet dream, menstruation or post-natal bleeding.

## Hadath aSghar حدث أصغر

Minor impurity

Minor ritual impurity means that one cannot pray or touch the Qur'an except after having ablution ("wuDuu'"). This type of impurity is caused by things like going to the bathroom, touching the private parts, passing wind and bleeding (from a wound, e.g.).

## Hadd 1 (pl. Huduud) حد 1 (حدود)

Limit set by Allah

Limit set in the Qur'an which should not be transgressed by a Muslim, or an act prohibited by Allah.

## Hadd 2 (pl. Huduud) حد 2 (حدود)

Specified punishment

Punishment specified in the Qur'an for a major crime, such as murder, stealing or fornication.

## Hadd al-qadhf حد القذف

Penalty for slander

The penalty specified for accusing a Muslim, male or female, of fornication, without producing four witnesses. (See the Qur'an, 24: 4).

## Haddatha (yuHaddith) حدث (يحدث)

To narrate a hadeeth

To report or narrate a prophetic tradition.

Hh

Hh

## Hadiith حديث

Prophetic tradition

A report about the Prophet Muhammad (PBUH) saying or doing something, or reacting to something (approving or disapproving of it). The authenticity of the report (hadeeth) depends on the reliability of the narrator(s).

## Hadiith al-ifk حديث الإفك

Story of the Slander

The slanderous rumour that was fabricated by some hypocrites about Aishah, the wife of the Prophet (PBUH), claiming that she committed adultery. The Qur'an declared her innocence of this slander, and Allah warns the Muslims of repeating it. (See the Qur'an, 24: 11-20).

## Hadiith 'aziiz حديث عزيز

Dear hadeeth

This is a Prophetic tradition narrated by two people and heard from two others.

## Hadiith Da'iif حديث ضعيف

Weak hadeeth

This means that there is doubt about the narrator suffering from bad memory or lack of integrity. So the text's authenticity becomes questionable.

## Hadiith ghariib حديث غريب

Strange hadeeth

A hadeeth is considered 'strange' if its text is unfamiliar, being reported by a single narrator, for example.

## Hadiith Hasan حديث حسن

Good hadeeth

The reference is to the degree of reliability of transmission of the text, not the text itself. "Hasan" is considered the second degree of reliability, the first being "SaHiiH" (sound).

## Hadiith maqTuu' حديث مقطوع

Disconnected hadeeth

A hadeeth attributed to a "taabi'iyy" (a second generation follower of Islam).

## Hadiith marfuu' حديث مرفوع

Attributed hadeeth

A hadeeth attributed to the Prophet (PBUH), but not proven to have a continuous chain of transmitters up to him.

## Hadiith mashhuur

حديث مشهور

Famous hadeeth

A Prophetic tradition reported by at least three people in each level of the chain of transmitters.

## Hadiith mawDuu'

حديث موضوع

Fabricated hadeeth

A tradition fabricated by the narrator and falsely ascribe it to the Prophet Muhammad (PBUH). Naturally, this is a grave sin.

## Hadiith mawquuf

حديث موقوف

Suspended hadeeth

A tradition ascribed to a companion of the Prophet (PBUH).

## Hadiith munqaTi'

حديث منقطع

Unconnected hadeeth

A tradition that has a discontinuous chain of transmitters (e.g., a second generation narrator is missing before the name of the Companion of the Prophet (PBUH).

## Hadiith mursal

حديث مرسل

Mursal hadeeth

A hadeeth attributed to the Prophet (PBUH) by a second generation narrator without mentioning the name of the first generation narrator (the companion of the Prophet (PBUH).

## Hadiith mutawaatir

حديث متواتر

Frequently reported hadeeth

A hadeeth that has been reported by many narrators and with different chains of transmission.

## Hadiith muttaSil

حديث متصل

Continuous hadeeth

A "Hadiith" that has a continuous chain of narrators.

## Hadiith qudsiyy

حديث قدسي

Divine hadeeth

A hadeeth whose text is attributed by the Prophet to Allah. So we read: "The Prophet (PBUH) said: Allah says: "...". Naturally, this should not be confused with the Qur'an, because the words in the hadeeth are of the Prophet, unlike the Qur'an which is the exact words of Allah.

## Hadiith SaHiiH

حديث صحيح

Sound hadeeth

A hadeeth whose transmission satisfies the conditions set by specialists, such as having a continuous chain of well-known narrators of high moral calibre and strong memories.

## Hadr حدر

Relatively fast recitation

The mode of reciting the Qur'an in a manner faster than usual, but without neglecting any of the rules of correct enunciation ("tajwiid"). See "tadwiir" and "tartiil."

## hady(un) هدي

Offering

An animal designated to be offered for sacrifice by a pilgrim.

## hajr al-qur'aan هجر القرآن

Abandoning the Qur'an

Neglecting the Qur'an or ignoring its teachings. (See the Qur'an, 25:30.)

## HafiiZ (al--) الحفيظ

The Ever-Protecting / Guarding

A Divine Attribute of Allah .The True Protector of His creation.

## Hajar (al--) al-aswad الحجر الأسود

The Black Stone

The blessed stone in the Northern corner of the Ka'bah nearest to the door, from which the circumambulating("Tawaaf")ofthe Ka'bah starts. A circumambulating person should try to kiss it, touch it or at least point to it every time he passes by.

## Hajara (yaHjur) حجر (يحجر)

To declare legal incompetence

To declare legal incompetence of a person. Naturally, this can only be done by a court of law.

## Haajib (pl. Hujjaab) حاجِب (حُجّاب)

Guard-secretary

In Islamic history, the job of screening visitors of a man of authority, such as a Caliph or governor, is done by the Haajib.

## Hajb حجب

Blocking inheritance

Preventing someone from inheriting. In Islamic law, the presence of a closer relative to the deceased, for example, may block a further relation from inheriting.

## Hajj حج

Pilgrimage to Mecca

It is the fifth corner-stone of Islam which should be performed by every able, adult Muslim once in his / her life time. It has to be performed in a very specific manner, at the time specified in the month of pilgrimage ("Dhul-Hijjah").

## Hajj al-bayt حج البيت

Pilgrimage to Mecca

Literally, the expression means going to the House (of Allah), the Ka'bah for pilgrimage.

## Hajj al-ifraad

## حج الإفراد

Hajj performed alone

Performing Hajj only, not preceded by or coupled with "'umrah" (lesser Hajj).

## Hajj al-qiraan حج القران

Hajj coupled with 'umrah

Performing both "Hajj" and "'umrah" (lesser pilgrimage) without changing one's pilgrim garb ("iHraam.("

## Hajj' aSghar حج أصغر

Lesser pilgrimage

This refers to the'" umrah", which may be performed any time around the year.

## Hajj at-tamattu' حج التمتع

Hajj of enjoyment

Performing "'umrah" then changing to regular clothes to enjoy a normal way of living until the eighth day of the month of pilgrimage. Then one wears the "iHraam" again to start the rituals of the hajj.

## Hajj mabruur حج مبرور

Pure pilgrimage

A pilgrimage in which the pilgrim observes all the rules of proper pilgrimage, including rituals and conduct, and not committing any violations.

## Hajr حجر

Declaring legal incompetence

Declaring legal incompetence of an adult. So he may not, for example, carry out any transactions, such as selling or buying, donating…etc.

## hajr az-zawjah هجر الزّوجة

Deserting the wife

To desert one's wife, usually by sleeping away from her, or not sleeping with her in the same bed.

## Hakam (al--)

## الحكم

Supreme Judge / Ruler

A Divine Attribute of Allah.The Absolute Ruler, Whose judgement no one can dispute or disregard.

**Hakam حَكَم**

Referee

In order to avoid divorce the Qur'an instructs that Muslims resort sometimes to settlements decided by referees from the husband' and wife's sides. (See the Qur'an 4: 35.)

**Hakiim (al--) الحكيم**

The All-Wise

A Divine Attribute of Allah. The One Whose wisdom has no limits.

**Halaal حلال**

Permissible, lawful

In Islam everything is considered lawful unless it is explicitly or implicitly forbidden by the religion.

**Halafa (yaHlif) حلف (يحلف)**

To swear, take an oath

A Muslim should never swear except to or by God.

**Halif حلف**

Swearing, taking an oath

See "Halafa" ("yaHlif").

**Haliim (al--)الحليم**

The Ever-Forbearing

A Divine Attribute of Allah. The One Who is always Tolerant of His servants' mistakes, and is never hasty in punishing them for their sins.

**hallala (yuhallil) هلّل (يهلّل)**

To say: "laa 'ilaaha 'ill-allaah."

To say the expression which means, "There is no deity except Allah." The verbal noun is "tahliil".

**Halq حلق**

Shaving

Removing the hair from any part of the body with a blade or the like, as opposed to "natf" (plucking) and "taqSiir" (shortening or cutting).

**Halq, Huruuf al- حلق ، حروف ال-**

Throat sounds

In Qur'anic phonetics, the term refers to the sounds produced in or near the throat: ء ، ع ، ح ، غ ، خ ، هـ The n sound is clearly enounced before them. (See "iZhaar".)

**Halq al-'aanah حلق العانة**

Shaving pubic hair

It is sunnah (recommended practice of the Prophet Muhammad

Hh

{PBUH}) to remove pubic hair by shaving or other means.

## Hamdalah حَمدلة

saying: "al-Hamdu lillaah"

Saying the expression which means" Praise the Lord "or "Thank God."

## Hamdu (al--) li-llaah الحمد لله

Praise the Lord ,Thank God

This is the expression often said by a Muslim to express his gratitude to Allah for all His favours of health ,provisions etc .Therefore, it is sometimes used to mean" I am fine "in answer to" How are you ,"?and it is said after eating or drinking.

## Hamida (yaHmad) حمد (يحمد)

To praise or thank

The verb has both meanings .This is true of its derivatives :Hamd, muHammad,Hamiid,maHmuud, aHmad...etc.

## Hamiid (al--) الحميد

The Ever-Praiseworthy

A Divine Attribute of Allah .The One Most Worthy of praise and thanks for His unlimited favours.

## hamzah همزة

Glottal stop

This is the first letter of the Arabic alphabet. It is called a glottal stop because the air coming from the lungs is temporarily stopped by the glottis (in the throat). This sound is significant in rules of tajwiid ('Qur'anic phonetics), as it affects the elongation or lengthening of the vowels before it.

## Hamzah حمزة

Hamzah

This was the name of a well-know paternal uncle of Prophet Muhammad (PBUH) who was called "asadu-llaah" ('God's lion') for his courageous defense of Islam and Muslims both in Mecca and in the battle fields. He was martyred in the Battle of Uhud at Medina, where his grave is.

## Hanafiyy (pl. 'aHnaaf) حنفي (أحناف)

Hanafi

Follower of Imam Abu Hanifah al-Nu'man school of Islamic law, which is one of the four major Sunni schools.

## Hanatha (yaHnath) حنث (يحنث)

To foreswear, break an oath

See "Hinth al-yamiin".

## Hanbaliyy (pl. Hanaabilah) حنبلي (حنابلة)

Hanbali

Follower of Iman Ahmad ibn Hanbal, founder of one the four major Sunni schools of Islamic law.

Hh

## Haniif (pl. Hunafaa') حنيف (حنفاء)

Upright

Many verses are found in the Qur'an that describe the Prophet Abraham (PBUH) as being "Haniif" meaning that he was in the right direction.

## Haniifiyyah (al--) الحنيفية

Hanifism, uprightness

In Islamic history the term often refers to the beliefs of the pre-Islamic believers in monotheism in Arabia.

## Haqq (al--)الحق

The Supreme Truth

A Divine Attribute of Allah. The One Whose existence and reality cannot be denied or doubted.

## Haqq 1 حق

True, truth

This word could be used as an adjective to mean 'true' (not false), real' or 'inevitable'. It can be used as a noun to mean 'truth'.

## Haqq 2 (pl. Huquuq) حق 2 (حقوق)

Right, due

Such as the right a parent has over his children.

## Haqq al-'abd حق العبد

Right of man

Any right that relates to people, moral or material. If violated, repentance to God alone is not sufficient. The transgressor has to seek forgiveness of the person whose rights have been infringed upon. This is the same as "Haqq al-insaan".

## Haqq al-'insaan حق الإنسان

Human's right

This is often used in contrast to "Haqq allaah". It means right of a person. For example, when a person steals he violates the injunctions of his religion and violates the right of the human (the person stolen from) by taking something from him. The former violation can be forgiven by Allah, but the human's right has to be returned as a necessary part of repentance. In Modern usage, we hear "Huquuq al-insaan" meaning 'human rights'.

## Haqq allaah حق الله

Allah's right

This is often used in contrast to "Haqq al-insaan" (human's right). It means the duty to Allah, such as performing prayers and paying poor due, as well observing other Divine injunctions.

## Haqq al-yaqiin حق اليقين

Absolute certainty

Certainty that comes after experiencing something.

## Haraam1 حرام

Forbidden, unlawful

Something forbidden in the Qur'an or the teachings of the Prophet Muhammad (PBUH).

## Haraam 2 حرام

Sacred

This meaning is found in expressions like "al-bayt al-Haraam" (the Sacred House - the Ka'bah) and "ash-shahr al-Haraam" (the sacred month).

## Haraj حَرَج

Blame

This word is often found in the Qur'an in the context of excepting certain people, such as the sick, from certain rulings. (See the Qur'an, 24: 61.)

## Harakah (pl. Harakaat) حركة (حركات)

Vowel

In "Tajwiid" the term means either a short vowel or the duration of a short vowel. So a vowel could, for example, have the duration of 4 or 5 Harakaat. Nasalization could have the duration of 2 vowels.

## Haram (al--)الحرم

The Sanctuary

This word is often used to refer to either the holy mosque of Mecca or the Prophet's mosque at Medina Technically, the word means a sanctuary; hence it could refer to the whole area surrounding both mosques within whose boundary no hunting is permitted.

## Harbiyy حربي

Hostile unbeliever

A disbeliever in Islam who is in a state of war with Muslims.

Hh

## Harf (pl. Huruuf)
## حرف (حروف)

Letter / sound

In Arabic grammar books and in tajwiid (Qur'anic phonetics) the word is used for both the written form of the sound and the sound itself, since there is a high degree of fit between sounds and their written representations in Arabic.

## Harfaan mutajaanisaan
## حرفان متجانسان

Two similar sounds

Two sounds are 'similar' if they are produced from the same place/ point of articulaltion, like /t/ and /d/.

## Harfaan mutamaathilaan
## حرفان متماثلان

Identical sounds

Any consonant occurring twice (at end of a word and the beginning of another, for instance) as in "min naar" in which case they become geminated (doubled in pronunciation) and the words are treated like one.

## Harfaan mutaqaaribaan
## حرفان متقاربان

Two almost similar sounds

Two sounds are considered almost similar if their places of articulation are the adjacent to each other and the sound have similar characteristics, like /r/ and /l/ and /q/ and /k/.

## Harrafa (yuHarrif)
## حرّف (يحرف)

To misinterpret ,misrepresent

To deliberately give wrong meaning or representation of a sacred text.

## Harrama (yuHarrim)
## حرّم (يحرم)

Make unlawful or sacred

The verb is used in both senses in the Qur'an; its meaning depends on the context. (See, e.g., the Qur'an: 27: 91 and 2: 275.)

## Haruuriyyah
## (sg. Haruuriyy)
## حرورية (حروري)

Harouris

The term is used to refer to khawaarij (kharijites) or a certain group of them.

## Hasad حسد

Envy, jealousy

This means feeling jealous of someone for a certain blessing (good fortune or wealth, e.g.)

and wishing that he be deprived of the blessing, which is strongly condemned by Islam. (See reference to this in the Qur'an 113:5.)

## Hasan حسن

Good

In the science of hadeeth, this term is used to describe the text of the hadeeth that has specific qualities, such as a reliable chain of narrators and logical acceptability.

## Hasanah (pl. Hasanaat) حسنة (حسنات)

Merit

The reward recorded for one on doing a good thing or abstaining from something wrong or bad. It is the opposite of "sayyi'ah" (demerit). (See the Qur'an, 6: 160.)

## Hasbiy-allaahu wa ni'ma al-wakiil حسبي الله و نعم الوكيل

Allah is sufficient for me, and He is the Best Trustee

This expression, mentioned in the Qur'an (3: 173), is said when a Muslim is in difficulty or under a threat, to seek Divine help and support.

## Hashr (al--)الحشر

The Gathering, Assembling

The resurrection and gathering of all creatures on the Day of Judgement.

## HaTiim (al--)الحطيم

Hateem

The half circular wall that encloses Hijr Ismael (the open area that complements the Ka'bah and is considered part of it). One should, therefore, walk outside it during the Tawaaf (circumambulation).

## hatk al-irD هتك العرض

Disgracing

Violating someone or causing him/ her to be disgraced, such as by raping a woman.

## hawaa (al--)الهوى

Whims and desires

One's desires and whims. This expression is commonly found in the expression "ittibaa' al-hawaa" (following one's whims). (See the Qur'an, 38: 26.)

## Hawaariyy (pl. Hawaariyyuun) حواري (حواريون)

Disciple

Often, this term is used to refer to

the disciples of the Prophet Jesus (PBUH).

### HawD (al--) al-mawruud الحوض المورود

The frequented basin

The reference is to the special basin of water / river which the Prophet (PBUH) has been promised by Allah in the Hereafter. Some scholars say that it is the River Kawthar mentioned in Chapter 108 of the Qur'an.

### Hawl 1حول

Lunar year

We often find the expression "Haala 'alayhi al-Hawl" meaning one year passed for it. The "zakaat" becomes required for certain things upon the passage of one lunar year.

### Hawl 2 حول

Power, ability

See "laa Hawla walaa quwwata illaa bi-llaah" for the common expression in which this word occurs.

### Hawqalah حوقلة

Saying: "laa Hawla"…

Saying what is translated as "There is no power or ability except with Allah's help". (See "Hawl 2").

### Hawwaa حواء '

Eve

Name of the mother of mankind and wife of Adam.

### Hayaa' 1 حياء

Modesty ,shyness

The opposite of vulgarity and boldness.

### Hayaa' 2 حياء

Fear of shame

The sense which makes one avoid wrong acts and words ;it is similar to the fear of God.

### Hayaat (al--) ad-dunyaa الحياة الدنيا

This life

Life in this world ,which is a transient and temporary one .It is the life where one should prepare for the Hereafter by doing good deeds and avoiding bad ones.

### HayD حيض

Menstruation ,menses

Regular monthly bleeding by females .There are certain rules to be observed by the woman during her period ,such as not performing regular prayers or fasting.

### Hayy (al--) الحي

The Ever-Living

A Divine Attribute of Allah .The One Whose life has no beginning nor an end.

## Hayyi' ala-falaaH
## حيّ على الفلاح

Hurry to success!

This is part of the" adhaan" (call to prayer), reminding believers that performing the prayer means success.

## Hayyi 'alaS-Salaah!
## حيّ على الصّلاة

Hurry to the prayer!

One of the utterances of the call to prayer, reminding believers that it is time to pray.

## Hidaad حِدَاد

Mourning

In Islam, mourning should not exceed three days except for the widow whose mourning period is four lunar months and ten days, during which period she has to observe certain restrictions in appearance and movements.

## hidaayah هداية

Guidance

Showing the right way.

## HifZ al-'ahd حفظ العهد

Upholding a pledge

Fulfilling an obligation, a promise or an agreement.

## HifZ al-farj حفظ الفرج

Being chaste

Literally, this means guarding one's genitals against committing illegal sex.

## HifZ al-lisaan حفظ اللّسان

Guarding the tongue

Guarding one's tongue against saying anything wrong or bad.

## Hijaab حِجَاب

Screen, covering the body

The word occurs once in the Qur'an in the context of male believers not to ask the wives of Prophet Muhmmad (PBUH) for anything except from behind a "Hijaab" (screen). According to Islamic teachings, an adult Muslim female should cover, as a minimum, her whole body, with the exception of the face and hands in the presence of "ajnabiyy" (stranger) or "non-maHram" men. (See the Qur'an, 24:31and 60; and 33: 59 for rulings in this regard).

## Hijaabah حجابة

Visitor screening

In Islamic history, the job of screening visitors of a man of authority, such as a Caliph or

Hh

governor. The person is called "Haajib."

## Hijaamah حِجامة

Cupping ,blood letting

A medical practice that was common in Muslim countries was making small cuts in certain parts of the body and using a cupping glass to let the' bad blood 'out.

## Hajjat al-wadaa حجّة الوداع '

Farewell pilgrimage

The pilgrimage performed by the Prophet (PBUH) in the tenth year of Hijra, during which he gave a comprehensive sermon known as "the Farewell Speech" (Khutabat al-wadaa').

## Hijr ismaa'iil حجر إسماعيل

Ishmael's enclosure

The enclosure adjacent to one side of the Ka'bah of which it is considered to be a part of it. Therefore, the person making "Tawaaf" should go around it (not inside it).

## Hijrah هجرة

Migration

In Islam, "hijrah" means migrating from a land of persecution and disbelief to a land of belief, normally to find freedom to practice Islam.

## hijriyy / hijriyyah هجري / هجرية

Of Hijra

Related to the hijrah (migration of the Prophet Muhammad (PBUH) from Mecca to Medina in 622 AD. (See "taqwiim hijrii").

## Hikmah (pl. Hikam) حكمة (حكم)

Rationale

Reason for a certain injunction ,for example .Naturally ,when we talk about religious injunctions we may give' possible 'explanations or reasons.

## Hikmah حكمة

Wisdom / discretion

## Hill حِل

Lawful ,permissible

It is a less common alternative to the word "Halaal". It occurs in the Qur'an a couple of times. (See, e.g., 5: 5.)

## Hill (al--)الحل

Outside the sanctuary

Beyond the boundaries of Mecca or Medina ,where hunting is permitted.

## Hilm حلم

Clemency ,forbearance

Lenience and toleration of others' wrong doings against one.

## Himaa (al--)الحمى

Sanctuary ,protected area

## Hinth al-yamiin

## حنث اليمين

Foreswearing ,breaking an oath

Not doing something one has sworn to Allah to do.

## Hiqq (Huquuq)

## حقّ (حقوق)

Four year camel

A male camel that has reached its fourth year .A female is called Hiqqah .The term is often used in the calculation of" zakaah" of camels.

## Hiraabah حِرَابة

Highway robbery

Highway robbery is considered a major crime for which one may lose a hand and a leg or even receive the penalty of death.

## Hisaab 1 حساب

Accountability

The Day of Judgement is also called "yawm al-Hisaab" (the Day of Accountability / Reckoning).

## Hisaab 2 حساب

Calculation

## Hisbah (al--)الحسبة

Inspection

Checking that people are behaving according to the rules of the religion, including the inspection of weights and measures used by tradesmen and merchants.

## Hizb (pl. 'aHzaab)

## حزب (أحزاب)

Sub-part

In its general sense the word means a party or group of people, but it is used as a technical term to mean half of the "juz'" in the Qur'an. So the Qur'an consists of 60 Hizbs.

## hubal هُبَل

Hubal

Name of a male idol that was stationed in the Ka'bah before the advent of Islam.

## Hubus

## حبس

Endowment

A building endowed for specific purposes or groups of people.

## hudaa هُدَى

Guidance

The right path or showing it to someone.

## Hujjah 1 (pl. Hujaj)

## حجّة 1 (حُجَج)

Hh

Conclusive evidence, execuse
This word originally comes from the verb Haajja which means to argue or ask for proof of the opponent's argument.

## Hujjah 2
## حجج (حجّة 2)

Authority
When used to refer to a person, the word means an authority in a certain field of learning.



## Hujrah (al--) an-nabawiyyah
## الحجرة النّبويّة

The Prophet's Chamber

The enclosure where we find the tombs of the Prophet (PBUH) and his friends, Abu Bakr and 'Umar. Originally, this was one of the rooms in which the Prophet (PBUH) used to live.

## Hukm (pl. 'aHkaam)
## حكم (أحكام)

Ruling
See "'aHkaam" (rulings).

## Hukm (al--) ash-shar'iyy
## الحكم الشّرعي

Legal decision, Shari'a ruling
The legal decision in Islam regarding an issue.

## Hukm takliifiyy
## حكم تكليفي

Defining law

A communication from the Lawgiver (e.g., God or His Messenger) to followers of the religion to do something or abstain from it, in the form of a demand or an option.

## Hukm waD'iyy حكم وضعي

Man-made law/ ruling

The term is often contrasted with "Hukm shar'iyy" (religious law or ruling). However, writers on the Principles of Islamic law may use it in other senses.

## Hulum (al--) الحلم

Puberty, physical maturity

See "buluugh".

## Huluul حُلول

Incarnation

The belief that God incarnates in a human body, such as Jesus or Ali ibn Abi Talib or 'saints', which is an obvious contradiction to the Qur'anic teachings about Allah and His Majesty. (See, for example, the Qur'an 6: 103 and 42: 11.)

## Hunayn حُنَين

Valley of Hunain

A valley between Mecca and Taif where a major battle between Muslims under the leadership of Prophet Muhammad (PBUH) and polytheists took place after the Prophet's capture of Mecca. (See ghazwat Hunayn.)

## Huquuq az-zawjiyyah حقوق الزّوجيّة

Nuptial rights

The rights a spouse has over his or her partner, or the duties of the spouse.

## Hurmah (pl. Hurumaat) حرمة (حرمات)

Sanctity, sacred thing

Either sacredness or the thing that is made sacred by the religion.

## Hurmah mu'aqqatah حُرمة مؤقّتة

Temporary prohibition

An example is marrying a sister-in-law. In the case of separation from the wife the prohibition no longer applies claim. In some contexts the word is also used to mean 'excuse'.

## Husn al-khuluq حُسن الخلق

Good manners / conduct

The word "khuluq" covers both moral character and good behaviour.

## Husn al-mu'aasharah حُسن المعاشرة

Good companionship

Living with mates in a fair and good way.

## Husnaa (al--)الحسنى

The best

Very often this word is used in the phrase "'asmaa' Allah al-Husnaa", which literally means the best names of Allah or simply "al-'asmaa' al-Husnaa" (the best names). Traditionally, this has been transalted "the Most Beautiful Names / Attributes of Allah".

## Husnayayn (al--)الحُسنَيين

The two best things

This refers to the two alternative outcomes a Muslim fighter for the cause of Allah gets in the battlefield: victory over the enemy or martyrdom (hence entering paradise in the Hereafter).

## huud هود

Hood

Name of a prophet that was sent to a tribe in the Arabian Peninsula. (See the Qur'an, 26: 123-40).

# Ii

## 'ibaadaat (sg. 'ibaadah) (عبادة) عبادات

Worship practices

Any act of worship, such as praying and fasting.

## 'ibaad allaah عباد الله

Servants of Allah

Male people. Sometimes, it may include both male and female people.

## 'ibaadah عبادة

Worship

Worship in Islam includes any act of the tongue (such as remembering Allah or saying a good word) or the body (such as praying or helping someone) with the purpose of seeking Divine pleasure. Therefore, charity can be a good deed or even a kind word.

## 'ibaadat al-awthaan عبادة الأوثان

Idol worship

Worshipping idols or inanimate deities, such as statues of different persons. See "wathaniyyah".

## ibaaDiyyah إباضية

Ibadis

An Islamic sect whose leader was Abdullah ibn AbaD. The followers of the sect are found in the Sultanate of Oman.

## ibaaHah إباحة

Permitting, making lawful

See "Hill".

## ibaaq إباق

Running away

The running away of a slave for no legitimate reason.

## ibliis إبليس

Satan

The name of Satan mentioned in the context of the story of the creation of Adam and Eve in the Qur'an. (See, for example, 15: 30-40).

## ibn as-sabiil ابن السبيل

Way-farer

In the Qur'an this term refers to the person on travel who needs help. He is one of the eight categories of people who deserve charity and to whom alms (zakaat) may be given. (See the Qur'an, 8:60).

## ibn maryam ابن مريم

Son of Mary

Obviously, the reference is to Jesus (PBUH) whose full name is "'iisaa ibn maryam", being fatherless.

## ibraahiim إبراهيم

Abraham

The name of the patriarch (father) of the prophets. He had two well-known sons: Ishamael and Isaac. It was he and his son Ishmael who built the Ka'bah in Mecca. (See the Qur'an, 2: 127.) He is frequently mentioned in the Qur'an. See, e.g., 21: 51-70, for his story of smashing his people' idols, their attempt to burn him and God's saving him miraculously from the fire.) Prophet Muhammad (PBUH) was a descendant of Ishmael.

Islam is the religion of Abraham who called its followers "Muslims" (the Qur'an, 22: 78), and it was he who instituted pilgrimage to Mecca at the command of God (the Qur'an, 22: 26-27).

## ibTaal إبطال

Invalidating, nullifying

The word is used to mean invalidating or nullifying any action, such as ablution, prayer, commercial transaction...etc.

## ibtidaa' ابتداع

Innovating in religion

The terms refers to making innovations (something not done by Prophet Muhammad (PBUH) or his companions), in worship practices especially.
See "bid'ah".

## ibtihaal ابتهال

Supplication

Usually, this implies imploring and earnestly seeking Divine help and guidance. (See the Qur'an, 3: 61.)

## ibtilaa' ابتلاء

Testing

We often find this word with reference to 'testing' a person's faith either with good or bad things. (See the Qur'an, 18:7, e.g.)

## iDaa'at aS-Salaah إضاعة الصلاة

Neglecting Salaah/
formal prayers

Literally, this means 'losing the Salaah', but it refers to ignoring and neglecting to perform it.

## 'iddah (pl. 'idad) عدة (عدد)

Waiting period

The period after which a divorced woman or a widow may marry again. (See "'iddat aT-Talaaq" and "'iddat al-wafaah").

## 'iddat aT-Talaaq

### عدة الطلاق

Divorce waiting period

The time that a divorced woman has to wait before she can remarry. It is either three menstrual periods, three lunar months or the duration of pregnancy, if she is pregnant. (See the Qur'an, 2: 228 and 65: 4).



## 'iddat al-wafaah

### عدة الوفاة

Widow's waiting period

The time a widowed woman has to wait before she can remarry. For a non-pregnant woman, it is four lunar months and ten days. (See the Qur'an, 2: 234).

## 'idghaam bighayri ghunnah

### إدغام بغير غنة

Unnasalized / full assimilation

When the /n/ sound is followed by /r/ or /l/ it is fully assimilated to it; i.e., it becomes /r/ or /l/, losing its own characteristics. For example, (min rabbihim) is pronounced (mir-rabbihim).

## 'idghaam bighunnah

### إدغام بغنة

Nasalized assimilation

When the /n/ sound is followed by /y/, /n/, /m/ or /w/ (as in man ya'mal) it is assimilated to it; i.e., it becomes like it, while the air still comes from the nose. The above example is pronounced ma(n)-yya'mal.

## idhn إذن

Permission

The term refers to actual or implied permission or consent, such as in the case of the woman's indication of consent to marry someone .In the" Hadiith", a previously married woman should indicate this explicitly, a virgin may indicate it implicitly through silence.

## idraak 1 إدراك

Catching, doing in time

Catching the "rak'ah", for example. This means a person joins the "imaam" in congregational prayer before the imaam raises his head from the "rak'ah" (bowing position). "'idraak aS-Salaah" means that one does the prayer before its specified time is over.

## idraak 2 إدراك

Maturing, coming of age

Reaching the age of puberty, which is the age of legal and religious responsibility in Islam. Another term is "buluugh."

## idriis إدريس

Idrees

A prophet of Allah mentioned in the Qur'an (See 19: 56-7).

## 'iffah' / afaaf عفة / عفاف

Chastity ,probity

The word refers to both chastity (of a woman, e.g.) and probity, meaning the avoidance of wrong doing.

## ifk إفك

Serious lie ,slander

A common phrase we have in Islamic history is" Hadiith al-ifk" (story of the slander) in which the enemies of Islam fabricated a rumour accusing Ayshah (wife of the Prophet Muhammad {PBUH}) of adultery! (See the Qur'an, 24: 11-18).

## ifraad allaah bi-l'ibaadah إفراد الله بالعبادة

Worshipping Allah alone

Worshipping God alone means that one's prayers or any form of worship should be made directly to God and for Him, since Islam strongly rejects the idea of intermediaries between God and man or taking partners with Him.

## ifshaa' as-salaam إفشاء السلام

Greeting

Greeting by saying "as-salaamu 'alaykum" ('Peace be with you').

## iftaa' إفتاء

Giving fatwaa (legal opinion)

Giving the Islamic legal position on an issue, normally by a religious scholar or authority.

## ifTaar إفطار

Breaking the fast

Breaking the fast or not observing it. It is also used to refer to the first meal of the day.

## iftaraa (yaftarii) افترى (يفتري)

To fabricate, lie

To make a false claim or story. (See, e.g., the Qu'an, 3: 94.)

## iftiraa' افتراء

False claim

Making a false claim or accusation of something wrong or bad. (See "iftaraa (yaftarii)".

## iftiraash افتراش

Sitting on left foot

In Salaah (formal prayer), this means sitting on one's left foot, while the right foot is in an upright position.

## ightaaba (yaghtaab) اغتاب (يغتاب)

To backbite

To say something bad (even if true) about someone in his absence, which is strongly condemned by the Qur'an. (See 49: 12). See "ghiibah".

## ightasala (yaghtasil) اغتسل (يغتسل)

To wash one's body

To wash the whole body, including the head.

## ightisaal اغتسال

Bathing, having a shower

Washing the whole body, including the head, with the intention of purification. The sunnah is for one to make ablution then wash the whole body, starting from the head

## iHdaad / Hidaad إحداد /حداد

Mourning

Showing sorrow over a deceased person by observing certain actions or customs. In Islam one should not do that for more than three days, except for the grieving widow who should observe it for four lunar months and ten days. (See "'iddat al-wafaah".)

## iHraam إحرام

Ritual consecration

A state in which a pilgrim to Mecca observes certain rules ,such as wearing the'" iHraam" dress and abstaining from acts forbidden for him such as having sex, hunting, wearing perfumes and cutting his hair.

## ighwaa' إغواء

Seduction, leading astray

The act of leading someone to do something wrong. (See the Qur'an: 15:39.)

## iHsaan 1 إحسان

Benefaction

Doing good or favours to others or showing them kindness.

## iHsaan 2 إحسان

Acting in the best way

The Prophet Muhammad (PBUH) defined this word by saying, "that you worship Allah as if you see Him, for even if you do not see Him He sees you."

## iHSaan 1 إحصان

Consummated marriage

In the punishment for fornication, there is a difference between a virgin, "bikr", and a person who was/ is married, "muHSan" ('having been married'.).

## iHSaan 2 إحصان

Being married

The concept is used in the passive participle form "muHSanah", e.g. (See the Qur'an 4: 24.)

## iHSaar إحصار

Hindering

The inability to perform "Hajj" rites due to unforeseen circumstances. The injunction regarding such a case in given in the Qur'an 2:192.

## iHtikaar احتكار

Monopoly

Monopolizing necessary food stuff is forbidden by Islam.

## iHtilaam احتلام

Wet dream, nocturnal emission

Having a dream that causes sexual arousal and ejaculation. This requires "ghusl" (washing the whole body) before one can pray or touch the Qur'an or even recite verses from it.

## iHtisaab
## احتساب

for the sake of God/ for free

Doing something good without expecting reward from a human being.

## iHtiyaaT احتياط

Precautionary measure

Doing something or refraining from it for fear of committing a sin.

## iHyaa' al-lyal إحياء الليل

Night vigil

Staying awake at night in devotions. Literally, the expression means enlivening the night.

## iHyaa' al-mawaat
## إحياء الموات

Cultivation of virgin land

According to some schools of Islamic law, the term means preparing a lot of un-owned land for use, such as residence, stables, or cultivation, by fencing or digging a well. By doing this the person can claim ownership of the land.

## 'iid al-aDHaa عيد الأضحى

Feast of Sacrifice

The feast that occurs on the tenth day of the month of pilgrimage. On this day and the next three days (ayyaam at-tashriiq) one may slaughter his sacrifice or animal offering.

## 'iid al-fiTr عيد الفطر

Feast of Breaking the Fast

The feast which marks the end of Ramadan, the month of fasting.

## iijaab إيجاب

Offer, proposition

Usually, this refers to a guardian offering his trustee (e.g., daughter) in marriage to someone, saying something like: "I give you my daughter X in marriage..."



## iilaa' إيلاء

Vowing continence

A man taking an oath not to have sexual relation with his wife. According to Islamic law, if he insists on doing so after the passage of four months the wife may seek divorce from him. (See the Qur'an, 2: 226.)

## iilyaa' إيلياء

Jerusalem

The name is found in early Islamic history.

## iimaa' إيماء

Implication, prerequisite

In the Science of Principles this means indirect reference to a certain opinion, e.g.

## iimaa' fiS-Salaah إيماء في الصلاة

Miming in prayer

Signaling the motions of the formal prayer (Salaah) with one's head, or even eyes, instead of going through the actual movements, bowing and prostration, for example. This is permissible if one cannot move his body to perform the prayer in the normal way.

## iimaan إيمان

Faith, belief

Firm conviction and belief in someone or something. See "arkaan al-'iimaan".

## iiman bil-qadar إيمان بالقدر

Belief in predestination

Belief that God has the final decision in all affairs and that He has prior knowledge of all that happens in the universe.

## iimaan bil-yawm al-aakhir

## إيمان باليوم الآخر

Belief in the Hereafter

Belief in the physical resurrection of the dead, Day of Judgment and life in the Hereafter.

## 'iisaa ibn maryam

## عيسى بن مريم

Jesus son of Mary

The Prophet Jesus (PBUH). There are many references in the Qur'an to his miraculous birth (3: 45-47; 19: 16-30), miracles (3: 49), and attempted crucifixion (4: 157), prophecy of the coming of Prophet Muhammad (PBUH) after hi (61: 6), among many aspects of his life.

## iitaa' az-zakaah

## إيتاء الزكاة

Alms-giving

Paying alms or what some call the poor dues. This is one of the five pillars of Islam. (See "zakaah").

## iithaar إيثار

Altruism, selflessness

Giving preference to others over oneself, which is a highly commended act. (See the Qur'an 59:9.)

## i'jaaz إعجاز

Miraculous nature; inimitability

Very often we have the expression "i'jaaz al-qur'aan" to refer to the miraculous nature of the Qur'an, aspects that prove its supernatural (Divine) origin. (See the Qur'an, 17: 88.) Linguistically, the word means challenging someone to something that is impossible for him to do.

## i'jaaz (al-) fi-lqur'aan

## الإعجاز في القرآن

miraculous aspects of the Qur'an. Thes aspects have been described as being linguistics/ stylistic, legislative, scientific and historical. Many works have been written on the subject by scholars in different disciplines.

## ijaazah إجازة

Licensing, giving permission

In the religious context, this means giving a student permission to teach what he has learnt from a certain scholar (his shaykh).

## ijmaa' إجماع

Consensus

The agreement of Muslim scholars over a certain issue. It is considered one of the main sources of Islamic jurisprudence

**ijmaa' Dimniyy إجماع ضمني**

Implicit consensus

The case when certain scholars express an opinion and it is widely spread. Yet, no contemporary scholar objects to it.

**ijmaa' SariiH إجماع صريح**

Explicit consensus

This is the case where scholars explicitly agree on a certain issue.

Ii

**ijmaa' sukuutii إجماع سكوتي**

Consensus by silence

Consensus achieved by the lack of objection to an opinion.

**ijtihaad اجتهاد**

Informed reasoning

Reasoning carried out by a Muslim, based on his knowledge of the Qur'an and teachings of the Prophet (PBUH), in a matter not specified by either.

**Ikhfaa' إخفاء**

Homorganic assimilation

Literally, the word means 'hiding', but in Qur'anic phonetics it refers to the fact that the sound /n/ becomes similar (' is assimilated') to the following consonant in its place of articulation ("makhraj") but maintains its nasality. For example, in the expression "man dhalladhii" the air for the /n/ consonant comes out between the teeth like the /dh/ which follows it.

**ikhlaaS إخلاص**

Sincerity, loyalty

This word is used in Islamic theology in the sense of devoting one's worship to Allah Alone and believing in His absolute oneness. Chapter 112 is called "suurat al-'ikhlaaS."

**ikhtilaaf اختلاف**

Divergence

In the context of juristic opinions, the term refers to divergence of views.

**ikraah إكراه**

Compulsion

Islam is agains compelling people to embrace it. We read in the Qur'an: "Let there be no compulsion in religion..." (the Qur'an, 2: 256.)

Forcing someone to do something against his/her will relieves the latter from liability and accountability. (See the Qur'an, 16: 106.).

## ilaah إله

God ,deity

## ilHaad 1 إلحاد

Atheism

The denial of the existence of God.

## ilHaad2 إلحاد

Deviation from the truth

The word is used in the Qur'an (25 :22)to refer to any serious sin.

## ilhaam إلهام

Inspiration

Normally ,this refers to Divine inspiration.

## ilHaaq إلحاق

Analogical extension

Treating an issue or matter like another one by analogy.

## 'illah (pl. 'ilal) (علل) علة

Reason ,cause

The reason behind a certain injunction or ruling.

## 'ilm al-faraa'iD علم الفرائض

Science of inheritance shares

The science which studies methods of distributing the inheritance and calculating the shares of different heirs according to Qur'anic injunctions.

## 'ilm al-fiqh علم الفقه

Science of jurisprudence

The field of knowledge that deals with issues related to worship matters as well as transactions.

## 'ilm al-firaasah علم الفراسة

Physiognomy

The word firaasah has many meanings usually related to keenness of the mind ,such as discernment ,having a keen eye… etc .As a field of knowledge) more an art than a science (it means the ability of judging character by the study of physical features.

## 'ilm al-Hadiith علم الحديث

Science of hadeeth

The science which studies the principles of authenticating the hadeeth text,such as the evaluation of the narrators ,chain of narration and methods of transmission.

## 'ilm al-kalaam علم الكلام

Dialectic theology

The study of theology in terms of logic and philosophy.

## 'ilm al-uSuul

## علم الأصول

Sciene of the Principles

Usually this refers to "'ilm uSuul

al-fiqh" ('science of the principles of jurisprudence') which is a special field of investigation that studies the principles of reasoning, inferncing and deduction of rules regarding different aspects of the religion.

## 'ilm al-yaqiin علم اليقين

Certainty of knowledge

The certainty one reaches through observation and logical deduction.

## 'ilm at-tajwiid علم التّجويد

Science of Qur'anic recitation/ Qur'anic phonetics

The science which studies the rules of correct recitation of the Qur'an, including enunication of sounds, elongation of vowels and assimilation of the /n/ consonant.

## 'ilm at-tawHiid علم التّوحيد

Theology

The study of issues related to God, His attributes, and other matters of belief, such as the belief in the Hereafter, the unseen…etc.

## 'ilmaaniyyah علمانيّة

Secularism

The denial of religious authority in our lives.

## imaam 1 (pl. a'immah) إمام 1 (أئمة)

Leading scholar

The term is used to refer to a leading scholar or a founder of a school of Islamic law, usually in religious subjects, like imaam Bukhaari or imaam Abu Haniifah…etc.

## imaam 2 (pl. a'immah) إمَام 2 (أئمّة)

Leader, head

Someone who leads the congregational worship or is a head of the Muslim community.

## imaam al-muslimiin إمَام المسلمين

Leader of the Muslims

Often, this term refers to the caliph or the ruler.

## imaam raatib إمام راتب

Regular imam / leader

The person who regularly leads congregational prayer in a mosque, whether officially appointed or not.

## imaamah إمامة

Imamate, leadership

Very often, the term refers to religious leadership. (See "imaam.("

## 'imaamah (pl. 'amaa'im) عمامة (عمائم)

Turban

A piece of cloth wound around the top of the head. Wearing it is a sunnah of the Prophet (PBUH).

## imaamiyyah إمامية

Imamis

Muslims who claim that Imam Aliyy ,the Prophet's cousin, should have been his successor.

## imhaal إمهال

Giving a grace period

Giving someone additional time to do something required, such as paying a debt.

## imsaak إمساك

Keeping, withholding

This comes from the verb "'amsaka" (to hold). The noun could mean 'holding, keeping, withholding or abstention' depending on the context. In the Qur'an (2: 229) it refers to keeping or retaining the wife.

## inaabah 1 إنابة

Delegating someone

To delegate someone to do something on your behalf. The person delegated is called "naa'ib".

## inaabah 2 إنابة

Turning in repentance

We find this sense of the word in the Qur'an (39:17) and in other verses, where we find the adjective "muniib."

## innaa lillaahi wa' innaa 'ilayhi raaji'uun إنا لله و إنا إليه راجعون

To Allah we belong and to Him we shall return.

This is the sentence a Muslim should say whenever any misfortune befalls him/ her. See the Qur'an, 2: 156-7, where the rewards for saying this with full conviction is mentioned.

## injiil إنجيل

Gospel

The Book originally revealed to

the Prophet Jesus) PBUH .(Now it is found in many forms ,which Muslims consider to be distorted or altered.

**'inniin عنّين**

Impotent

A man who cannot perform sexual intercourse especially due to inability to reach erection of his organ.The husband's impotence is considered a legitimate ground for the wife to seek divorce.

Ii

**inshaa 'allaah إن شاء الله**

God willing

If Allah wills (it). A Muslim is advised to say this expression whenever he talks about doing something in the future, out of humility and recognition of Divine Will being above all wills and circumstances.

**intiqaal انتقال**

Changing

In the Science of Principles ,this means changing the school of thought one is following ,such as changing from Hanafi to Hanbali school.

**inzaal إنزال**

Ejaculation

Ejaculation requires major ablution (ghusl), regardless of its cause.

**inZaar إنظار**

Grant of respite

Giving someone the chance to fulfill an obligation at a later time or date .Another word of similar meaning is" imhaal" ('giving a grace period').

**iqaalah إقالة**

Releasing from obligation

Allowing a party in a transaction to cancel the deal.

**iqaam aS-Salaah إقام الصلاة**

Performing salat (formal prayer)

This is the second of the five pillars of Islam. It means observing the five daily prayers.

**iqaamah (al--) الإقامة**

Readiness call

The call which announces that the imam is ready for congregational worship. Its text is similar to the "'adhaan", except that there is an additional sentence which translates, "prayer is being performed".

**iqaamat al-Hadd إقامة الحد**

Carrying out the Hadd

See "Hadd".

## iqlaab إقلاب

Labialization

The labialization of the /n/ sound; i.e., making it /m/, when it is followed by the /b/ sound. (e.g., min ba'd becomes mim-ba'd).

## iqraar 1 إقرار

Acknowledgement

Acknowledging someone else's right over something or simply of being right.

## iqraar 2 إقرار

Confession

Confessing to something or a belief.

## iqraar 3 إقرار

Approving

Indicating approval of an action or saying by somebody else, or at least not expressing disapproval.

## iqT إقط

Dried yogurt

Yogurt paste that is dried in the sun. It is one of the categories of food that may be given in "Sadaqat al-fiTr."

## iqtadaa (yaqtadii) bi اقتدى (يقتدي) بـ

To emulate

To follow someone as a model for his actions, such as emulating the Prophet (PBUH) or following the imam in congregational worship.

## iqtara'a (yaqtari') اقترع (يقترع)

Cast lots

See "iqtiraa'".

## iqtidaa' اقتداء

Emulation

Following someone's actions.

## iqtiDaa' an-naSS اقتضاء النص

Presumed meaning

A meaning that has to be presumed for a correct understanding of a text.

## iqtiSaaS اقتصاص

Seeking retaliation (qiSaaS)

Seeking retaliation, such as the killing of a person who murdered a relative.

## iraadah إرادة

intention or will

In the expression "'iraadatu-llaah" it means Divine Will.

## 'iraafah عرافة

Soothsaying, divination

The practice of fortune telling and claiming knowledge of the unseen, which strongly denounced by Islam.

## iram إرم

Iram

The name of a nation that used to live in the Arabian Peninsula long before the advent of Islam. They are also known as 'aad. (See the Qur'an, 84: 6-7).

## 'irD (pl. 'a'raaD) عرض (أعراض)

Honour

Though this word is used often to refer to honour in the sex related matters, it covers one's name and the reputation of his family as well.

## irDaa' إرضاع

Breast feeding

Technically, this means suckling a baby, as opposed to "riDaa'(ah)". If this is done five or more times, then the woman becomes a 'foster mother'. Both she and her children become like blood relations to the baby in matters of marriage.

## irdabb (pl. araadib) أردب (أرادب)

A unit of dry measure. It is estimated to be between 66 to 80.5 liters.

## irtadda (yartadd) (ارتد (يرتد

To apostasize

To reject Islam after having accepted it. According to Islamic law, a person who does so deserves capital punishment.

## irtidaad ارتداد

Apostasy

Rejecting the faith of Islam after having accepted it. (See "riddah").

## iSaabat al-l'ayn إصابة العين

Evil eye effect

Being affected by an evil eye, usually of someone jealous of the affected person (al-maHsuud). Another word is "Hasad".

## isbaagh al-wuDuu' إسباغ الوضوء

Careful ablution'

Properly washing every required member of the body in the "wuduua'" (ablution).

## isbaal إسبال

Letting fall

Making one's garment ("thawb") or "izaar" (loin cloth) too long, below the heel. This is forbidden for men, since it is considered a sign of vanity.

## 'ishaa' (al--) العشاء

Late evening

The time that begins with the disappearance of the red dusk after sunset. This is the time of the fifth prayer of the day in Islam.

## isHaaq إسحاق

Isaac

The second son of the Prophet Abraham (PBUH), born to him after Ishmael. (See the Qur'an, 37: 101-112). He is the father of the Prophet Jacob.

## ish'aar إشعار

marking

Marking a camel for sacrifice.

## ishaarat an-naSS إشارة النص

Alluded meaning

Meaning that is inferred from a certain text, but not explicitly stated.

## ishtaraTa (yashtariT) اشترط (يشترط)

To stipulate, set conditions

## iSlaaH dhaat al-bayn إصلاح ذات البين

Peace making

Bringing peace and reconciliation between ftghting parties, which is a highly recommended act of charity.

## ism (al--) al-a'Zam الاسم الأعظم

The Supreme Name

The Special Name of Allah which comprehends all His Attributes.

## Ismaa'iil إسماعيل

Ishmael

The first son born to the Prophet Abraham (PBUH). His mother was Hager. It was Ishmael who helped Abraham to build the Ka'bah in Mecca, and it was he who was offered for sacrifice, not Isaac, as claimed by some people. (See the Qur'an, 37: 100-112). The Prophet Muhammad (PBUH) is a descendant of the Prophet Abraham (PBUH) through his son Ishmael.

## ismaa'iiliyyah إسماعيلية

Ismaelis

A shi'ite group who claim to be followers of Ismael ibn Ja'far. They are found especially in some East African countries.

## 'iSmah 1 عصمة

Infallibility

Protection provided by Allah against sinning, which is normally given to prophets and messengers of Allah.

## 'iSmah 2 عصمة

right to divorce

A term used in modern times to mean the right to divorce, which is normally in the hands of the husband, but the wife may ask for it in the marriage contract.



## isnaad al-Hadiith إسناد الحديث

Citing chain of narrators

Giving the names of the persons involved in transmitting a certain prophetic tradition up to the Prophet(PBUH).

## isqaaT إسقاط

Abortion

Normally this refers to natural abortion. Induced abortion is forbidden by Islam, except under specified conditions such as saving the life of the mother.

## israa' إسراء

Night journey

The night journey of the Prophet Muhammad (PBUH) from Mecca to Jerusalem. (See the Qur'an, 17: 1). Both the night journey and the 'ascension' ("mi'raaj") occurred on the same night.

## israaf إسراف

Wasting, extravagance

Using or spending more than necessary, which is condemned by Islam.

## israafiil إسرافيل

Israfeel

The angel who will blow / sound "al-Suur" (the trumpet) on the Day of Judgment. (See the Qur'an, 27: 87.)

## Israa'iil إسرائيل

Israel

This is said to be a name of Prophet Jacob; hence his descendants are called "banii israa'iil" ('children of Israel' or 'Israelites'), an expression used in the Qur'an to refer to early Jews. But we have to know that the majority of today's Jews are not Israelites (descendants of Jacob), since almost all Jews of Western origin are actually descendants of Central Asia Khazars who had converted to Jewdaism about a thousand years ago, being ruled by Jewish kings.

## Israa'iiliyyaat إسرائيليات

In the science of the principles of Qur'anic exegesis ("tafsiir"), this terms refers to information obtained from Jewish sources (based on the Old Testament), which has to be carefully evaluated in light of Islamic teachings. For example, Muslim scholars would reject stories alleging that Prophets of God committed immoral things or would object to ascribing human qualities to God the Almighty.

## ista'aadha (yasti'iidh)

## استعاذ (يستعيذ)

Seek refuge

Usually, this verb is used in the expression "ista'aadha billaahi" (He sought refuge in Allah) from something bad, such as Satan or Hell fire.

## ista'dhana (yasta'dhin)

## استأذن (يستأذن)

Ask permission

See "isti'dhaan'.

## istakbara (yastakbir)

## استكبر (يستكبر)

To be conceited

This verb means that a person to be conceited, suffering from "kibr" (vanity and arrogance), hence does not accept the truth. (See, e.g., the Qur'an, 2: 34.)

## istarja'a (yastiarji')

## استرجع (يسترجع)

Seek Divine solace

To say "'innaa lillaahi wa 'innaa 'ilayhi raaji'uun" (To Allah we belong, and to Him we shall return). This is the expression a Muslim should say when misfortune (such as death in the family) befalls him. (See the Qur'an, 2: 156).

## istataaba (yastatiib)

## استتاب (يستتيب)

To ask sb. to repent

See "istitaabah."

## isti'aadhah (al--)

## الاستعاذة

Seeking refuge

Often this means seeking refuge in Allah from Satan by reciting: "a'uudhu bi-llaahi min ash-shayTaanir-rajiim" (I seek refuge in Allah from the cursed Satan). A Muslim is required to recite this before reading the Qur'an. (See the Qur'an 16: 98).

## istiHsaan استحسان

Juristic preference

In the absence of clear rulings on certain matters in the main sources of Islamic law ,the jurist may resort to what is considered preferable in terms of the general good" ,maSlaHaH mursalah."

## istibraa استبراء '

Ascertaining purity

Making sure that one is clean from impurities like urine or stool .It is also used to mean ascertaining that a woman is not pregnant.



## isti'dhaan استئذان

Asking permission

The verb "ista'dhana" is used in the Qur'an in the sense of 'execusing oneself' (See the Qur'an, 9: 44-45.) It is also used to mean asking permission to enter a house or room, by knocking and announcing oneself and waiting for permission, which is an Islamic rule of conduct. (the Qur'an, 24: 58.)

## istidlaal استدلال

Reasoning

## istiftaa استفتاء '

Seeking legal opinion on religious matters .The person who gives such opinion is called a" mufti".

## istighfaar استغفار

Asking for forgiveness

Asking Allah for forgiveness. The simplest prayer is "astaghfiru-llaah" (I ask Allah for fogiveness). There are many longer and more elaborate versions. The Prophet (PBUH) recommended this form of prayer, pointing out that he said it more than seventy times every day.

## istiHaaDah استحاضة

False menstruation

Vaginal bleeding other than regular menses.

## istiHbaab استحباب

Recommending something.

Literally, the word means liking'. Technically, it means considering something commendable or plausible, but not required.

## istiHdaad استحداد

Removing pubic hair

This could be done through plucking or shaving. It is one of the hygienic practices to be observed by a Muslim.

## istihlaal استهلال

Indicating life

Anything on the part of the new

born baby medicating that it is alive, at the time of birth.

## istiHsaan استحسان

Considering sth. better

As a source of Islamic law, the acceptance of a rule because of its superior equity in comparison with an already established law.

## istiHyaa' استحياء

Shyness, bashfulness

See also "Hayaa."'

## istiilaad استيلاد

Impregnating a slave

The master's impregnating his bondswoman or slave girl.

## istijmaar استجمار

Cleansing with pebbles

Cleansing the private parts (after the call of nature) with pebbles or any other solid object ,such as toilet paper .Bones are to be avoided.

## istikbaar استكبار

Arrogance ,being arrogant

This is the verbal noun from "istakbara ."Technically ,it has been defined as rejecting truth.

## istikhaarah استخارة

Seeking Divine guidance

Seeking Divine guidance in an important matter .The usual procedure is praying two" rak'ahs" after which one says some prayers asking Allah's guidance in the affair ,by facilitating it if it is good, and by making it unattainable if it is bad for the supplicant.

## istikhlaaf استخلاف

Appointing a successor / trustee

Appoint someone to be successor. In the Qur'anic context ,the word would be best translated as appointing a trustee or vicegerent.

## iSTilaaH اصطلاح

Technical term

A word or expression used by specialists with a specific meaning, other than the one in common usage.

## istimnaa' استمناء

Masturbation

Masturbation is forbidden in Islam ,and if ejaculation occurs one has to have" ghusl" (wash the whole body) before he can pray or touch the Qur'an.

## istinbaaT استنباط

Deduction, inference

Ii

The process of deriving certain rules or meanings from a text.

**istinjaa' استنجاء**

Washing the private parts

Washing the private parts of the body to remove the urine or stool.

**istinshaaq استنشاق**

Sniffing water

Sniffing water and squeezing it out of the nose in order to cleanse the nostrils, in the process of ablution.



**istiqaamah استقامة**

Uprightness

Living according to the teachings of Islam, carefully observing its injunctions and prohibitions in one's actions. This word is found in its verbal form "istaqaama" (See the Qur'an 41: 30.) The imperative forms ("istaqim, istaqiimuu" 'Be upright and straight'!), is found more frequently in the Qur'an. (See, e.g., 41:6 and 42:15.)

**istiqbaal al-qiblah**
**استقبال القبلة**

Facing the Ka'bah

Facing the Ka'bah is required in formal prayers ("Salaah") and recommended when making supplications.

**istiqraa' استقراء**

Induction

Studying instances to reach a conclusion regarding a certain act.

**istiSHaab استصحاب**

Presumption of continuity

In the Science of Principles, this means presuming that a case or condition that was there earlier still exists unless proven otherwise.

**istiSlaaH استصلاح**

Considering public interest

In the Science of Principles, taking public good into consideration in deciding matters not specified in the main sources of Islamic law.

**istishhaad استشهاد**

Martyrdom

Dying for the Cause of Allah, such as while fighting the enemies of the faith or defending a Muslim territory.

**istislaam استسلام**

Submission, surrender

In the Islamic religious context this refers to submitting totally to Allah's Will.

**istisqaa' استسقاء**

Praying for rain

See "Salaat al-istisqaa."'

## istitaabah استتابة

Ordering sb .to repent

To instruct somebody that he or she should repent from some sinful act, such as neglecting formal prayers ("Salaah") or saying blasphemous things, or giving him/ her the chance to repent before punishing him/ her.

## i'taaq إعتاق

Manumission

See "'itq".

## i'tanaqa (ya'taniq) al-islaam

## اعتنق (يعتنق) الإسلام

Embrace Islam

To convert to Islam.

## i'tamar (ya'tamir)

## اعتمر (يعتمر)

To make 'umrah (lesser pilgrimage)

See "'umrah".

## 'iTbaaq إطباق

Velarization

Raising the rear part of the tongue while producing a certain sound. (See "tafkhiim" too).

## 'ithm (pl. 'aathaam)

## ( إثم (آثام

Sin, wrong doing

Any act that violates the teachings of Islam.

## ithnaa 'ashariyyah اثنا عشرية

Twelvers

A sub-sect of the Shi'ites who believe in twelve "imaams'.

## i'tibaar اعتبار

Learning a lesson

Taking a lesson from what happened to others, e.g. (See the Qur'an, 59:2)

## i'tidaad اعتداد

Being in waiting period

To be in the waiting period before getting married again, such as the duration of pregnancy of a divorced woman.

## i'tikaaf اعتكاف

Retreat (in mosque)

Staying (usually, a few days) in a mosque for devotions, and going out only for necessary things.

## i'tiSaam اعتصام

Holding fast

May mean putting one's faith in someone.

## iTmi'naan fiS-Salaah اطمئنان فى الصلاة

Proper performance of prayer

One of the conditions to be observed while performing the prayer is the observance of propriety in the sense of standing, bowing, prostrating, and sitting in a slow, respectful manner, remembering that one is in the presence of the Almighty Allah.

## 'itq raqabah عتق رقبة

Manumission of a slave

Setting a slave free, which is a very highly recommended act of charity. Sometimes, it is required in expiation of certain sins. A synonym of the expression is "fakku raqabah".

## 'itrat an-nabiyy عترة النبي (ص)

Family of the Prophet

Descendants of the Prophet Muhammad (PBUH).

## ittaqaa (yattaqii) اتقى (يتقي)

To fear God

The word means both to fear God and to seek protection (from Hell fire)

Many scholars have translated the word "be righteous". The idea here is probably that one seeks protection from Allah's wrath and punishment by obeying and fearing Him. (See example of use of this word in the Qur'an, 2:203 and 92:5).

## ittaqi-llaah اتق الله

Have fear of God

This a frequently heard expression in Islamic preaching (e.g, teachings of Prophet Muhammad (PBUH) and even in daily conversations until today.

Basically, it is a reminder to the listener that he should be good and fair, because God is watching him. In a famous Hadiith, we find: "ittaqi-llaaha haythumaa kunta…" ('Have fear of God wherever you are…') The form of addressing more than one (male) person is: "ittaquu allaaah". (See, e.g., the Qur'an, 2: 206). It is worth noting that the verb is found in its different imperative forms very frequently in the Qur'an.

## ittibaa' اتّباع

Following others

The term often refers to following

the teachings or practices of certain scholars or religious leaders.

## ittibaa' al-hawaa

## اتباع الهوى

Following whims

A Muslim is instructed to follow the teachings of the religion, rather than follow his own whims and desires. (See the Qur'an, 6: 56.)

## ittikaal اتكال

Trusting in, depending on

The word is often used to refer to leaving matters in the Hands of God. The most common expression used by Muslims is, "tawakkaltu 'ala-llaah" which means, "I leave the matter in the Hands of God".

## 'iyaadat al-mariiD

## عيادة المريض

Visiting the sick

Visiting a sick Muslim is a recommended act of charity.

## izaar (pl. 'uzur) رازإ (رزأ)

Loin-cloth

A piece of cloth worn around the loins to cover the lower part of the body. It is like a skirt, worn by men.

## 'iZah (pl. 'iZaat)

## عظة (عظات)

Sermon, exhortation

A religious talk given in preaching.

## iZhaar إظهار

Clear enunciation

The clear enunciation of the /n/ or /m/ sounds in the recitation of the Qur'an, which is done when these consonants are followed by certain sounds, such as "hamza" (glottal stop) and "haa'" (/h/).

## 'izraa'iil عزرائيل

Izraa'eel

The name of the angel of death, according to popular Islamic traditions.

# J j

## jaabii (pl. jubaah) جابي (جباة)

Tax collector

The person in charge of collecting taxes and alms on behalf of the government.

## jaahara (yujaahir) جاهر (يجاهر)



To publicize

This term is often used with wrong acts and sinning ,to mean doing them in public or boast of them.

## jaahiliyyah (al--) الجاهلية

Dark ignorance ,pre-Islamic era
The time of ignorance is used to refer to the historical era in Arabia before Islam .The term is sometimes used to refer to any un-Islamic practices.

## jaa'iz جائز

Permissible

The opposite of" Haraam" (forbidden). It is synonymous to "Halaal."

## jaaluut جالوت

Goliath

The tyrant king of the disbelievers who was killed by the Prophet David. (See the Qur'an, 2: 250-251).

## jaami' (al--) الجامع

The Gatherer

A Divine Attribute of Allah. The One Who brings all beings and things (including the opposites) together.

## Jaami' (al--) aSSaHiiH الجامع الصحيح

Authentic collections

This term is used to refer to the Hadiith book compiled by imam Al-Bukhaarii, since it is considered the most authentic book of its nature.

## jaami' (jawaami') جامع (جوامع)

Central mosque

The word is short for al-masjid al-jaami' (the mosque that brings people together). It is often used to refer to a mosque where Friday services are held, since in many Muslim countries not all mosques are used for that purpose.

## jaaza (yajuuz)
## جاز (يجوز)

To be permissible
Not be forbidden.

## jaann (sg. jinniyy)
## جان (جني)

Jinn

Beings created from fire, and not normally visible to humans. It is believed that they may assume different visible forms. The message of Islam is directed to them just as it is to human beings. (See the Qur'an, 72; 46: 29-32; 55: 15).

## jaariyah (pl. jawaarii)
## جارية (جواري)

Young girl, bondswoman
The word was used for both meanings: a young girl or a bondswoman. But nowadays it is often used in the second sense, literally or figuratively.

## jaar(un) junub جار جنب

Far neighbour

A neighbour who is not next door. It could also mean a neighbour who is a relative.

## jabbaar (al--) الجبار

The Highest Potentate

A Divine Attribute of Allah. The One Who makes everyone and everything obey His will.

## jabal ar-raHmah

## جبل الرحمة

Mountain of Mercy

The mountain in the Plain of 'arafah from which the Prophet Muhammad (PBUH) gave his farewell speech ("khuTbat al-wadaa'").

## jabriyyah (al--) الجبرية

Predeterminism / predeterminists

The denial of all forms of free will, or the followers of such a belief.

## jadha' aD-Da'n

## جذع الضأن

One year old sheep

A sheep that has completed one year of age. Jadha' is also used with goats with same meaning.

## jadha' al-'ibil

## جذع الإبل

Four year old camel

A camel that has completed four years of age.

## Ja'farii جعفري

Jaffari

A follower of a Shi'ite sect who claim to follow imam Ja'far al-Sadiq, a descendant of Imam Ali, the Prophet Muhammad's cousin and son-in-law.



## jaHada1 (yajHad)

## جحد 1 (يجحد)

To reject, deny

In the context of religious precepts and rituals, the word means to reject them or deny their importance.

## jaHada2 (yalHad)

## جحد 2 (يجحد)

To show ingratitude

With reference to favours, the verb means to deny them and be ungrateful.

## jahannam جهنم

Hell

The word is found in many parts of the Qur'an where it is mentioned as the punishment for those who reject the truth and and fight it. (See, e.g, the Qur'an, 2: 206.)

## jaHiim جحيم

Hell-fire

In the Qur'an we find many references to this word which mentioned as the abode of arrogant disbelievers in the Hereafter. (See, for example, 79: 36-39.)

## Jahr bi-lqiraa'ah

## جهر بالقراءة

Reciting aloud

Reciting the Qur'anic verses aloud in the standing position in the "Salaah" performed during the night (sunset, late evening and dawn.)

## jahriyyah (Salaah --)

## جهرية (صلاة)

Loud prayers

The term refers to the mode of reciting the Qur'an in the standing position of the" Salaah". The prayer during which this is done aloud is called "Salaah jahriyyah", as opposed to "sirriyyah" (secret, softly) in which the recitation of the Qur'an is done softly in a manner, heard only by the person reciting. The prayers done during the night (sunset, late evening and dawn) fall under this category.

## jald جلد

Flogging

See "jaldah".

## jaldah (pl. jaldaat) جلدة (جلدات)

Lash

In the punishment by flogging, usually the number of lashes is determined by the kind of crime, such as 80 or 100 lashes.

## jaliil (al--) الجليل

The Ever-Majestic

A Divine Attribute of Allah. The One Whose Majesty is incomparable.

## jamaa'ah جماعة

Group, congregation

We find this word in expressions like "Salaat al-jamaa'ah" (congregational prayer) and "jamaa'at al-muslimiin" (the Muslim community)…etc.

## jamaa'ah 'uduul جماعة عدول

Men of integrity

Good Muslim men who observe their religious duties and have moral integrity.

## jamaraat (sg. jamrah) جمرات (جمرة)

Stoning sites

The sites where a pilgrim throws seven pebbles at each pillar (symbolizing Satan). There are three such sites at Mina, near Makkah: the major, the middle and the minor.

## jam' جمع

Combining

Combining two prayers (noon and afternoon or sunset and late evening) by performing them at the time of either.

## jam' Salaatayn جمع صلاتين

Combining two prayers

See "jam'".

## jam' ta'khiir جمع تأخير

Delayed combining

In the context of the "Salaah", this means combining either "Zuhr" and "'aSr" (noon and afternoon) or "maghrib" and "'ishaa'" (sunset and late evening) prayers and performing them at the time of the second of the pair (afternoon and late evening).

## jam' taqdiim جمع تقديم

Advanced combining

In the context of the "Salaah", this means combining either noon and afternoon or sunset and late evening prayers and performing them at the time of the first of the pair (noon and sunset).

## jamrah (pl. jamaraat / jimaar)

## جمرة (جمرات / جمار)

Stoning pillar

The pillar which people believe to symbolize Satan at Mina. There are three pillars which a pilgrim has to stone as a part of the Hajj ritual. The stoning means throwing seven pebbles, one by one, at the pillar while saying "Allahu akbar."

## jamrah (al--) aS-Sughraa

## الجمرة الصغرى

The small stoning pillar

The third of the pillars pilgrims have to stone (by throwing seven pebbles, one by one) as a part of the Hajj rituals.

## jamrah (al--) al-wusTaa

## الجمرة الوسطى

The middle stoning pillar

The second of the pillars pilgrims have to stone (by throwing seven pebbles, one by one, at it) as a part of the Hajj rituals.

## jamrat al'-aqabah

## جمرة العقبة

'Aqabah stoning pillar

The largest of the three pillars pilgrims have to stone by throwing seven pebbles ,one by one ,at them.

## janaabah جَنابة

State of major impurity

The state of ritual impurity as a result of having sex or a wet dream. A Muslim is not supposed to pray or touch the Qur'an or even recite it until he / she has "ghusl" (a full shower, washing the whole body).

## janaazah (pl. janaa'iz)

## جنازة (جنائز)

Funeral

The word is used to refer to a funeral procession too.

## jannah (pl. jannaat)

## جنة (جنات)

Garden ,paradise

Originally, the word means a garden. But it is often used to refer to the Garden of Eden or Paradise. It is found in contrast to "an-naar" ('Hell-fire'), as we can see, e.g., in the Qur'an, 59: 20. The term may be modified by "'adn" ('Eden'-the Qur'an, 9: 72)), or "firdaws" ('Paradise'-the Qur'an, 18: 107), probably indicating different types or classes.

## jannah / jannaat 'adn

## جنة / جنات عدن

Garden(s) of Eden

Some Qur'an exegesists say that '"adn "means' stay and eternity.'

## jarH (al--) (wat-ta'dill)

## الجرح و التعديل

Discrediting and endorsement

A procedure in the science of hadeeth authentication in which the transmitters or reporters of the text are evaluated on the basis of their merits of piety ,memory and general moral integrity.

## jawaaz جواز

Lawfulness ,permissibility

See" jaa'iz."

## jazaa' جزاء

Repayment ,requital

Good or bad repayment, reward or punishment. (See the Qur'an, 25: 15 & 54: 14.)

## jazaakum / jazaak allaahu khayra(n)

## جزاكم / جزاك الله خيرًا

May Allah reward you!

An expression usually said to express gratitude. A common mistake is saying: "jazaakum Allaah" only, because this does not specify the reward. (See "jazaa'").

## jazaa (yajzii)

## جزى (يجزي)

To give one his due

The verb is neutral in the sense that what one is given could be good ("khayr") or bad ("sharr"), whichever one deserves. Therefore, if we want to thank someone we should say: "jazaak Allahu khayran."

## jazuur جَزور

Slaughtered camel

Usually ,we see" laHm al-jazuur" (camel meat), the eating of which may require one to have ablution before praying according to the Hanbali school of Islamic law.

## jibaayah جِباية

Collecting taxes

The act of collecting taxes and alms.

## jibriil جبريل

Gabriel

According to Islamic teachings, Gabriel was the angel who used to bring down the revelations from Allah to His messengers.

## jibt جِبت

Idol

Something worshipped by polytheists.

## jihaad جهاد

Striving, holy war

The term means exerting a great effort, but it has come to mean exerting a great effort in the Cause of Allah, more specifically in the form of fighting.

## jihaad an-nafs جهاد النفس

Fighting the tempting self

The term refers to controlling oneself by forcing it to do righteous deeds and shun wrong ones. A similar expression is "mujaahadat-an-nafs".

## jilbaab (pl. jalaabiib) جلباب (جلابيب)

Overgarment

For women, this refers to a garment normally worn over regular garments such as dresses. Reference to this word is found in the Qur'an (33: 59).

## jimaa' جماع

Copulation, sex act

Copulation leads to "janaabah" which requires washing the whole body to attain ritual purity, even if there is no ejaculation .

## jinnah (sg. jinniyy) جنة (جني)

Jinn

See "jaann".

## jizyah جِزية

Protection tax

The head tax paid by non-Muslim citizens to the Islamic state which is responsible for their protection. See "ahl adh-dhimmah".

## ju'l (pl. ju'uul) (جُعل جعول)

Payment, wage

## juHfah (al--) الجُحفة

Juhfah

Name of the place where people coming from west the Red Sea to start their status of "iHraam" on their way to Mecca for "'umrah" or "Hajj". Today it is in the neighborhood of the town of Raabigh in Saudi Arabia.

## juluus جلوس

Sitting

In formal prayers, this is the position in which a person bends his knees and sits on his legs, with the right foot in vertical position, its toes touching the ground. This is similar to genuflection except that one's buttocks rest fully on the legs.

## jumu'ah (al--) الجمعة

Friday

Friday is a special day in Islam. We are told by the Prophet (PBUH) that Adam was created on this day and entered Paradise on this day.

## Jumaadaa al-uulaa

## جمادى الأولى

Jumada the First

The name of the fifth month of the Islamic calendar.

## jumaadaa ath-thaaniyah

## جمادى الثانية

Jumada the Second

The name of the sixth month of the Islamic calendar. Another name is jumaadaa al-aakhirah.

## jumhuur جمهور

Dominant majority

The term is used to refer to the majority of scholars, short for "jumhuur al-'ulamaa'" .

## junaaH جُناح

Sin, wrong

This word is usually found with the negative particle "laa" (no): "laa JunaaH" ('There is no sin or anything wrong with sth'.) See the Qur'an, 2: 233-236.

## junub جُنُب

In a state of major ritual impurity

See "janaabah."

## juz' (pl. 'ajzaa')

## جزء (أجزاء)

Part

The Holy Qur'an is divided into 30 'ajzaa' (roughly equal parts), each consisting of two "Hizbs".

# Kk

## kaafir (pl. kuffaar / kaafiruun) كافر (كفار / كافرون)

Unbeliever, infidel

Someone who does not believe in Islam and its teachings.

## kaahin (pl. kuhhaan / kahanah) كاهن (كهان / كهنة)

Diviner, soothsayer



A person who claims knowledge of the future. A Muslim is warned against resorting to him for advice.

## kaatib (pl. kuttaab) al-waHy كاتب (كتاب) الوحي

Revelation scribe

A companion of the Prophet (PBUH) who used to write the Qur'anic revelations as dictated by the Prophet (PBUH).

## kaaZim al-ghayZ كاظم الغيظ

Suppressor of anger

Someone who controls his tempter and does not allow rage to take control of him. Controlling one's temper is a highly recommended act. (See the Qur'an, 3: 134.)

## ka'bah (al--) الكعبة

Ka'bah

The cubic building in the centre of the Holy Mosque of Makkah, originally built by the Prophet Abraham and his son Ishmael. (See the Qur'an, 2: 127.) It is the first house of Allah ever known to mankind. It is also referred to in the Qur'an as "al-bayt" (the House) or "al-bayt al-'atiiq" ('the Old House').

## kabbara (yukabbiru) كبر (يكبر)'

To say "Allaahu 'akbar"

Originally ,the word means to magnify or enlarge .But it is normally used in the first sense given above.

## kabiirah (pl. kabaa'ir) كبيرة (كبائر)

Major sin

Any sin that is punishable by "Hadd" ('prescribed punishment') (, such as murder, fornication, stealing …etc.

## kabiir (al--) الكبير

The Ever Great

A Divine Attribute of Allah. The One Whose greatness surpasses that of every other being.

## kadhaba (yakdhib) كذب (يكذب)

To lie

Not to tell the truth. Lying is strongly condemned in Islam, and it its considered a sign of hypocrisy.

## kadhdhaba (yukadhdhib) كذب (يكذب)

To disbelieve, belie

To reject the truth of someone or something. ( See the Qur'an, 25: 11 and 37.)

## kadhib 1 كذب

Telling lies

Not telling the truth.

## kadhib 2 كذب

Falsehood

Opposite of truth.

## kafaalat an-nafs كفالة النفس

Guarantee of person

Taking the responsibility of making sure that the bailed person will be present when so required.

## kafaalat ad-dayn كفالة الدين

Guarantee of debt

This means the guarantor is responsible for making sure that debt is paid back one way or another.

## kafaalat al-yatiim كفالة اليتيم

sponsorship of an orphan

Taking care of an orphan, especially in the material sense. Regarding treatment of orphans, see for example, the Qur'an, 4: 2, 6 and 10.

## kafan (pl. akfaan) كفن (أكفان)

Shroud

The cloth used to enshroud the corpse of a person.

## kafara (yakfur) كفر (يكفر)

To disbelieve

To disbelieve or announce the rejection of faith in Allah or any of His commandments.

## kaffaarah (pl. kaffaaraat) كفارة (كفارات)

Atonement, expiation

An act to be carried out by a Muslim

for committing a wrong (such as involuntary man- slaughter) or not observing an obligation (such as not observing the fast during Ramadan by certain excused people). It includes, among others, feeding a number of poor people or fasting a number of days.

## kaffaarah (pl.kaffaaraat) al-yamiin كفارة (كفارات) اليمين

Atonement of an oath

The atonement one should do for violating an aoth.

## kaffara 1 (yukaffir) كفر 1 (يكفر)

To declare sb. unbeliever

To declare that someone is an unbeliever or has disbelieved, because of a certain deed or words said by him, such as denying the oneness of Allah or denying the necessity of performing the five daily prayers.

## kaffara 2 (yukaffir) كفر 2 (يكفر)

To atone, expiate

To do something in order to atone for a sin or for not doing something one is required to do, such as fasting in the month of Ramadhan. (See "kaffaarah").

## kahaanah كهانة

Soothsaying

Soothsaying is considered a form of polytheism ,since the soothsayer claims knowledge of the unseen. A Muslim is forbidden from visiting a soothsayer or to believe in his words.

## kalaam كلام

Speech ,words

Any utterance ,oral or written .It could also mean language.

## kalaam-al' ,ilm علم الكلام-

Theology

In classical usage, the science which deals with issues related to Divine Attributes and beliefs in general. Now many people use the word "tawHiid" or "'ilm at-tawHiid" ('study of monotheism').

## kalaam allaah كلام الله

Words of Allah ,the Qur'an

The Qur'an is considered the exact words of Allah revealed to the Prophet Muhammad (PBUH) through Archangel Gabriel.

## kaliim allaah كليم الله

Speaker to Allah

Literally, this means the one spoken to by Allah. It refers in

Islamic writings to Prophet Moses to whom Allah spoke at Mount Sinai. (See the Qur'an 4:164.)

## kalimat ash-shahaadah كلمة الشهادة

Declaration of Faith

Saying: "ashhadu an-laa ilaaha illa-llaah wa ashhadu anna muHammadan rasuulu-llaah." (I bear witness that there is no deity except Allah, and I bear witness that Muhammad is the messenger of Allah).

## Kalimah (al--) aT-Tayyibah الكلمة الطيبة

Good Word

Any good word or reciting: "There is no deity except God". (See the Qur'an 14:24.)

## kalamat at-tawHiid كلمة التوحيد

Utterance of monotheism

Testifying that there is no deity except God.

## karaahah كراهة

reprehensibility ,aversion

Considering something reprehensible or distasteful.

## karaamah (pl. karaamaat) كرامة (كرامات)

Extraordinary act

This term literally means' a sign of honour 'and refers to supernatural acts) like walking on water .(It is used in conjunction with saints or men of God other than the prophets ,for whom the word "mu'jizah" (miracle) is used.

## kariim (al--) الكريم

The Most Generous

A Divine Attribute of Allah .The One Whose bounties and favours know no limits.

## karrama allaahu wajhahu كرم الله وجهه

May Allah honour his face

This expression is often used instead of "raDiya allaahu 'anhu" ('May Allah be pleased with him') especially when Muslims speak of Ali, cousin and son-in-law of the Prophet (PBUH) . It has been said that he was the only early convert to Islam who never prostrated to an idol, since he adopted Islam at a very young age. This expression presumably refers to that fact.

## kataba (yaktub) allaah 1 كتب (يكتب) الله 1

Allah enjoined ,decreed

This is one of the senses of the

word as used in the Qur'an and other Islamic texts. We may find this verb in the passive form "kutiba 'alaykum" meaning "it has been ordained upon you (by Allah)."

## kataba (yaktub) allaah 2
## كتب (يكتب) الله 2

Allah destined, foreordained

In Islamic text we find cases where this verb (active and passive forms)
is used in the sense of predestination.

## katama (yaktum) al-Haqq
## كتم (يكتم) الحق

To conceal the truth
To withhold information in order to hide the truth. The Qur'an warns us not to do that (See the Qur'an, 2:42).

## katm / kitmaan ash-shahaadah
## كتم / كتمان الشهادة

Concealing testimony

Not giving testimony, when asked to give it. This is considered a sin, as we can see from the Qur'an (2: 283.)

## kawthar (al--) الكوثر

River of Abundance

The river promised by Allah to the Prophet Muhammad) PBUH( in the Hereafter) .See Chapter108 of the Qur'an.)

## kaZm al-ghayZ
## كظم الغيظ

Controlling temper

Literally, this means suppressing rage. This act is considered one of the qualities of a good believer. (See "kaaZim al-ghayZ"). In the hadeeth we are advised to change our position (from standing to sitting) and even make ablution as a measure to fight loss of temper.

## khaafiD (al--)الخافض

The Supreme Debaser

A Divine Attribute of Allah .The One Who debases and brings humiliation to sinners.

## khaala'at (tukhaali')
## خالعت (تخالع)

To seek khul'

A woman may seek divorce from her husband through the procedure known as" khul'" or "mukhaala'ah". In .this type of agreement the wife may have to pay back the dower given to her by the husband and agree to pay for other expenses as well.

K k

## khaaliq (al--) الخالق

The Creator

A Divine Attribute of Allah. The One Who created everything and everyone from nothing.

## khaashi' خاشع

Humble, submissive

An attribute of the good believer is to be humble and submissive in his prayers. (See the Qur'an, 23: 2).

## khaatam al-'anbiyaa' / an-nabiyyiin
## خاتم الأنبياء / النبيين

Seal of the Prophets

The reference is to the Prophet Muhammad (PBUH) who has been the last and most important in a chain of prophets and messengers sent by God. So there would be no prophet after him. (See the Qur'an, 33: 40).

## khaatam an-nubuwwah
## خاتَم النبوة

Seal of prophecy

A special mark between Prophet Muhammad (PBUH)'s shoulders, which was a sign of him being the Prophet foretold in some scriptures.

## khaaTib (pl. khuTTaab) خاطب (خطاب)

suitor

A man who is asking for someone's hand.

## khaaTibah خاطبة

Female matchmaker

A woman who helps in selecting future grooms and brides for people.

## khabar (pl. akhbaar)
## خبر (أخبار)

Report ,hadith

Though the word simply means a report or piece of new ,in specialized writings it is used to mean a" Hadiith ) "tradition of the Prophet Muhammad) PBUH.(

## khabar al'-aaHaad
## خبر الآحاد

Uniquely reported

A tradition that has been reported by a single narrator ,as opposed to" khabar mutawaatir" (reported by many).

## khabar mutawaatir
## خبر متواتر

Well attested report

A report or tradition reported by a large number of transmitters.

Kk

## khabiir (al--) الخبير

The Ever-Cognizant

A Divine Attribute of Allah. The One Who is knowledgeable of the most secret of things and affairs.

## khabiith خبيث

Bad, wicked, impure

Sometimes, the word "al-khabiith" is used to refer to Satan.

## khalaf (al--) الخَلَف

Succeeding generation(s)

The generations that came later.

## khaliifah 1 (pl. khulafaa') خليفة 1 (خلفاء)

Caliph, successor

Originally, someone who succeeded the Prophet (PBUH). Later, it came to be used to refer to all the heads of the Islamic State, until the last Ottoman ruler.

## khaliifah 2 (pl. khulafaa') خليفة 2 (خلفاء)

Vicegerent, viceroy

In the Qur'an, the term is used to refer to a vicegerent, someone who rules on earth, so to speak, on behalf of Allah. So Adam was made a "khaliifah". (See the Qur'an, 2: 30). And so was David (See the Qur'an, 38: 26).

## khaliifah (al--) ar-raashid الخليفة الراشد

The righteous caliph

The righteous successor to the Prophet (PBUH), Abu Bakr as-Siddiiq or any of his three successors. (See "al-khulafaa' ar-raashiduun").

## khaliil allaah خليل الله

Friend of Allah

This was a title given to the Prophet Abraham .The term" khaliil" implies close relationship, as opposed to "Sadiiq", which does not have this connotation.

## khalq خلق

Physical form, looks

The structure and form of the various parts of the body. It could also mean the general appearance of a person, as opposed to "khuluq" ('manners and morals').

## khalwah (pl. khalaawii) خلوة (خلاوي)

Secluded place

Sometimes, the term is used to refer to a (secluded) area in a mosque, for example, where religious teaching takes place.

## khalwah (pl. khalawaat) خلوة (خلوات)

Being alone, solitude

The term could mean being alone with oneself or with someone. For example, it is forbidden in Islam for a man to be in "khalwah" with a woman who is a stranger to him.

## khamr (pl. khumuur) خمر (خمور)

Wine, alcoholic drink

Any alcoholic drink that may cause intoxication is called "khamr", and it is forbidden for a Muslim to consume or even deal with (such as buying and selling).

## kharaaj خراج

Land tax

Land tax paid to the Muslim treasury which was paid by non-Muslims.

## khashyat allaah خشية الله

Fear of Allah (God)

Reverence to Allah and fear of His punishment.

## khaSiyy (pl. khiSyan) خصي (خصيان)

Eunuch, castrate

A man whose testicles have been removed.

## khaTii'ah (pl. khaTaayaa/ khaTii'aat) خطيئة (خطايا / خطيئات)

Sin

Something forbidden by the religion.

## khaTiib (khuTabaa') خطيب (خطباء)

Public speaker

Often, the word is used to refer to the person who gives the Friday sermon.

## khaTiibah خطيبة

Fiancée

A female who has been engaged, but not married yet. According to Islamic law, her fiance is considered a 'stranger' in all regards. She has to observe the "Hijaab" (veil) with him.

## khatm an-nubuwwah 1 ختم النبوة

sealing/ finality of prophethood

Indicating that Muhammad (PBUH) is the last prophet and messenger of Allah. No prophet of messenger would ever come after him, and anyone who claims prophecy has to be false. (See the

Qur'an 33:40.) Besides the Qur'an there are many authentic prophetic traditions that emphasize this point.

## khatm al-qur'aan ختم القرآن

Finishing the Qur'an

Finishing the recitation or reading of the whole Qur'an. Many pious Muslims observe the practice of reading the whole Qur'an in a specific number of days, weeks or months.

## khawaarij (al--) الخوارج

Kharijites (rebellious dissedents)

A fanatic group of Muslims who claimed that the Caliph Ali ibn Abi Taleb and Mu'aawiyah as well others were all unbelievers, and should be killed. They were responsible for the assassination of the fourth Righteous Caliph Ali (RAA).

## khawaatiim al-'a'maal خواتيم الأعمال

The last deeds / actions

The last thing one does in this life, for example.

## khawaatiim as-suurah خواتيم السورة

Concluding verses

The last verses of a chapter in the Qur'an, such as the last two or three verses of Chapter 2, which are highly recommended to be recited by a Muslim at dawn and sunset.

## khayr al-quruun خير القرون

The best generation(s)

Quruun literally means 'centuries', but the "Hadiith" which says: "khayr al-quruun qarnii thumma al-ladhiin yaluunahum thumma al-ladhiina yaluunahum…" has been translated as: "The best generation is mine, then the following one, then the next…"

## khayr 1 (pl. khayraat) خير 1 (خيرات)

Good deed or thing

## khayr 2 خير

Better, superior

The word means both good and better. The expression "bi-khayr" means 'well' or 'in good condition'.

## khayshuum خيشوم

Nose

In Qur'anic phonetics, this

Kk

term is used to refer to the nose; two consonants are produced there: m and n.

## khazraj (al--) الخزرج

Khazraj

One of the two main Arab tribes of Medina at the time of the Prophet Muhammad (PBUH).

## khiDr (al--)

## الخضر

The Khidr

Muslim scholars say that this is the name of the pious man of knowledge referred to in the Chapter of the Cave in the Qur'an from whom the Prophet Moses sought to learn. (See the Qur'an, 18: 66-83).

## khilaafah خلافة

Caliphate

Succession in heading the Muslim community, as a ruler. Originally, it meant succeeding the Prophet (PBUH) in heading the Muslim community. The first "khaliifah" was a successor to the Prophet, and each one was successor to the preceding one.

## khimaar (pl. khumur)

## خِمَار (خُمُر)

Veil ,head cover

Any scarf- like piece of cloth used to cover the whole head and neck and may also be used to cover the bosom of a woman. (See the Qur'an, 24:31(. (C.f. "niqaab".)

## khitaan خِتان

Circumcision

Circumcision or removing the foreskin of the penis is required by Islam for all males.

## khiTbah خِطبة

Betrothal, asking to mary

Asking for someone's hand in marriage.

## khiyaanah خيانة

Treachery, infidelity

This involves deception breach of agreements and promises and failing a trust as well as infidelity.

## khiyaant al-'ahd/ al-'amaanah

## خيانة العهد/الأمانة

Breach of a trust, betrayal

In the "Hadiith" it is considered one of the four signs of a hypocrite.

Kk

## khubth (al--) wa al-khabaa'ith

## الخبث و الخبائث

Evil male and female spirits

The Prophet (PBUH) instructed Muslims to seek refuge in Allah from these spirits whenever they enter a bathroom.

## khuff (pl. akhfaaf) خف (أخفاف)

Light boot

This was like a sock made of leather, similar to boots.

## khul' خُلْع

Khul'

The arrangement in which the wife seeks divorce through making a deal with her husband, such as returning his dower and paying for the wedding expenses.

## khulafaa' (al--) ar-raashiduun

## الخلفاء الراشدون

The Righteous Caliphs

The four heads of the Muslim community who succeeded the Porphet Muhammad (PBUH): Abu Bakr aS-Siddiiq, 'umar ibn al-Khattaab, 'uthmaan ibn 'affaan and 'aliyy ibn abii Taalib.

## khuluq (akhlaaq) خلق (أخلاق)

Manners, morality

The term is a comprehensive one that covers the moral and behavioural aspects of a person. It is reported that the Prophet Muhammad (PBUH) whenever he looked in a mirror he used to pray: "O Allah, make my khuluq (manners and morals as good as You have made my khalq (looks)".

## khumus (al--) الخُمُس

The fifth

This refers to the portion of the war booty that reserved for the Cause of God, His messenger and his near relatives as well for the orphans, the needy and the way farers. (See the Qur'an 8:41.)

## khunthaa (pl. khanaathii) خنثى

Hermaphrodite, bisexual

A person whose gender cannot be determined due to having both male and female sexual organs or neither of them.

## khushuu' خشوع

Submissiveness, humility

The attitude one should show when praying or supplicating.

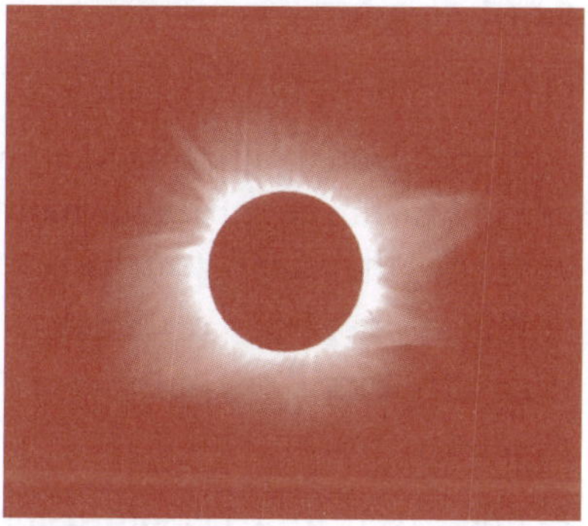

## khusuuf

خسوف

Lunar eclipse

## khuTbah (pl. khuTab)

خطبة (خطب)

Sermon, speech

## khuTbat al-'iid

خطبة العيد

Eid sermon

The sermon given on the day of the Feast of Breaking the Fast, or of Sacrifice. Unlike Friday, the sermon is given after the prayer.

## khuTbat al-Haajah

خطبة الحاجة

Wedding sermon

See "khuTbat an-nikaaH".

## khuTbat al-jumu'ah

خطبة الجمعة

Friday sermon

The sermon given by the imam on Friday congregational service. The service consists of a two-part sermon, followed by two "rak'ahs" of prayer.

## khuTbat an-nikaaH

خطبة النكاح

wedding sermon

A sermon given on the occasion of a wedding ceremony. Sometimes, it is called "khuTbat al-Haajah".

## khuTbat al-wadaa'

خطبة الوداع

The Farewell Sermon

The sermon given by the Prophet Muhammad (PBUH) on the ninth day of the month of pilgrimage at 'Arafah to the largest crowd of pilgrims ever seen until then. It was a comprehensive speech, declaring, among many other issues, oneness of mankind and their equality in the sight of Allah.

## kibr كبر

Arrogance, self conceit

The feeling that one is superior to others; hence, they do not deserve his respect nor his accepting their advice. (See the Qur'an, 40: 56.)

## kibriyaa' كبرياء

Pride, self-respect

Greatness and self-respect. For Allah, this includes majesty. (See the Qur'an, 45: 37).

## kitaabiyy (pl. ahl al-kitaab) كتابي (أهل الكتاب)

Member of the people of the Scripture

A Christian or Jew, who are called in the Qur'an "ahl al-kitaab".

## kitaabiyyah كتابيّة

Christian or Jewish woman

According to Islamic law, a Muslim man may marry a chaste "kitaabiyyah". (See the Qur'an 5:5.).

Kk

## kufr كفر

Disbelief

The word means denying Allah's favours or rejecting His authority.

## kufrun bawaaH كفر بواح

Clear blasphemy

An act that is definitely contrary to Islamic teachings.

## kulliyyaat-al al-khams كليات-ال الخمس

Five universals

It seems that some writers use this term for the more common one "aD-Daruuriyyaat al-khams" ('the five essentials').

## kuhl كُحل

Black antimony

A black semimetallic powder in use in Muslim countries for more than one thousand year for eye lining.

## kunyah كنية

Agnomen

A title given to a person, using the words "abuu" (father of) or "'umm" (mother of), followed by a son's or daughter's name.

## kuswat al-ka'bah كسوة الكعبة

Ka'bah cover

The cloth used to cover the Ka'bah. It is made of black silk and decorated with Qur'anic verses embroidered with gold threads.

# L l

## laa Hawla wa laa quwwata illaa bi-llaah
## لا حول و لا قوة إلا بالله

No power nor might except from Allah

This expression is a highly recommended form of prayer. It is often said by a Muslim to find solace, especially when faced with difficulties.

## laa ‘ilaaha ill-allaah
## لا إله إلا الله

There is no deity except Allah

This is a negation of the existence of any type of deity with the exception of Allah (God). It is the motto of Islam.

## laahuut لاهُوت

Theology

## laat (al--) اللات

Lat

Name of an idol that was worshipped by pagans in Arabia.

## la‘nah لعنة

Curse, damnation

Dismissing from the mercy of God, or depriving one of Divine blessing.

## labbayk allaahumma
## لبيك اللهم

I dutifully answer you, my Lord

I am responding dutifully to Your command or call. This is the expression often repeated by pilgrims.

## laghw لَغو

Idle talk

In the case of an oath, this means an oath said unintentionally.

## laHd (pl. luHuud)
## لحد (لُحُود)

Grave

Technically, this is the hollow part of a grave where a corpse is placed. Whenever possible, a side cavity is dug in the grave for the corpse.

## laHm al-khinziir لحم الخنزير

Pig's meat

Pig's meat as well as any part of a pig's body is considered impure and forbidden for Muslims to eat or even use.

## lahw al-Hadiith لَهْوُ الحديث

Vain talk, futile discourse

Islam discourages its followers from wasting their time in useless things, including vain talk. (See the Qur'an, 31: 61.) In this sense it is similar to "laghw".

## lamam لَمّم

Minor offences

Unintentional minor offences or mistakes, which contrasted with "kabaa'ir" and "fawaaHish" (major sins).

## lamaza (yalmiz) (لَمَز (يلمز

To slander

To find fault with others or speak ill of them, directly or by insinuation, which is condemned by the Qur'an (49: 11).

## laqiiT لَقِيط

foundling

A baby whose parents are unknown.

## laTiif (al--) اللطيف

LI

The Ever-Kindly

A Divine Attribute of Allah. The One Who is Kind to His creation, or Who is too Subtle for people to know His identity.

## lathawiyy لثوي

Alveolar

This refers to sounds for the production of which the tongue touches or comes close to the alveolar ridge, such as t, d, s.

## lawH (al--) al-maHfuuz اللوح المحفوظ

Divine-Protected Tablet

The Depository of all the Divine decrees and willed events, ordained by Allah, since the beginning of creation. (See the Qur'an, 85: 22).

## laylat al-qadr ليلة القدر

The Night of Power / Esteem

The night of the 27th of Ramadan is believed to be the night called "laylat al-qadr" referred to in the Qur'an, Chapter 97.

## li'aan لِعان

Mutual cursing

See "mulaa'anah". Reference to this is found in the Qur'an (24: 6-9).

## libaas al'-iHraam لباس الإحرام

Pilgrim's dress

The special clothing worn by a pilgrim. For men, two sheets of seamless white cloth, one for the upper half of the body ("ridaa'") and the other for the lower half ("'izaar"); for women, a plain proper dress.

## liin al-mu'aamalh لين المعاملة

Gentleness in dealing

Dealing with others in a gentle fashion.

## liin al-qalb لين القلب

Softness of heart

It may refer to kindness as well.

## liin al-qawl لين القول

Mildness in speech

Speaking to people in a nice way, with kind words.

## liin, Harf -- لين ، حرف

Semivowel

The two consonants w and y, as in /nawm/ ('sleep') and /bayt/ ('house').

## lukhuf / likhaaf (sg. lukhfah)

## لخف / لخاف (لخفة)

White slates

White slates were sometimes used in the early days of Islam for writing.

## luqmaan لُقْمان

Luqman

A sage ,pious man to whom reference is made in the Qur'an, Chapter.31

## luqaTah لُقَطَة

Found object

There are certain rules to be observed by a Muslim in handling a found object ,be it animate or inanimate ,such as announcing about it for a certain period of time before keeping it.

## luuT لُوط

Lot

Name of the prophet who was a nephew of the Prophet Abraham (PBUH), we are told. He was sent to a people that practiced homosexuality and were severely punished by Allah. (See the Qur'an, 26: 160-174).

## luuTiyy لُوطي

Homosexual ,sodomite

## liwaaT لِوَاط

Homosexuality ,sodomy

Homosexuality is considered a major sin in Islam. (See the Qur'an, 26: 160-174).

## luzuum لزوم

Implication ,prerequisite

Generally ,this means necessity or obligation .But in the Principles of Islamic Law this means something being a prerequisite, hence is implied by it .The term is synonymous to" mulaazamah" ('accompaniment').

# Mm

## maajid (al--) الماجد

The Glorious

A Divine Attribute of Allah. The One Who deserves real glorification.

## maal (pl. 'amwaal) مال (أموال)

Money ,property

It is often used to mean possessions.

## maalik 1 مالك

Master ,owner

The word comes from the verb "malaka "to possess .We find this word in this sense in" suurat al-faatiHah" (Opening Chapter) as well as in many other parts of the Qur'an.

## maalik 2 مالك

Malik

The name of the guard of Hell. ( See the Qur'an, 43: 77).

## maalik 3 مالك

Malik

Imam Malik was one of the four founders of the major schools of Islamic law. He was born in and taught at Medina, and is known as a traditionalist. His school of thought ("madhhab") is commonly followed in Africa.

## maalik al-mulk مالك الملك

The Ruler of the Dominion

A Divine Attribute of Allah. Master of the universe or the King of kings.

(See the Qur'an, 3: 26.) Sometimes we hear the expression "maalik al-mulk wa al-malشkuut".

## maalikiyy (pl. maalikiyyah) مالكي (مالكية)

Malikite

Follower of Imam Malik.

## maalikiyyah (sg. maalikiyy) مالكية (مالكي)

Malikites ,Malliki school of thought

See" maalikiyy ."This school of thought is widely spread in Africa.

## maani' مانع

Preventing cause ,obstacle

Something that makes another

disallowed ,such as the state of ritual impurity which prevents a Muslim from praying or touching the Qur'an.

## maani' (al--) المانع

The Protector or Withholder

A Divine Attribute of Allah .The One Who protects His servants ,or Who withholds what He wills.

## maa shaa 'allaah ما شاء الله

God bless!

Literally ,this means" What God has willed ."It is usually used to express admiration of something, while indicating the real Causer of this ,Allah .It is a good practice to say this expression every time a Muslim likes something.

## mabruur مبرور

Perfect ,well performed

The term is usually used with "Hajj" to mean pilgrimage which a person performed very well, by avoiding all the actions that nullify or invalidate it, for example.

## madd مد

Elongation

Lengthening of a vowel.

There are different types of elongation mentioned in the books of tajweed: "'aSlii, far'ii, jaa'iz, laazim, Harfii, kalimii" (See these terms in their proper places).

## madd 'aSliyy مد أصلي

Intrinsic elongation

The normal elongation of a long vowel. It is considered equivalent to two short vowel lengths. For example, the vowel in Arabic "laana" (He became soft) is twice as long as the vowel in "lan" (will not).

## madd 'aariD lis-sukuun مد عارض للسكون

Elongation occasioned by finality

Extra elongation of a long vowel when it comes before a word final consonant. If the said consonant is vocalized (followed by a vowel), then there is no extra elongation. For example, for the word "raHiim" one elongates the /ii/ twice or three times ("raHiiiiiim"), but if we say "raHiimun" the /ii/ should not be elongated more than usual.

## madd al-farq مد الفرق

Discrimination elongation

The extra elongation of a long vowel in a word initial position in order to distinguish the word in an interrogative mode from the word in a declarative mode, such as "'aaaaaal'aana?" (Now?) as opposed to "'aal'aana" (Now).

## madd al-liin مد اللين

Elongation of a glide

The two glides /w/ and /y/ are made long when they occur before a word final consonant, such as "khawf" (fear) and "bayt" (house) if we stop on these words. So the above words may be pronounced "khawwwwf" and "bayyyyyyt".

## madd aS-Silah مد الصلة

Liaison elongation

Extra elongation of a vowel after the pronominal suffix- hi/u) him( if the/ h /is preceded by a vowel and the pronoun is followed by any word .Unless the following word begins with a glottal stop ")hamzah ,("the vowel of- hi and -hu is made twice as long ,such as "'inda-hu 'ilmun" which is pronounced "'inda-huu 'ilmun". If the followiing word begins with a glottal stop, then this same vowel is made four or five times longer, as in "'inda-huuuu illaa"

## madd at-tamyiiz مد التمييز

Distinguishing elongation

See "maddal-farq" (discrimination elongation).

## madd far'iiyy مد فرعي

Incidental elongation

The extra elongation of a vowel due to some linguistic factors, such as occurrence before a glottal stop, as in "maa'" (water) which is pronounced maaaaa' (with a fairly long vowel).

## madd Harfiyy مد حرفي

Letter elongation

The extra elongation of a long vowel in the name of a letter, which is found at the beginning of a "suurah" of the Qur'an, such as "SaaD" (the 14th letter in the Arabic alphabet) which should be pronounced "SaaaaaaD", because the vowel is followed by a word final consonant, /d/.

## madd Harfiyy mukhaffaf مد حرفي مخفف

Light letter elongation

The extra elongation of a long vowel in the name of a letter, which is found at the beginning of a "suurah" of the Qur'an, such as "kaaf" (the equivalent of k) which should be pronounced "kaaaaaaf", because the double vowel is followed by a word final consonant, /f/. The above example is also called 'light', because the vowel is followed by a single consonant, not followed by a geminate consonant (i.e., double consonants).

## madd Harfiyy muthaqqal

## مد حرفي مثقل

Heavy letter elongation

This type is called Harfiyy (related to a letter / sound) because it occurs with the letters / sounds whose names are pronounced in the "muqaTTa'aat" (disjoined letters) that occur at the beginning of some chapters in the Qur'an , such ALM (pronounced 'alif-laaaaaaam-miiiiiim). In this example, we find that /aa/ in the middle is followed by /m/ with double value. Since the /m/ is repeated (geminated), we say that it is 'heavy', and the elongation is called heavy.

## madd jaa'iz مد جائز

Optional elongation

The optional extra elongation of a long vowel, when it is word final and the following word begins with the glottal stop ("hamzah"), as in "qaaluu 'innaa". In such a case, the /uu/ can be pronounced with extra elongation (/uuuu[u]/) or at normal length /uu/.

## madd jaa'iz munfaSil

## مد جائز منفصل

Optional separated elongation

See "madd jaa'iz" for an example. It is called "munfaSil" (separated) because the long vowel is in a word while the glottal stop ("hamzah") is in another (following) word.

## madd kalimiyy مد كلمي

Word elongation

The extra elongation of a long vowel which affects the pronunciation of a word, such as "daabbah" (animal) which should be read as "daaaaaabbah" because the long vowel /aa/ is followed by a double consonant, /bb/.

## madd kalimiyy muthaqqal

## مد كلمي مثقل

Heavy word elongation

This is called 'heavy' because it occurs before a geminate consonant, and 'word' because it occurs in words, such as the /aa/ in "daabbah" (animal), which is pronounced obligatorily with extra elongation due to its occurrence before the double 'b' letter / sound. So the above word is pronounced in the Qur'an with six vowel length, "daaaaaabbah."

## madd laazim مد لازم

Required elongation

An obligatory type of extra elongationofavowel.Thisincludes the two" madd kalimiyy" and two "madd Harfiyy" mentioned in their places in this dictionary.

## madd Tabii'iyy مد طبيعي

Normal elongation

It is a two-short- vowel length, as in "yakuunu" where the first /u/ is twice as long as the second /u/ in the word. (See "madd 'aSliyy" 'intrinsic elongation').

## madd waajib muttaSil مد واجب متصل

Obligatory ,connected elongation

Extra elongation of the vowel which precedes a glottal stop ("hamzah") in the same word, such as "maa'" (water) and "suu'" (something bad). In Qur'anic recitation, the vowels should be made extra long (4 or 5 times the length of a short vowel); the above words should be pronounced maaaaa' and "suuuuu'.

## madhhab (pl. madhaahib) مذاهب (مذهب)

School of thought

A school of thought ,usually in matters of Islamic law .There are four major schools of thought recognized by Sunni Muslims: Hanafi ,Maliki ,Shafi'i and Hanbali.

## ma'dhuun مأذون

Justice of the peace ;registrar

This refers to a man who has been authorized to perform religious weddings.

## ma'dhuur معذور

Excused ,excusable

A person may be excused if he is compelled to do something wrong or forgets to do a required act, under certain circumstances.

## madhy مذي

Arousal genital fluid

Fluid that comes out of the penis upon a male's being sexually aroused. It is considered ritually impure, and should be removed by washing the penis. It also invalidates the ablution, but doen not require "ghusl" ('washing whole body').

## maDmaDah مضمضة

Rinsing the mouth

Rinsing the mouth ,preferably with tooth brushing ,usually during the" wuDuu'" (ablution).

## maghaazii مغازي

The term is used by some historians to refer to the campaigns led by the Prophet Muhammad (PBUH). It is always found in the plural form.

## maghrib (al--) المغرب

Sunset

Technically, as a prayer time, "maghrib" means the time between actual sunset and the disappearance of the evening dusk.

## maHiiD محيض

Menstruation

State of menstruation. Regarding approaching a wife during her period, see the Qur'an 2: 222.

## mahmuus مهموس

Voiceless

The vocal chords are open; so they do not vibrate. Voiceless consonants include: f, t, s, sh and k.

## majhuur مجهور

Voiced

The vocal chords are closed; so they vibrate when air goes through them. Voiced consonants include: b, z and gh.

## mahr (pl. muhuur) مهر (مهور)

Dower

It is the money or gift one has to give a woman upon marrying her. See "Sadaaq."

## mahr al-mithl مهر المثل

Normal dower

The dower given to women of a similar social status.

## maHram (pl. maHaarim) محرم (محارم)

Unmarriageable relation

A relative who cannot be married to a female ,such as a father, brother ,uncle ,etc ,.as opposed to "ajnabiyy" (stranger). He can act as a chaperon, and she does not have to cover up in his presence.

## maHZuur (pl. maHZuuraat) محظور (محظورات)

Forbidden act

An act forbidden, especially due to certain circumstances, such as wearing sewn garments for a male or hunting in the state of "iHraam" during pilgrimage.

## majiid (al--) المجيد

The Ever-Glorious

A Divine Attribute of Allah. The One Who is glorified and honoured the most. The word is also used to describe the Qur'an (5: 1).

## majlis (pl. majaalis) adh-dhikr

مجلس (مجالس) الذكر

Meeting of remembrance

A group of people sitting together to remember Allah in different ways, such as studying the Qur'an.

## majuusiyy (pl. majuus) مجوسي (مجوس)

Magian

An adherent of Mazdaism, worshipper of fire.

## majuusiyyah (al--) المجوسية

Mazdaism

The Persian religion of fire worship.

## makaarim al-'akhlaaq مكارم الأخلاق

Good morals and conduct

Teaching these is one of the main duties of Prophets of God. In the hadeeth, the Prophet (PBUH) says: "I have been sent but to perfect good morals and conduct."

## makhiiT مخيط

Sewn garment

Any piece of garment that is sewn (shirt, trousers…), as opposed to a seamless sheet of cloth. A male pilgrim should not wear such a garment during pilgrimage.

## makhraj al-Harf (pl. makharij al-Huruuf) مخرج الحرف (مخارج الحروف)

Place of articulation

In phonetics, this means the point where the air escapes when we pronounce a certain "Harf" ('letter/ sound'), such as /b/ where the place of articulation is the lips; hence /b/ is called a bilabial consonant.

## makruuh (pl. makruuhaat) مكروه (مكروهات)

Reprehensible, hateful (act)

An act that is considered reprehensible or hateful, though not forbidden by the religion, such as many distasteful actions.

## malaa'ikah (sg. malak) ملائكة (ملك)

Angels

See "malak."

## malak (pl. malaa'ikah) ملك (ملائكة)

Angel

A Muslim believes that these are pure creatures, created of light who never disobey Allah. Many of them are assigned specific jobs, such as recording the good and bad deeds of people or guarding Paradise or Hell…etc. The best known among them are Gabriel, Michael, "israafiil", and "'izraa'iil" (the Angel of Death).

## malak al-mawt ملك الموت

Angel of Death

'"izraa'iil" is believed to be the name of the Angel of Death who is assigned to take away people's souls from them, causing their death.

## malakuut ملكوت

Kingdom, dominion

As a religious term this refers to the Kingdom (of both Heaven and Earth) which belongs to Allah Alone. A common expression is "maalik al-mulk wa al-malسkuut" (The possessor of the Sovereignty and the Dominion).

## malik (al--) الملك

The King

A Divine Attribute of Allah. The Absolute Ruler of the universe.

## mal'uun ملعون

Cursed, damned

Someone who is being dismissed from or deprived of Divine mercy.

## ma'muum مأموم

Follower

A person who follows the leader in congregational prayer.

## manaasik (sg. mansak) مناسك (منسك)

Rituals

See "mansak ."We often hear the expression" manaasik al-Hajj" (Haj rituals).

## manduubiyyah مندوبية

plausibility
See "manduub."

## manhduub (pl. manduubaat) مندوب (مندوبات)

Plausible recommended act

An act that is considered plausible or recommended, but neither required nor regularly observed by the Prophet (PBUH).

## maniyy مني

Semen

Though ejaculation makes a Muslim in a condition of major impurity (requiring full washing of body), Semen by itself is not considered "najaasah" (impure).

## mann منّ

Showing grace/ favour

The act of reminding a person we do favour to of the favour to humiliate him. (See the Qur'an, 2: 264 for prohibition of such an act.)

## mansuukh منسوخ

Abrogated

A decree or commandment that has been abrogated by another more recent one or modified by it.

## maqaam (al--) al-maHmuud المقام المحمود

The honoured status

The special status given by Allah to one person only on the Day of Judgement. All indications point to the fact that this would be the Prophet Muhammad (PBUH). Many scholars say that the reference in the Qur'an (17: 79) is to the "Greatest Intercession" or "ash-shafaa'ah al-kubraa".

## maqaam ibraahiim مقام إبراهيم

Maqam Ibrahim

The standing post of Abraham is a rock believed to have been used by the Prophet Abraham to stand on during the building of the Ka'bah .It is now encased in a crystal housing ,near the Ka'bah. The area adjacent to it is also called" maqaam ibraahiim ,"and a Muslim would normally pray two" rak'ahs" in the area after the "Tawaaf."

## maqaaSid ash-shar' ash-sharii'ah مقاصد (مقصد) الشرع / الشريعة

Objectives of Sharii'ah

The purposes for which Islamic Law is instituted ,such as preservation of human life and protection of honour and property.

Mm

## marHalah (pl. maraaHil) مَرحَلَة (ج مراحل)

Stage

A distance covered by laden camels in one day .It has been estimated to be around 45 kilometers.

## Maryam مريم

Mary

This is the name of the mother of Prophet Jesus. It is also the name of Chpter 19 of the Qur'an. Mary is well praised in the Qur'an where she is given as a model of believing women (the Qur'an, 66: 12).

## ma'ruuf معروف

Kindness, good deed

A good, common practice, including kindness and other good deeds.

## maSaadir at-tashrii' مصادر التشريع

Sources of Islamic law

The sources upon which the "sharii'ah" is based. Four main sources are recognized: the Qur'an, the sunnah, analogy and consensus of Muslim scholars.

## maSaaliH mursalah مصالح مرسلة

General good

The term has been defined as "public welfare neither commanded nor prohibited in any source of Islamic law."

## masaHa (yamsaH) مسح (يمسح)

To wipe

To wipe something, like the head or footwear, with a wet hand in the process of ablution.

## masbuuq (al--) fii aS-Salaah المسبوق في الصلاة

Missing part of prayer

The person who missed part of the congregational prayer.

## masH 'alaa al-khuffayn مسح على الخفين

Wiping over footwear

Wiping over a shoe or a heavy stocking. It is permissible for a Muslim who wears a footwear, before making ablution, to wipe its upper part with wet hands instead of washing the feet, for 24 hours as long as he does not remove it. If he is on travel, he may do so for three days.

## mash'ar (al--) al-Haraam المشعر الحرام

Sacred site

A place in Muzdalifah, near Mecca, where pilgrims are supposed to stop during the night preceding the tenth of Dhul-Hijjah and say prayers. (See the Qur'an, 2: 298).

## mashhuur, Hadiith

## مشهور ، حديث

A well known hadeeth

A Hadiith narrated by more than two narrators.

## mashruu' مشروع

Permissible, legitimate

Something allowed by the religion.

## mashruu'iyyah مشروعية

Legality, lawfulness

The state of something being legal or permissible.

## masiih (al--)

## المسيح

The Messiah

Unless specified, this term refers to Jesus son of Mary.

## masiiH (al--) 'iisaa ibn maryam

## المسيح عيسى بن مريم

Jesus son of Mary

Literally, the Messiah Jesus son of Mary.

## masiiH (al--) ad-dajjaal

## المسيح الدجال

Antichrist, false messiah

In the traditions of the Prophet (PBUH) there are references to a false messiah who comes in the latter days of this world and pretends to be the true messiah, or even as God, in order to mislead people into disbelief.

## masiiHiyy مسيحي

Christian

A relatively new word for the Islamic word "naSraaniyy."

## masiiHiyyah (al--)

## المسيحية

Christianity

This is a modern synonym for "naSraaniyyah."

## ma'Siyah (pl. ma'aaSii)

## معصية (معاصي)

Sin

Literally ,an act of disobedience to Allah.

## masjid (al--) al-aqSaa

## المسجد الأقصى

TheAqsa Mosque

Literall ,it means the Furthest Mosque ,the reference is to the main mosque of Jerusalem ,built on the site to which the Prophet Muhammad) PBUH (went in his night journey") al-israa'") and from where the Prophet (PBUH) ascended to heaven. (See the Qur'an, 17: 1).

## masjid (al--) al-Haraam المسجد الحرام

The Holy Mosque

The mosque that encloses the Ka'bah at Mecca.

## masjid al-khayf مسجد الخيف

al-Khayf Mosque

The mosque at Mina.

## masjid (al--) an-nabawiyy المسجد النبوي

The Prophet's Mosque

The mosque at Medina, which was first built by the Prophet Muhammad (PBUH) and where he is buried.

## masjid Diraar مسجد ضرار

Mosque of harm

The mosque that was built by the hypocrites in Medina, during the early days of the Prophet in that town, in order to detract the worshippers from joining the Prophet in their prayers. (See the Qur'an 9: 107)

## masjid namirah مسجد نمرة

Namirah Mosque

The mosque at 'Arafah, where the pilgrims perform both noon and afternoon prayers together on the ninth day of Dhul-Hijjah.

## masjid qubaa' مسجد قباء

The Mosque of Qubaa'

The name of the first mosque ever built in Islamic history, since the Prophet (PBUH), upon his arrival at Medina, first stayed at Qubaa', then moved to Medina proper. (See the Qur'an, 9: 108).

## maSlaHah مصلحة

Public good

This is short for "maSlaHah 'aammah" which means what is good for the general public, something to be taken into consideration in legislation.

## masnuun (pl. masnuunaat) (مسنونات) مسنون

Sunnah practice

Practice observed and/or recommended by the Prophet Muhammad (PBUH).

## mass (min al-jinn / ash-shyTaan) مس من الجن / الشيطان

Possession (by Satan or a jinni)

The state of being controlled by an evil spirit or jinn.

## ma'Suum معصوم

Infallible

A person, usually a prophet, protected by Allah from committing wrong acts or sins.

## mataa' al-Hayaat ad-dunyaa متاع الحياة الدنيا

Worldly pleasures

The reference is to the temporary pleasures of this life, as opposed to the eternal pleasures of the Hereafter.

## maTaaf (al--) المطاف

Circumambulation path

The path which is followed by the person that circumambulates (walks around) the Ka'bah.

## mathaanii مثاني

Oft-repeated

In the Qur'an, the term refers to the verses that are frequently repeated. The Opening Chapter is referred to as "assab' al-mathaanii" ('the seven repeated verses').

## ma'thuur مأثور

Reported

This word means something (prayer or saying, for example) that was reported from the past, generally accepted by Muslims. (See 'athar).

## matiin (al--) المتين

The Ever Strong

A Divine Attribute of Allah. The One Whose strength has no limits.

## matn al-Hadiith متن الحديث

Hadeeth text

The main text of the tradition of the Prophet Muhammad (PBUH), giving his words, for example.

## mawaalii (sg. mawlaa) (مَولى) موالي

See mawlaa 1-3.

## maw'iZah (pl. mawaa'iZ) (مواعظ) موعظة

Sermon

A general term used for any type of a talk giving religious advice.

## mawaaqiit (sg. miiqaat) مواقيت (ميقات)

Appointed times or places

See "miiqaat".

## mawDuu' موضوع

Forgery

The term refers to a hadeeth fabricated by someone and falsely ascribed to the Prophet (PBUH).

## mawlaa 1 (pl. mawaalii) مولى 1 (موالي)

Lord, master, protector

In the Qur'an we often find the word in these senses referring to Allah.

## mawlaa 2 (pl. mawaalii) مولى 2 (موالي)

Paternal relatives

According to some scholars, the term "mawaalii" found in Chapters 4 (verse 33) and 19 (verse 5) of the Qur'an refers to the paternal kinsfolk, technically called "'aSabah" in the laws of inheritance.

## mawlaa (pl. mawaalii) 3 مولى 3(ج موالي)

Former bondsman

The term is usually used in the context of sb being a former bondsman of a certain person (e.g. X mawalaa Y), who may have some legal rights due to this relationship.

## mawlid (al--) an-nabawiyy المولد النبوي

The Prophet's birthday

The birthday of the Prophet Muhammad (PBUH) is assumed to be most probably on Monday the 12th of Rabi' al-Awwal. It was in the year 570 AD. The term is also used to mean the celebration of the same.

## mawqi'ah (pl. mawaaqi') موقعة (مواقع)

Battle

In Islamic history, the term is used to refer to all battles, both during the days of the Prophet Muhammad (PBUH) and at other times.

## mawquudhah موقوذة

Dead through beating

An animal whose meat is normally edible, but dies as a result of beating; hence, its meat becomes forbidden for a Muslim to eat, due to the fact that it is not properly slaughtered. (See the Qur'an, 5: 3).

## maysir ميسر

Gambling ,game of chance

Gambling is forbidden by Islam. (See the Qur'an, 5: 90-91).

## maytah ميتة

Carrion

The meat of the animal that dies a natural death .Such meat is forbidden for a Muslim to eat even if it is edible when the animal is properly slaughtered.

## mazaamiir daawuud مزامير داود

Psalms of David

The book that was revealed to Prophet David (PBUH).

## maZlamah) pl .maZaalim( مظلمة (مظالم)

Complaint, Grievance

Complaint usually made to the regular authorities or higher authorities in some cases.

## miHraab (pl. maHaariib) محراب (محاريب)

prayer nitch

An enclave made in a worship place ,in the front for the" imam" who leads the congregation.

## miikaa'iil ميكائيل

Michael

The angel who is in charge of dispensing the provisions decreed by Allah for different creatures. The name is given as" miikaal" too ,in the Qur'an.

## miil ميل

Islamic mile

It is said that the Islamic mile is equivalent to 1848 meters.

## miiqaat (pl. mawaaqiit) ميقات (مواقيت)

Appointed time or place

For the pilgrims, "miiqaat" usually means the place where they should wear the "iHraam" (pilgrim's garb) and make the intention for "Hajj" or "'umrah".

## miithaaq (pl. mawaathiiq) ميثاق (مواثيق)

Covenant ,pledge

Fulfilling the covenant (not breaking it) is considered an important quality in believers. (See the Qur'an 13:20, e.g.)

## mikHalah (pl. makaaHil) مكحلة (مكاحل)

Kohl container

A small container in which "kohl" (antimony powder) is placed.

## millah (pl. milal) ملة (ملل)

Religion

The term is sometimes contrasted with "niHlah" (a sect).

## minaa منى

Mina

The valley next to Mecca where pilgrims stay the eighth and the tenth through the thirteenth days of the month of pilgrimage ,Dhul Hijjah.

## manaarah منارة

Minaret

The tower in a mosque from which the" adhaan) "call to prayer (was made by the muezzin .Nowadays, loud speakers are put there while the call is actually made inside the mosque itself in front of a microphone.

## minbar (pl. manaabir) منابر (منبر)

pulpit

A pulpit or speaking forum ,from where a speech or sermon is delivered.

## mansak (pl. manaasik) منسك (مناسك)

Pilgrimage rite

A rite or ritual observed when one performs pilgrimage to Mecca.

## miqdaar al-madd مقدار المد

Duration of a vowel

Literally, the duration of the elongation. Normally, a typical elongation is two short vowels length. A vowel, however, may be four, five or six times long in certain contexts, such as in the case of the vowel being followed by a "hamzah" (glottal stop).

## mi'raaj (al--) المعراج

The Ascension

The ascension of the Prophet Muhammad (PBUH) from Jerusalem to the seven Heavens after the "israa'" , believed to be in the night of the 27th of Rajab.

## mirwad (p. maraawid) مرود (مراود)

Kohl stick

A thin cylindrical metallic stick which is dipped in the "kohl" (antimony powder) by inserting the stick inside the container of the kohl. It is then used for putting the kohl inside the eyes or used for eye lining.

## misbaHah (pl. masaabiH) مسبحة (مسابح)

Prayer beads

Beads strung together in specific numbers ,usually 33 or ,99 and are used to count how many times one has said a certain prayer ,such as" subHaana allaah" (Glory be to Allah'), "al-Hamdu li-llaah" (Thank Allah) and "allaahu 'akbar" (Allah is the Greatest).

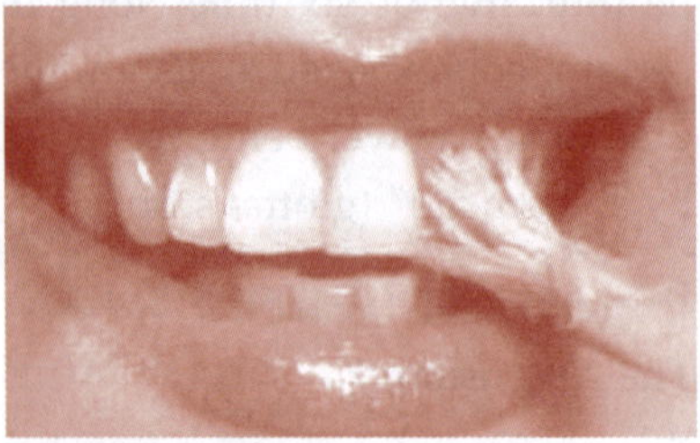

## miswaak (pl. masawwiik) مسواك (مساويك)

Tooth stick

The original tooth brush used by the Prophet Muhammad (PBUH) more than 1400 years ago, and is still being used by some Muslims, is a tooth brush in the form of a stick taken from a tree known in Arabia as "al-araak", which has medicinal value and a good smell.

## mithqaal (pl. mathaaqiil) 1 مثقال 1 (مثاقيل)

Mithqaal

It is said to be the weight of a dinar, the equivalent of 72 grains of barley (approx. equals 4.5 grams). It may be somewhat less or more.

## mithqaal (pl. mathaaqiil) 2 مثاقيل (مثقال 2)

Mithqaal

weight of

This is the literal sense of the word, and it is used in this sense in the Qur'an (e.g., 99: 7-8).

## mu'aahad معاهد

protected

Literally, the word means someone with whom we have made a covenant. Technically, it refers to the people of the Scripture who have been promised protection by the Muslim State. It is similar to the word "dhimmiyy."

## mu'aamalaat مُعامَلات

Transactions ,dealings

Any activity that involves others, as opposed to'" ibaadaat"(worship practices).

## mu'aasharah bil-ma'ruuf معاشرة بالمعروف

Consorting/ living with fairness

The reference is to husband wife relations. (See, e.g., the Qur'an, 4:19.)

Mm

## mu'adhdhin مؤذن

Muezzin

The person who makes the "adhaan" (call to prayer) to inform people that the time for a certain "Salaah" has come.

## mu'akhkhar aS-Sadaaq مؤخر الصداق

Deferred dower

Often, a part of the dower paid by the groom to his wife is deferred, to be paid upon separation or at the request of the wife.

## mu'akhkhir (al--) المؤخر

The Supreme Retarder

A Divine Attribute of Allah. The One Who delays things and postpones affairs at His Will.

## mu'allafah (al--) quluubuhum المؤلفة قلوبهم

Newly won friends

One of the definitions of this term says that they are a group of people whose hearts the Muslim community tries to win to encourage them to accept Islam and show loyalty to it.

## mu'allaqah معلقة

Suspended

A wife in a state of indetermination. She is not treated like a wife, nor is she divorced, which is prohibited by Islam (the Qur'an, 4: 129).

## mu'awwadhataan (al--) المعوذتان

Chapters 113 and 114 of the Holy Qur'an

The two chapters of the Qur'an which begin with the words "qul A'uudhu" (Say: I seek refuge…), which are recommended by the Prophet (PBUH) to be recited for protection from various types and sources of evil.

## mubaaH (pl. mubaaHaat) مباح (مباحات)

Permissible (act or thing)

Something permitted by the religion, or not forbidden by it. The general rule is that things are permissible unless they are explicitly or implicitly forbidden in the Qur'an or sunnah of the Prophet (PBUH).

## mubaahalah مباهلة

Mutual supplication

This word comes from the verb "'ibtahal" (to supplicate or pray to Allah). The term refers to the incident in which Allah ordered

His Prophet Muhammad (PBUH) to challenge some leading Christian figures of his time regarding their view of God versus the Islamic view. In this verse the Prophet was to challenge those Christians by both praying to Allah to curse the person not telling the truth among them. (See the Qur'an , 3: 61).

## mubaarak مبارك

Blessed

Someone or something that has received Divine blessing; therefore, could be a source of blessing. This word is used in congratulating others, such as "zawaaj mubarak" (blessed wedding), "'iid mubaarak" (blessed Eid), "shahr mubaarak" (blessed month). A related (colloquial) word is "mabruuk" which has the same meaning, though slightly different in use.

## mubaasharah مباشرة

Enjoyment by physical contact

This refers to a man enjoying his wife's body through physical contact other than sexual intercourse. The practice is resorted to, for example, during her menstruation.

## mubdi' (al--) المبدئ

The Commencer

A Divine Attribute of Allah. The One Who initiated the creation of everything from nothing.

## mubtadi' مبتدع

Innovator

Someone who introduces practices not approved by the religion, and considers them part of the faith.

## mubTil (pl. mubTilaat) مبطل (مبطلات)

Nullifier

Something that nullifies or invalidates an act of worship or the like, such as bleeding which nullifies one's ablution, making it necessary for the person to do the ablution again in order to pray, or laughing aloud while praying, which nullifies one's prayer, making it necessary to do it again.

## muDaarabah مضاربة

Silent partnership

Partnership of two people, one with the capital and the other with labour. Profits are divided between them.

## mudabbar مُدَبَّر

Promised freedom

A slave promised to become free upon death of the master.

## mudd مد

Mudd

A dry measure for grains, roughly equivalent to the amount that fills the two hands cupped together (appr. 1.032 litres).

## mudhill (al--) المذل

The Supreme Humiliator

A Divine Attribute of Allah. The One Who brings humiliation to His enemies and the enemies of truth, with degradation in this life and punishment in the Hereafter.

## mufakhkham مفخّم

Velarized

The center of the tongue is raised towards the velum (back of mouth) at the production of the sound. Some consonants are velarized by nature, such as D, T and Z. Two consonants are velarized under certain conditions, r and l. For example, the r is velarized if it is followed by a or u; the l in the word Allah is velarized if preceded by a or u.

## mufaaraqah fiS-Salaah مفارقة في الصلاة

Parting the Imaam

Acting independently from the leader in a congregational prayer, under certain conditions.

## mufaSSalaat (al--) / al-mufaSSal المفصلات / المفصل

Shorter chapters

Literally, this means the 'detailed ones'. The reference is to chapters of the Qur'an from suurat Qaaf (chapter 49) to the end of the Qur'an (chapter 114).

## mufassir مفسر

Interpreter, exegete

The person who interprets the Qur'an and explains its meanings, according to the rules and conditions stipulated for the task.

## mufliH مفلح

Successful, prosperous

This word is used in the Qur'an in the plural form ("mufliHuun") to describe the believers (the Qur'an, 2: 5). It is also a promise from Allah that they are the ones who will achieve success and salvation as well as spiritual prosperity.

## muftii مفتي

Mufti

Expounder of the law, or a religious

authority officially assigned the job of expounding the laws of Islam and giving official opinion on various religious and legal matters.

## mufTir مفطر

Not fasting

This refers to someone who is not observing the fast for whatever reason. It is the opposite of "Saa'im."

## mughallaZah (yamiin / 'aymaan --) مغلظة (يمين / أيمان --)

Very emphatic oath(s)

Swearing, for example, to Allah and many of His Attributes to emphasize or confirm something.

## mughnii (al--) المغني

The Supreme Enricher

A Divine Attribute of Allah .The One Who makes others self-sufficient.

## muhaajir (pl. muhaajiruun) مهاجر (مهاجرون)

Immigrant

Someone who migrates from a place (usually of disbelievers) to a place (of believers). The term "muhaajiruun" (immigrants) usually refers in Islamic history to the early followers of Islam who migrated from Mecca to Medina, as opposed "al-anSaar".

## muHaasabat an-nafs محاسبة النفس

Examination of conscience

scrutinizing one's own actions and deeds in the light of the teachings of the religion.

## muHaddith محدث

Hadeeth teacher

A scholar who teaches prophetic traditions.

## muHallil محلل

Legalizer

Somebody who does something to make legal an illegal act. The typical example is when a man marries an irrevocably divorced woman so that after divorcing her she may be remarried to her first husband.

## muHammad محمد

Muhammad

Name of the Prophet of Islam. He was the first to be given this name, which means "someone who is praised and praiseworthy". Reference to prophet Muhmmad by this name is found in many

Mm

verses of the Qur'an, though he is often referred to as "an-nabiyy" (the Prophet) and "rasuul-allaah" (the Messenger of God). (See, e.g., the Qur'an, 33: 1, 6, 21, 28, 30) The three words occur together in Chapter 33, verse 40 whch translates: "Muhmmad is not the father of {any} one of your men, but (hes is) the Messenger of God and seal (last) of the prophets, and God is Ever knowledgeable of all things." Today, the name Muhammad is the most common name ever found among Muslims. Many, in fact, use it as the first of a double name (e.g., Muhammad X or Muhammad Y…etc.)

## muHarram 1 محرم

Forbidden

Something forbidden by the religion.

## muHarram 2 محرم

Sanctified, sacred

It is also the name of the first month of the Islamic calendar. The correct name is "al-muHarram" (the sanctified month).

## muHarram 3 (pl. muHarramaat) محرم 3 (محرمات)

Forbidden act, thing

Something forbidden by the Qur'an or the Prophet Muhammad (PBUH).

## muhaymin (al--) المهيمن

The Supreme Controller

A Divine Attribute of Allah. The One Who controls all things in the universe and watches over them.

## muHdith 1 محدث

Ritually impure / unclean

Someone who has done something that makes him ritually impure or unclean. (See "Hadath 'akbar" and "Hadath 'aSghar").

## muHdith 2 محدث

Innovator

A person who introduces innovations into the religion.

## muHkam (muHkamaat) محكم (محكمات)

Exact in meaning

Usually, this word is used in contrast to "mutashaabih" (see word). It means tight. With reference to Qur'anic verses, the word refers to the verse(s) which have exact or unequivocal meanings. (See the Qur'an, 3: 7).

## muHrim محرم

Wearer of iHraam

A pilgrim wearing the pilgrimage garb, "iHraam".

## muHSan محصن

married man

A man previously married.

## muHSar مُحصَر

Hindered

The term refers to a pilgrim hindered from continuing his journey.

## muHSanah 1 محصنة

Married woman

In the Qur'an, the term is used to refer to a married, free or virtuous woman (the Qur'an, 4: 24-25).

## muHSanah 2 محصنة

Chaste / virtuous woman

This is one of the three main senses of the word found in the Qur'an and Islamic writings. (See the Qur'an, 4: 24-25).

## muHSanah 3 محصنة

Free female

This is one of the three main senses of the word found in the Qur'an and Islamic writings. (The Qur'an 4: 24-25).

## muHSii (al--) المحصي

The Numberer

A Divine Attribute of Allah. The One Who keeps record or takes account of everything.

## muHtaDar محتضر

Dying person

A person on his death bed. Usually, we should try to prompt him to say "ash-shahaadataan" so that they would be his last words.

## muHtasib 1 محتسب

Not expecting reward

Someone who does not wait for rewards from people, but does things for the sake of God Alone.

## muHtasib 2 مُحتسب

Market inspector

Someone appointed by the state to make sure that merchants and tradesmen are honest in their dealings. In modern times the term is used to refer to a morality policeman.

## muHyii (al--) المُحْيِي

The Quickener, Giver of life

A Divine Attribute of Allah. The One Who gives life.

## mu'iid (al--) المُعِيد

The Supreme Restorer

A Divine Attribute of Allah. The One Who returns the living to their former existence and gives life to the dead.

## mu'izz (al--) المُعِز

The Supreme Honourer

A Divine Attribute of Allah. The One Who gives honour and esteem to His servants.

## mujaahid مُجاهد

Fighter for the Cause of Allah

Someone who fights for the Cause of God.

## mujaahrah bil-ma'Siyah مجاهرة بالمعصية

Sinning in public

Sinning in public or making a public announcement about sins committed by self.

## mujaahir مُجاهر

Bold sinner

A sinner who does sinful acts publicly or announces them, without a sense of shame.

## mujiib (al--) المجيب

The Supreme Answerer

A Divine Attribute of Allah. The One Who answers the prayers and calls of His servants.

## mu'jiz مُعجز

Miraculous

Clearly superhuman and extraordinary, such as the Qur'an's content, language and style.

## mu'jizah مُعجزة

Miracle

Something supernatural performed by a prophet, for example, such as the changing of the rod into a snake by the Prophet Moses (PBUH).

## mujmal مجمَل

Ambivalent, ambiguous

Has more than one possible meaning.

## mujtahid مُجتهد

Independent legist/Jurist

A legist formulating independent decisions in legal or theological matters, based on the interpretation and application of the main principles of derivation of Islamic law.

## mukaatab مُكاتَب

Self-ransomer

A slave who makes arrangements with his master to buy his freedom from him.

## mukaatabah مُكاتَبَة

Self-ransoming

The arrangement which allows a slave to ransom him/ herself, such paying a sum of money to the master to set him/ her free. Such a slave is one of the eight categories of people to whom zakaah (obligatory charity or poor tax) may be given. See the Qur'an, 9: 60.

## mukaatib مُكاتِب

Owner of self-ransomer

The master of the slave who agrees to set his slave free upon fulfillment of certain conditions.

## mukallaf مكلف

Competent, accountable

Usually, a sane adult who is charged with religious and other duties and is accountable for carrying them out.

## mukarrar/ takriir مكرر/ تكرير

Trill

This refers to the tip of the tongue tapping the alveolar ridge. The Arabic r is similar in this regard to Scottish and Spanish r.

## mukhaala'ah مخالعة

Seeking divorce

The woman seeking divorce from her husband, often by compensating him, for example, for the expenses he had incurred. Another term is "khul' "

## mu'kil ar-ribaa مؤكل الربا

Feeder of usury

The person who borrows money with interest / usury is considered a culprit in the crime of usury; therefore, he is called the feeder of usury.

## mukrah مُكرَه

Forced, coerced

Someone who is forced to do something against his/ her will. He will not be accountable for the act according to Islam.

## mulaa'anah ملاعنة

Mutual cursing

A procedure in which a husband who accuses his wife of adultery, without having witnesses, swears four times to Allah that he is telling the truth, and fifth time that he deserves Allah's wrath if he is telling a lie. The wife then may, if she claims innocence, swear four times that he is telling a lie, and the fifth time that she deserves Allah's wrath if he is not telling the truth. (See the Qur'an, 24: 6-9).

## mulHid (pl. malaaHidah) ملحد (ملاحدة)

Atheist

A person who does not believe in the existence of Allah.

## multazam (al--) الملتزم

The Multazam

The area adjacent to the portal of the Ka'bah (between the black stone and the portal).

## multazim (pl. multazimuun) ملتزم (ملتزمون)

Conservative / committed person

This is a fairly recently coined term, meaning someone who tries to meticulously observe the teachings of Islam.

## mumiit (al--) المميت

The Supreme Death-Causer

A Divine Attribute of Allah. The One Who actually controls life and death.

## mu'min (al--) المؤمن

The Source of Security

A Divine Attribute of Allah. The One Who provides His righteous servants with security and safety from Hell Fire, and provides all His creation with security from injustice to them.

## mu'min (pl. mu'minuun) مؤمن

Believer

In Islamic terms, this means someone who believes in Islam with firm conviction.

## munaafiq (pl. munaafiquun) منافق (منافقون)

Hypocrite

Someone who pretends to be a believer, while he is not, in order to deceive others.

## munaajaah مناجاة

Intimate talk

Usually the word is used for the pious person's talking (praying) to God in a fervent manner in a state of solitude.

## munajjim منجم

Astrologer

Islam teaches its followers not to

resort to astrologers nor believe what they say.

## munfatiH منفتح

Open

The sound is produced with the mouth open and the tongue in lowered position.

## munfiq منفق

Spender

As a term this usually refers to someone who spends money for the sake of God.

## munkar (pl. munkaraat) منكر (منكرات)

Abominable act, evil

Anything that is forbidden by Islam may be considered "munkar", and it is a Muslim's duty to fight or correct it.

## munkar wa nakiir منكر و نكير

Munkar and Nakeer

The two angels assigned to interrogate the dead in their graves upon their burial.

## muntaqim (al--) المنتقم

The Supreme Avenger

A Divine Attribute of Allah.

The One Who punishes the persistent wrong doers or sinners.

## muntasib منتسب

Affiliated

A person affiliated to a certain school of thought.

## muqaaDaah مقاضاة

Suing

Taking someone to court.

## muqaayaDah مقايضة

Bartering

Giving something and receiving another for it at the same time.

## muqaddim (al--) المقدم

The Supreme Advancer

A Divine Attribute of Allah. The One Who advances and brings people and things nearer to each other.

## muqallid مقلّد

Imitator

Someone who follows others' opinions and/or practices

## muqaTTa'aat (al--) المقطعات

Disconnected letters

These are the letters that are found at the beginning of some chapters of the Qur'an, such as ALM (alif-laam-miim) and YS (yaa'- siin). They are called disconnected because we read the letter (their names) separately, rather than treat the combinations as single words.

## muqayyad مقيَّد

Qualified, restricted

A term that is accompanied by another qualifying or limiting term (an adjective, for example).

## muqiit (al--) المقيت

The Supreme Nourisher

A Divine Attribute of Allah. The One Who provides nourishment, or Who is in control of everything.

## muqsiT (al--) المقسط

The Supreme Equitable

A Divine Attribute of Allah. The One Who is never unjust or unfair.

## muqtadii مقتدي

Follower

A person who follows a certain "imaam" or school of thought.

## muqtadir (al--) المقتدر

The Most Efficient

A Divine Attribute of Allah. The One Who has total command over His creation.

## muraabaHah مرابحة

Profit sharing

Technically, this term is used short "bay' al-muraabaHa", which means a transaction in which one party sells something to another indicating the amount of profit he is making in the sale. Nowadays, this is applied to installment sales, where the buyer pays an extra amount of money or percentage of the sale price for the installments.

## muraabiT مرابط

Muslim frontier guard

The person who is posted at the borders of Muslim lands to protect them from the enemy.

## muraaqabat an-nafs مراقبة النفس

self monitoring, watching

Watching oneself in order to prevent it from doing wrong things.

## muraqqaq مرقق

unvelarized

The two consonants r and L are produced with the center of the tongue in normal position (not raised towards the velum), if the former is followed by /i/ and if the word Allah is preceded by the vowel /i/ (as in bi-llaah). The term is contrasted with "mufakhkham" (velarized).

Mm

## murDi'ah (pl. murDi'aat) مرضعة (مرضعات)

Wet nurse

A woman who breast feeds a baby that could be other than her own.

## muriid مريد

Sufi disciple

A person who is under training as a Sufi.

## mursal (Hadiith) مرسَل (حديث)

Of discontinuous chain

In the study of Prophetic traditions, the term refers to a "Hadiith" whose chain of narrators is interrupted.

## murtadd مرتد

Apostate

A Muslim who leaves the fold of Islam.

## murtashii (al--) المرتشي

Seeker of a bribe

Someone who asks for bribery. Both the seeker and the giver ("raashii") are sinners. So is the mediator or the go between person ("raa'ish"), if there is any.

## muruu'ah مروءة

Nobility

Nobility of character, including integrity and generosity.

## musaafir مسافر

Traveler

A person is considered 'on travel', technically, if he is about 80 kilometers (according to some scholars) away from his normal place of residence.

## musaakanah مساكنة

Sharing a dwelling

It could be same house or room.

## musaaqaah مساقاة

watering partnership

This is the arrangement in which the farm owner makes a deal with someone to take care of the plants, and they share the produce or crops.

## muSallaa مُصلّى

Prayer place

Any place designated for "Salaah", including a small area (for a limited number of people) or a big area for masses (such as an open space for Eid prayers).

## muSawwir (al--) المصور

The Supreme Fashioner

A Divine Attribute of Allah. The One Who fashions or gives perfect shape to His creation.

## mushabbihah مشبهة

Assimilators

Misguided Muslims who draw resemblances between Allah and His creatures, which is a clear contradiction to the Qur'anic statement: "Nothing is similar unto Him." (the Qur'an 42:11)

## muSHaf (al--) المصحف

Written text of the Qur'an

The written / printed text of the Qur'an.

## muSHaf (al--) al-'uthmaaniyy المصحف العثماني

Othman's copy of the Qur'an

The standard copy of the Qur'an which was compiled upon instructions from the third Righteous Caliph 'Uthmaan in order to protect Muslims from fighting among themselves regarding their modes of recitation of the Qur'an and the correct order of its chapters.

## muSHaf (al--) al-'imam المصحف الإمام

The standard copy of the Qur'an

The copy of the Qur'an compiled at instructions by the Caliph Othman, whose rules of dictation are observed in other copies printed up to the present time.

## mushrik مشرك

Polytheist, pagan

A person who worships more than one god, or associates partners with God.

## muskir (pl. muskiraat) مسكر (مسكرات)

Intoxicant

Anything that causes intoxication to a person. Alcoholic beverages and narcotic drugs are typical examples.

## musnad1 (Hadiith) مُسنَد (حديث)

Of continuous chain of transmitters

For a Prophetic tradition this means that it has a continuous chain of reporters/ narrators up to the Prophet Muhammad (PBUH).

## musnad 2 مسند

Book of hadeeth

A book of hadeeths collected by one person, such as "musnad al-'imaam aHmad ibn Hanbal" (The book of hadeeths compiled by ibn Hanbal).

## mustafiiD (Hadiith) مستفيض

Famous

For a Hadiith, it means well received by people, regardless of the chain of narrators. Another term is "mashhuur."

## mustafil مستفل

Low

The sound is produced with the tongue in a lowered position ,such as in the case is with unvelarized consonant like/ s /and/ f./

## musta'lii مستعلي

High

The sound is produced with the tongue in raised position ,such as in the case of velarized consonants, such as/ T /and/ S./

## mustaHaaDah مستحاضة

Female with false menses

A female that has vaginal bleeding other than her regular period.

## mustaHabb (pl. mustaHabbaat) مستحب (مستحبات)

Recommended act

An act recommended by Islam, not required nor regularly observed by the Prophet (PBUH).

## muSTalaH al-Hadiith مصطلح الحديث

Science of hadeeth

This term, which literally means "terminology of the hadeeth", is used to refer to the science of hadeeth text criticism and evaluation. It is the method of ascertaining the authenticity of the tradition ascribed to the Prophet Muhammad (PBUH).

## musta'man مُستأمَن

Promised immunity

Historically this meant a member of an un-Islamic hostile area who entered a Muslim territory and claimed safe conduct and immunity from hostilities. In modern terms, this might be compared to asking for an entry or transit visa. If the Muslim state agrees, then he becomes a "musta'man" and receives the promised treatment.

## musta'min مستأمن

Immunity seeker

See "musta'man".

## mustaTiil مستطيل

Lateralized

The sound is produced with the side of the tongue touching the molars. The only consonant which is given this characteristic is the Dad.(ض).

## muta'aalii (al--) المتعالي

The Supremely Exalted

A Divine Attribute of Allah. The One Who is above any reproach.

## mutabarrijah (pl. mutabarrijaat) متبرِّجة (متبرّجات)

Unveild orimproperly dressed woman

The term refers to an adult female who does not observe the rules of Islamic dress in the presence of male strangers, by showing parts of the body that are supposed to be covered as well as adornments on her body. Typically, this would be a person who violates the injuctions in the Qur'an (e.g., Chapter 24: 31). The term is used in the Qur'an (24: 60).

## mu'taddah معتدة

Woman in waiting period

A woman in a waiting period, upon divorce or death of a husband.

## mutaHajjibah متحجّبة

Veild, properly dressed woman

The term is commonly used to refer to a Muslim female who observes the rules of Islamic "Hijaab", which means covering the whole body, including the hair of the head, in the presence of strange men. (See the Qur'an, 24:31and 60; and 33: 59 for some rulings in this regard). The opposite of this word is "mutabarrijah".

## mutakabbir (al--) المتكبر

The Supremely Proud

A Divine Attribute of Allah. The One Who is above every type of deficiency or imperfection.

## mu'takif معتكف

In a state of "i'tikaaf"

A person who retreats in the mosque for devotions.

## mutamatti متمتع'

Pilgrim at leisure

A pilgrim who makes "'umrah" and wears his regular clothes to live a normal life until the eighth day of the month of pilgrimage, when he wears the "iHraam" again for the "Hajj". (See "tamattu'".)

## mu'tamir معتمر

Performer of " 'umrah"

Someone who performs the lesser pilgrimage ,which can be done any time of the year.

## mutaraddiyah مترديّة

Dead from a fall

An animal whose flesh is edible, but dies from a fall; hence, it is not slaughtered. It is forbidden for a Muslim to eat its meat. (See the Qur'an, 5: 3).

## mutaSawwif متصوف

Sufi

A follower of a Sufi order ,or simply someone who is living a simple way of life full of devotions.

## mutashaabih (pl. mutashaabihaat) متشابه (متشابهات)

Polysemous ,with many meanings

The word is used to refer to verse(s) of the Qur'an which have more than one possible interpretation or application. (See the Qur'an, 3: 7).

## muTbaq مطبق

Velarized

This means the center of the tongue is raised towards the back of the mouth (the velum), giving the sense of a full mouth. (See "mufakhkham").

## muTlaq مُطلَق

Absolute

This means there are no restrictions or limitations.

## mutawaatir متواتر

Well reported

A hadeeth is considered "mutawaatir" if it has a good chain of narrators: continuous, many sources, high reliability.

## mu'tazilah (al--) المعتزلة

Mu'tazilites

A sect of Muslims who called to the imposition of human rationalization on theological issues, such as predestination, Divine attributes, the Qur'an, etc. Their views often contradicted those of Islamic orthodoxy.

## mu'Tii (al--) المعطي

The Supreme Giver

A Divine Attribute of Allah. The One Who gives with no bounds or limits.

## muttafaq 'alayh متفق عليه

Agreed upon

This refers to a "Hadiith" that has been reported by both al-Bukhari and Muslim; hence, agreed upon or approved by them both. This would make the hadeeth text attain the highest degree of authenticity and reliability.

## muttaqii (pl. muttaquun) متقي (متقون)

God-fearing ,pious

Someone who remembers that God is watching him all the time; therefore, he conducts himself in the best manner that pleases God. He is also someone who fears Divine punishment, and seeks to protect himself from it. The related verb "ittaqaa (yattaqii)" is found in the Qur'an and Prophetic traditions (See, e.g. the Qur'an, 92: 5).

## muttaquun (sg. muttaqii) متقون (متقي)

God-fearing

See muttaqii.The word is also found in Islamic texts in its accusative and genitive forms "muttaqiin", depending on its grammatical case. (See, e.g., the Qur'an, 2: 2, which says that the Qur'an is a guidance for "al-muttaqiin".)

## muubiqaat (al--) (sg. muubiqah) الموبقات (موبقة)

Destructive sins

Major sins that cause the destruction of the person who commits them ,both in this world and the Hereafter.

## muujib (pl. muujibaat) موجب (موجبات)

Necessitating cause

Something that makes something else necessary ,such as menstruation that makes it necessary for a woman to have "ghusl" (wash the whole body) before she can pray or touch the Qur'an.

## muusaa موسى

Moses

A prophet of Allah sent to the Israelites. The Qur'an is full of references to the Prophet Moses (PBUH), his encounters with the Pharaoh of Egypt and his story with the the Israelites. (See, for instance, the Qur'an, 20: 9-98 and 26: 10-66.)

## muwaalaah 1 موالاة

Befriending, showing loyalty to

Befriending and showing loyalty to somebody or some people.

## muwaalaah 2 موالاة

Immediate succession

Doing things after each other immediately, such as washing the hands, rinsing the mouth, sniffing water and rinsing the nostrils ...

immediately after one another, without any appreciable pause in between them, when we do the ablution.

## muwaalat al-a'daa' موالاة الأعداء

Alliance with enemy

Alliance with the enemy, especially against Muslims.

## muwaaqa'ah مواقعة

Copulation

Having sexual intercourse.

## muwaHHId موحد

Monotheist

Someone who does not recognize nor worship anyone except the One God, Allah.

## muwakkal مُوَكَّل

Representative, agent

Someone appointed by another to represent him/ her.

## muwakkil مُوكِّل

Represented party

A person who appoints another to act on his/ her behalf.

## muwaTTa' (al--) الموطأ

The Muwatta

The book of hadeeths compiled by imam Malik ibn Anas of Medina.

## muzaabanah مزابنة

Indefinite for definite sale.

A forbidden type of sale, where a measured item is exchanged for an unknown one.

## muzaara'ah مزارعة

Farming partnership

An arrangement in which the owner of a land provides the land while another takes care of the farming, and they share the crops.

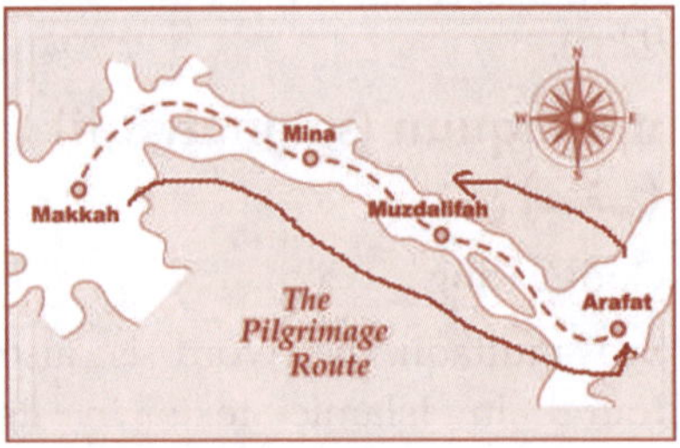


## muzdalifah مزدلفة

Muzdalifah

A place between 'Arafah and Mina, where pilgrims spend the night before the tenth day of Dhul-Hijjah ("'iid al-aDHaa").

Mm

# Nn

## naafi' (an--) النافع

The Benefit Giver

A Divine Attribute of Allah. The Only One Who can give benefits or withhold them.

## naafilah (pl. nawaafil) نافلة (نوافل)

Optional practice

Optional practice, usually of worship, such as extra prayers or fasting.

## naajiyah (al-firqah an--) الناجية (الفرقة ---)

The saved group (sect)

The reference is to the Muslims that will gain salvation on the Day of Judgment as a result of following the Qur'an and the teachings of Prophet Muhammad (PBUH) meticulously, as opposed to those groups that strayed from the path in different ways.

## naashiz ناشز

Insubordinate wife

A wife who rebels against her husband unjustifiably. She may be deprived of "nafaqah" ('financial support').

## naasikh (pl. nawaasikh) ناسخ (نواسخ)

Abrogating

A decree or revelation that abrogates a previous one or modifies it.

## naaZir al-waqf (pl. nuZZaar -) ناظر (نظار) الوقف

Steward of endowment

A person in charge of managing the affairs of an endowment.

## nabiyy (pl. 'anbiyaa') نبي (أنبياء)

Prophet

A man chosen by God to guide a group of people to the ways of God and teach them His message. According to some scholars ,a prophet may be a messenger of God ;he may not be a messenger.

## nabiyy (an--) al-'ummiyy النبي الأمي

The illiterate prophet

The reference is to Prophet Muhammad (PBUH) who could not read nor write. Some scholars say that the word "'ummiyy" may also mean gentile (non-Jewish). In fact, both descriptions apply to the Prophet Muhammad (PBUH). (See the Qur'an, 7: 157-8).

## nadb 1 ندب

Wailing

Wailing is prohibited by Islam, but not weeping ,in the event of death of a dear person.

## nadb 2 ندب

Recommendation

The term is similar to" istiHbaab;" something" manduub "means it is recommended but not required.

## nadhara (yandhur) نذر (ينذر)

To vow

To make a promise to God to do something.

## nadhr (pl. nudhuur) نذر (نذور)

Vow

A promise one makes to Allah to do something ,usually good.

## nafaqah (pl. nafaqaat) نفقة (نفقات)

Alimony ,expenses

The money usually paid by a former husband to his divorcee for her support during the' waiting period 'or for the support of his children from her ,who are in her custody .The word also means expenses or financial support in general.

## nafrah (an--) min 'arafah النفرة من عرفة

Rush from' arafah

Pilgrims 'move immediately after sunset of the ninth day of hajj from the plain of' arafah to Muzdalifah where they spend the night before going to Mina on the tenth.

## nafs نفس

Self ,soul

The word is used sometimes to mean a human being ,in the expression" qatl an-nafs" ('murder').

## nafs (an--) al-'ammaarah النفس الأمارة

The tempting self

The side of the human self that keeps tempting him/ her to do bad things, usually to find pleasure in them. (cf. "an-nafs al-lawwaamah" 'the blaming self / conscience').

## nafs (an-) al-lawwaamah النفس اللوامة

Conscience

Literally, this means the blaming self which prevents one from doing wrong things, as opposed to the tempting self that prompts one to do bad things.

## nafs (an--) al-muTma'innah النفس المطمئنة

The soul at peace

The soul of a believer. We find reference to this term in the Qur'an, 89: 27-30.

## nahaar (pl. anhur) نهار (أنهر)

Day

Day, as opposed to night, which begins with sunrise and ends with sunset.

## naHara (yanHar) نحر (ينحر)

To slaughter a camel

To slaughter a camel, usually while it is in standing position.

## naHr نحر

Sacrifice

Originally, the word means slaughtering a camel. But in the expression "yawm an-naHr" (the day / feast of sacrifice) it means sacrifice of any cattle.

## nahy 'an al-munkar نهي عن المنكر

Forbidding the wrong

Forbidding or stopping wrong actions, including sinful deeds and words. This can be done in action and through words.

## najaah (an--) النجاة

Salvation, deliverance

The case of being saved from something bad or evil. Often we hear the word in expressions like "an-najaah min an-naar" (being saved from Hell-Fire).

## najaasah (pl. najaasaat) نجاسة (نجاسات)

Ritually unclean / impure thing

Something that has to be removed from the body or the clothing of a Muslim before he can pray.

## najaashii (an--) النجاشي

The Negos

The Ethiopian Emperor during the time of Prophet Muhammad (PBUH). He welcomed the early Muslim immigrants to his country, and Muslim historians report that he actually embraced Islam.

## najas نجس

Ritually unclean / impure thing

Something that has to be removed from the body or the clothing of a Muslim before he can pray.

**najash نجش**

Deceitful outbidding

Outbidding with the sole purpose of leading others to pay a higher price for something. Naturally, this is forbidden in Islam according to the Prophetic hadeeth on the subject.

**najis نجس**

Ritually unclean

See "najas."

**najjasa (yunajjis) نجس (ينجس)**

To defile ,impurify

To make something ritually unclean or impure.

**nakaHa (yankaH) نكح (ينكح)**

To marry

**nakiir نكير**

Nakeer

The name of one of the two angels who come to the dead person in his grave for questioning .See "munkar wa nakiir."

**namiimah نميمة**

Talesbearing ,calumny

Reporting bad things said by someone against another person, which is strongly condemned by Islam.

**nammaam نَمّام**

Talebearer ,telltale

A person who reports bad things said against someone to another person.

**namruud نَمْرُود**

Nimrod

The tyrant pagan king who ordered Prophet Abraham (PBUH) to be thrown in the fire built for the purpose. In the Qur'an we read one of his encounters with Abraham (2: 258). In Arabic the name is used to indicate rebellion and arrogance.

**naqD1 نقض**

Invalidating

Doing something that makes something invalid, such as passing water which makes the ablution invalid, or breaking a promise... etc.

**naqD 2 نقض**

Breach, unfulfilling

In terms of covenants and promises, this means breaking the promise or breach of a contract.

## naqiib (pl. nuqabaa') نقيب (نقباء)

Leader

A person leading six persons in an expedition; a tribal leader.

## naql (an--) النقل

The Text

The text of the Qur'an and prophetic traditions. A contrasting word is "'aql" (reasoning).

## naqliyy نقلي

Transmitted (proof)

Usually, this refers to the Qur'an and traditions of the Prophet (PBUH).

## naSaaraa (sg. naSraaniyy) نصارى (نصراني)

Christians

See "naSraaniyy."

## nasab (pl. 'ansaab) نسب (أنساب)

Having same blood relationship, ancestry.

## nasab (shajarat an-) شجرةالنسب

Family tree

The family tree of a person ;i.e. names of his forefathers.

## nasakha (yansakhu) نسخ (ينسخ)

To abrogate

This refers to a verse of the Qur'an that was revealed after another one with a different ruling .The latter is called" naasikh "and the earlier" mansuukh."

## nasii'ah نسيئة

Postponed debt

A debt whose payment is postponed at the request of the indebted person .The interest charged for the postponement is called" ribaa an-nasii'ah."

## naSiiHah (pl. naSaa'iH) نصيحة ( ج نصائح)

Advice

Advice ,a piece of advice or offering it.

## naSiiHah li-a'immat al-muslimiin نصيحة لأئمة المسلمين

Advice to Muslim leaders

Offer of sincere advice to Muslim leaders.

## naSiiHah li-llaahi ta'aalaa نصيحة لله تعالى

Sincerity to God the Almighty

Being sincere in one's relationship with God.

## naskh نسخ

Abrogation

The process by which a new decree ,e.g ,.abolishes or modifies an earlier one.

## nasr نسر

Nasr

The name of a deity worshipped by the people of Prophet Noah. (See the Qur'an 71:23)

## naSraaniyy (pl. naSaaraa) نصراني (نصارى)

Christian

Afollower(orrather,aworshipper) of the Prophet Jesus (PBUH).

## naSraaniyyah (an --) النصرانية

Christianity

Originally ,the religion of Jesus, but now refers to the beliefs of Christians ,which Muslims believe contradict his teachings.

## naSS (pl. nuSuuS) نصّ (نصوص)

Clear injunction ,explicit textual ruling

The term literally means 'text'; In the Science of Principles "'ilm al-uSuul") it is used to mean 'text of the law'.

## naSuuH نصوح

Pure, sincere

Usually this adjective is used with the word "tawbah" (repentance).

## naTiiHah نطيحة

Dead by goring

An animal that is dead due to being gored by horns of another animal or its head. The meat of such an animal is forbidden to be eaten by a Muslim, because it is not properly slaughtered. (See the Qur'an, 5: 3).

## nawaaqiD (sg. naaqiDah) نواقض (ناقضة)

Invalidators, invalidating acts

Acts, including verbal ones, that make a certain state (such as ritual purity) invalid. So we hear of "nawaaqiD al-wuDuu'" (invalidators of ablution), "nawaaqiD aS-Salaah" (invalidators of prayer)…

## nawaasikh (sg. naasikh) نواسخ (ناسخ)

Abrogators

See "naasikh."

## nifaaq نفاق

Hypocrisy

Nn

In Arabic the word means showing what you do not believe in.

## nifaaq akbar نفاق أكبر

Major hypocrisy

Pretending to be a believer while harbouring disbelief. A description of this type of hypocrites is found in the Qur'an, for example ,in Chapter8-20 :2 and in the Chapter entitled" the Chapter of the Hypocrites(63) "

## nifaaq aSghar نفاق أصغر

Minor hypocrisy

Acts that may negatively affect the faith proper but does not make one an unbeliever ,such as lying and breaking promises.

## nifaas نفاس

Childbirth ,confinement

See" nufasaa."'

## niHlah 1 (pl. niHal) نحلة 1 (نحل)

Sect ,creed

In Islamic writings we sometimes find the term "niHal" (sects) to refer to different sects, as opposed to "milal" (religions).

## niHlah 2 (pl. niHal) نحلة 2 (نحل)

Free gift

This term is found in the Qur'an in this special sense in one verse (Chapter 4: 4.)

## nikaaH ('ankiHah) نكاح (أنكحة)

Marriage

## nikaaH faasid نكاح فاسد

Invalid marriage

Marriage that violates the basic requirements of proper marriage, such as marrying a first degree relative.

## nikaaH al-mut'ah نكاح المتعة

Temporary marriage

Literally ,this means' marriage for pleasure .'The marriage arrangement in which both parties agree to stay married for a specified time .This is forbidden according to main stream Islam.

## nikaaH ash-shighaar نكاح الشغار

Mutual marriage arrangement

An arrangement in which a person gives a female in his trust to someone who does the same, without either paying the" Sadaaq." This is forbidden in Islam.

## niqaab ('anqibah) (نقاب (أنقبة

Veil

A veil which covers the whole face with the exception of the eyes .It should not be worn by a woman on pilgrimage to Mecca.

## niSaab (pl. 'anSibah) (نصاب (أنصبة

Minimum taxable amount

The minimum amount of anything for which one should pay "zakaah". For example, forty sheep is the minimum number of sheep for one to pay alms. If one has less than forty, then he is not required to pay alms ("zakaah") on them.

## niyaaHah نياحة

Wailing

Wailing is forbidden in Islam .A Muslim woman may weep for losing someone ,but she should not wail nor tear her clothes or the like.

## niyyah (pl. niyyaat) (نية (نيات

Intention

Intention is a prerequisite for any act of worship. In fact, according to the Prophet (PBUH), deeds are judged by the intentions behind them.

## nubuwwah نبوة

Prophethood ,prophecy

The state of being a prophet; something foretold.

## nufasaa' نفساء

New mother ,confined woman

A woman who has recently given birth to a baby .The term is used mainly to refer to her during the post partum bleeding period, when she is not supposed to pray or fast or touch the Qur'an. Normally ,this could take up to40 days.

## nuSayriyyah نصيرية

Nusayris

An extremist group of Shi'ites who ascribe divinity to Imam Ali ,the Prophet 'cousin .More recently, they have been given the name of Alawiyyiin .The followers of this group are especially found in Syria.

## nushuur (yawm an--) (...نشور (يوم الـ

Day of Resurrection

## nushuuz نشوز

Wife insubordination

Insubordination or refusal to give the husband his marital rights. We also find this word with reference to husbands to mean ill-treatment. (See the Qur'an, 4: 34 and 128). (See also "naashiz").

## nusuk (pl. 'ansaak) نسك( أنساك)

Rite ,ritual

Religious ritual to be observed. Very often we find the synonymous word" mansak) "pl .manaasik( used.

## nuuH نوح

Noah

A major prophet of Allah who lived more than 950 years preaching the message of Allah to his people. They were drowned in the Flood, while he and the few believers with him were saved in the ark he built. (See the Qur'an, 11: 35-48 and 71).

## nuun at-tanwiin نون التنوين

' n 'of nunation

The /n/ which is pronounced but not written in Arabic, as an indication of indefiniteness for noun, such in كُتُبٌ (pronounced / kutubun/. In vocalized texts, there is a sign called nunation sign, which is doubling the diacritic sign of the short vowel.

## nuun mutaHarrikah نون متحركة

Vocalized 'n'

The /n/ which is followed by a vowel,as opposed to "nuun saakinah" (unvocalized n).

## nuun saakinah نون ساكنة

Unvocalized 'n'

The /n/ which is not followed by a vowel in any word.

## nuur (an--) النور

The Light

A Divine Attribute of Allah. The Source of all light in the universe.

## nuzuul al-qur'aan نزول القرآن

Revelation of the Qur'an

The process by which the Qur'an reached the Prophet Muhammad (PBUH) from Allah, through Archangel Gabriel.

# Qq

## qaabiD (al--) القابض

The Restrainer

A Divine Attribute of Allah. The One Who withholds whatever He likes, or the One Who takes life.

## qaabiil قابيل

Cain

A son of Adam and brother to Abel who killed him.

## qaaDii (pl. quDaat) قاض (قضاة)

Judge

Nowadays, we hear the expression "qaadii shar'iyy" to mean a judge according to Islamic law. But in Islamic history, the word itself meant a Muslim judge.

## qaadir (al--) القادر

The Ever Able

A Divine Attribute of Allah. The One Whose ability is unlimited.

## qaa'if قائف

Physiognomy specialist

Someone who has the skill of identifying the father of a child based on its physical features.

## qaanit قانت

Submissive, humble

Normally, this is used with reference to a person, being submissive and humble in his supplications or prayers.

## qaari' (pl. qurraa') قارئ (قراء)

Reader

Someone who is a professional reader of the Qur'an, normally a "HaafiZ" (who knows the Qur'an by heart, according to the rules of tajweed).

## qaarin قارن

Coupling hajj and 'umrah

Someone who performs both "'umrah" and "Hajj" without changing his pilgrimage garb. (cf. "mutamatti'" and "mufrid").

## qaaruun قارون

Korah

The ungrateful Israelite who was known for his great prosperity, but boasted "I have been given it only on account of knowledge I possess." Allah caused earth to "swallow him and his dwelling". (See the Qur'an 28: 76-82).

## qaaSir (pl. quSSar) قاصر (قصر)

Under age

Someone who is below the age of legal responsibility ;therefore, requires a guardian.

## qaaTi 'raHim قاطع الرحم

Severer of kinship relations

Someone who does not respect kinship relations.

## qaaTi 'Tariiq قاطع طريق

Highway robber

Someone who stops travelers to rob them.

## qabuul قبول

Acceptance

The term is usually used in conjunction with'" iijaab" (offer in marriage), and it means the groom's accepting the offer, normally made by the guardian of the bride.

## qaDaa' (al--) القضاء

The judiciary

People or system involved in making legal judgments.

## qaDaa 1 (yaqDii) قضى 1 (يقضي)

To rule ,decree

To make a ruling. For God, it usually means 'to decree / ordain'. (See, e.g., the Qur'an, 17: 23 and following verses.)

## qaDaa 2 (yaqDii) قضى 2 (يقضي)

To pay (a debt)

It is considered a sin for an able person not to pay back a debt.

## qaDaa 3 (yaqDii) bayna قضى 3 (يقضي) بين

To arbitrate

To settle a dispute between two parties.

## qaDaa 'ad-dayn قضاء الدين

Paying back

Paying back money borrowed from someone.

## qaDaa 'al-Haajah قضاء الحاجة

Relieving oneself

Going to the toilet.

## qaDaa 'al-Hajaat / al-Hawaa'ij قضاء الحاجات / الحوائج

Fulfilling the needs

Doing things ,usually for others in the way of helping them.

## qaDaa 'aS-Salaah
## قضاء الصلاة

Making up the prayer

Praying a" Salaah" which one missed to perform at the specified time for some reason or another.

## qaDaa' wa qadar
## قضاء و قدر

Divine decree, predestination

Something decreed by God beforehand, and one could not do anything about it.

## qadar (pl. 'aqdaar)
## قدر (أقدار)

Predestination, exact measure

Allah's assignment of ends to all processes of life and existence on earth. In this case, the term is conjoined with qaDaa'. The word is also used in the Qur'an (45: 49) to mean exact measure.

## qaddara 1 (yuqaddir)
## قدر 1 (يقدر)

To give measure

In this sense the word originally means to calculate or estimate. But when it refers to Allah in the Qur'an it is used to mean to give exact measure as well as 'decree'. (See below).

## qaddara 2 (yuqaddir)
## قدر 2 (يقدر)

To decree, to predestinate

In this sense the word is used with reference to Allah's decree or predestination of the things that happen in the universe.

## qadariyy قدري

Believer in absolute free will

Someone who believes in absolute free will; therefore, he denies any form of Divine predestination. He is the opposite of the fatalist.

## qadhf قذف

Slander

Technically, this means slander by accusing someone of fornication (sexual intercourse out of wedlock). The ruling regarding this is given in the Qur'an, 24: 4.

## qadH قدح

negation of a cause

In the Science of Principles, this means proving inadequacy of grounds for a ruling or opinion.

## qadr قدر

high esteem

## qahhaar (al--) القهار

The Supreme Vanquisher

A Divine Attribute of Allah. The One to Whose power everyone and everything has submitted and submits.

## qalqalah قلقلة

Slight vocalization

Adding a very brief vowel-like sound to certain consonants when followed by other consonants or in word final positions, while reciting the Qur'an, to make their enunciation clearer. For example, the word "yabda'u" has a very brief /a/ like vowel after it in pronunciation. The consonants subject to this feature are: /q/, /t/, /b/, /j/, /d/.. There are two degrees of "qalqalah", "Sughraa" and" kubraa" (minor and major), depending on the position of the sound.

## qanna'ah قناعة

Contentment

Accepting whatever comes to one or is given to him.

## qanaTa (yaqnuT) قنط (يقنط)

To despair

The Qur'an instructs believers not to despair of Allah's mercy and forgiveness. (See the Qur'an, 39: 53).

## qanata (yaqnutu) قنت (يقنت)

To humble one's self

To show humility and submission, or to supplicate with such a spirit. (See the Qur'an, 3: 43.)

## qaraamiTah (sg. qurmuTiyy) قرامطة (قرمطي)

Karamathians

A Shi'ite sect who ransacked the holy mosque in Mecca and took away the black stone, to be returned only at the orders of the Fatimite ruler of the time.

## qarD Hasan قرض حسن

Good loan

Loan according to the rules of Islam; that is, without interest, but for the sake of Allah.

## qariin (pl. quranaa') قرين (قرناء)

Constant companion

The companion referred to could be an angel, a human or a genie.

## qariinah (pl. qaraa'in) 1 قرينة (قرائن) 1

Context

It could be linguistic or situational.

## qariinah (qaraa'in) 2 قرينة (قرائن) 2

Circumstantial evidence

Evidence that can be drawn from the temporal, spatial and any other circumstances.

## qarn al-manaazil قرن المنازل

Qarn al-Manazil

Name of a place in the Arabian Peninsula where prospective pilgrims from Najd or those who pass by that location should start their "iHraam" status.

## qasaamah قسامة

Taking an oath

Technically, this means swearing to Allah when accusing or being accused of murder in order to confirm or deny the accusation.

## qasam قسم

Oath

Swearing to God.

## qasm (bayn az-zawjaat) قسم (بين الزّوجات)

division of time

Equitable allotting of time (especially at night) among one's wives.

## qaSr قصر

Shortening

Shortening a four-"rak'ah" prayer by performing two "rak'ahs". This is permissible for someone on travel.

## qaT' ar-raHim قطع الرحم

breaking family ties, alienation of relatives

To treat relatives as strangers, or to ignore one's duties to his relations, sometimes by mistreating them, which is a great sin. This is the opposite of "Silat ar-raHim."

## qaT 'aT-Tariiq قطع الطريق

brigandry ,highway robbery

This is a major crime in Islamic law. The Qur'anic ruling regarding the punishment is given in Chapter:5 .33

## qaT 'al-yad قطع اليد

Chopping off the hand

The punishment for stealing worthy objects from a safe place for the sake of stealing or making money is chopping the right hand off from the wrist .If any of the preconditions is not fulfilled ,such as stealing out of hunger ,then the thief's hand may not be chopped off.

## qaTaa'i' قطائع

Land grants

Land grants usually given by the

ruler to some of his subjects.

## qaTii'at ar-raHim قطيعة الرحم

Alienation of relatives

See" qaT' ar-raHim."

## qaT'iyy قطعيّ

Definitive

A ruling ,e.g ,.which is definitive, not speculative.

## qatl al'-amd قتل العمد

Murder

Intentionally killing someone. This is considered not only a major crime but also a major sin. Capital punishment or payment of" diyyah" (blood money) may be applied, depending on the wish of the family of the victim.

## qatl al-khaTa' قتل الخطأ

Manslaughter

Unintentional killing of a person. For the ruling on this, see the Qur'an, 4: 92.

## qatl an-nafs قتل النفس

Murder

Killing a human being, including committing suicide.

## qawad قود

Retaliatory punishment

See "qiSaaS."

## qawiyy (al--) القوي

The Omnipotent

A Divine Attribute of Allah .The One Whose power knows no limits.

## qayyim (pl. qayyimuun) قيّم

Custodian

See" qiwaamah."

## qayyuum (al--) القيوم

The Ever-Subsisting

A Divine Attribute of Allah .The One Who is Eternal and ever supports the existence of others.

## qiblah قبلة

Direction

When the term is used in anunqualified manner ,it usually refers to the direction of the Ka'bah ,which a Muslim should face when praying.

## qiil wa qaal قيل وقال

Rumours

Muslims are warned against following rumours, and they are instructed to verify allegations made against each other. (See the Qur'an, 49: 6.)

## qiiraaT(pl. qaraariiT) (قراريط) قيراط

Kerat

In Islamic writings, this term has many meanings: (1) unit of weight for precious stones and gold (0.195 g.), (2) a dry measure and (3) a square measure (175.035 square meters.)

## qimaar قمار

Gambling

Gambling is forbidden by Islam, and it is considered a work of Satan. (See the Qur'an, 5: 90).

## qinTaar (pl. qanaaTiir) (قناطير) قنطار

talent

A weight equivalent to 1200 ounces of gold.

## qiraa'aat (al--) as-sab' القراءات السبع

Seven modes of recitation

Specialists in tajweed talk of seven and ten modes of recitation of the Qur'an. These are simple variations in the pronunciation of certain words, attributed to the different dialects. (See "sab'at 'aHruf").

## qiraan قران

Wedlock ,coupling

## qiSaaS قصاص

Retaliatory punishment

Punishment ,both retributive and compensatory .It includes killing the murderer ,the ruling of" an eye for an eye "as well as compensatory payment of money.

## Qiwaamah1 قوامة

Custody ,guardianship

Providing protective care to somebody or something.

## qiwaamah 2 قوامة

Charge of family

Being in charge of and responsible for supporting a family.

## qiyaafah قيافة

Physiognomy

The term refers to an old practice which was used to identify fatherhood on the basis of physical features of a child and possible father.

## qiyaam قيام

Standing position

In formal prayers ,the standing position ,as opposed to bowing, prostrating or sitting.

## qiyaam al-layl قيام الليل

Night vigil

Spending the night in devotions, usually praying.

## qiyaamah (al--) القيامة

The Resurrection

Islam emphasizes the concept of physical resurrection, when the whole creation will be brought back to life in body and soul. (See the Qur'an, 22: 1-7; 75: 1-13; 78: 17-40; 80: 33-34, 42).

## qiyaas قياس

Analogy

Literally ,it means' measuring,' but technically it means analogy, which is one of the main sources of Islamic law.

## qiyaas iqtiraaniy قياس اقتراني

Circumstantial analogy

Analogy based on similarity of circumstances of a case to those of the original ruling.

## qubaa' قباء

Quba'

A suburb of modern Medina (al-Madinah al-Munawwarah) in Saudi Arabia, which lies to the south of the town. Prophet Muhammad stayed there upon his arrival to Medina from Mecca

in the "hijrah". The first mosque in Islam was built there, and it is frequented by visitors to Medina. (See the Qur'an 9:108)

## qubul قبل

Genitalia

The male or female sex organ.

## qudduus (al--) القدوس

The Most Holy

A Divine Attribute of Allah. The One Who is All-Pure and Blemish less.

## qudwah قدوة

Role model

A person we follow or imitate in behaviour and character. A similar word is "uswah."

## qunuut قنوت

humility ,submission

A common expression with which this term is associated is" du'aa 'al-qunuut "which is often said in the "witr "prayer ,the last voluntary prayer performed during the night.

## qur' (pl. quruu') قرء (قروء)

Menstrual period

Qur'anic commentators have differed whether this word means the time of menstruation or the time between two menstruations in their interpretation of verse228 of Chapter.2

## qur'aan (al--) القرآن

The Qur'an

The Exact Words of Allah revealed to the Prophet Muhammad (PBUH) through Archangel Gabriel. (See the Qur'an, 10: 37-38; 26: 192-5; 17: 88.) It consists of 114 chapters. The word "qur'aan" means reading or recitation.

## qur'ah قرعة

Casting lots

Usually ,we hear the expression "yujrii qur'ah "or the verb "yaqtari) "'to cast lots (for permissible things ,not gambling.

## quraysh قريش

Quraysh tribe

The noblest of Arab tribes, who livedinMeccaandwereconsidered the guardians and keepers of the Ka'bah. The Prophet Muhammad (PBUH) belonged to this tribe.

## qurbaan (pl. qaraabiin) قربان (قرابين)

offering

Usually, an animal slaughtered as an offering to God. A portion or all of the meat is normally given to the poor and needy.

## qurbah (pl. qurubaat) قربة (قربات)

Good deed

A deed performed by a Muslim to become nearer to Allah.

## qurraa' (sg. qaari') قرّاء (قارئ)

Reciters ,readers

Usually ,this refers to people who know the Qur'an by heart and recite it well.

## qu'uud قعود

sitting

Sitting position ,synonymous to "juluus."

# R r

## raafi' (ar-- ) الرّافع

The Raiser

A Divine Attribute of Allah .The One Who raises the position or status of those who obey His commands.

## raafiDah (sg. raafiDiyy) رافِضَة (رافضي)

Rejectionist

A term used to refer to Shi'ites who reject the right of the first three righteous caliphs to the caliphate, claiming that Ali (RAA) was supposed to be the first successor to the Prophet (PBUH).

## raahib (pl. ruhbaan) راهب (رهبان)

Monk

Though the word may be translated as' monk 'in general ,in Islamic terminology it is used to refer to a Christian monk who led a life of devotion in monasteries.

## raa'ii (pl. ru'aat) راعي (رعاة)

Person in charge

Lexically ,the word means a 'shepherd ,'but it is used to mean anyone in charge of others ,father, ruler etc.

## raa'ish رائِش

Bribery mediator

The person who mediates between the bribing and bribed persons. He is a sinner like them.

## raaHilah راحلَة

Riding-camel

A female camel used for a ride.

## raaki' راكع

Bowing (in prayer)

A person in the bowing position. See "rukuu'" (bowing).

## raaqii (ar--) الرّاقي

Reader of "ruqyah"

The person who reads Qur'anic verses and prayers over a sick person for healing purposes.

## raashii (ar--) الرّاشي

Briber

A person who offers a bribe to another .He is a partner in the crime ,which is a great sin .The other two sinners are the culprits: "al-murtashii" (the seeker of the bribe), and "ar-raa'ish" (the go-between).

## raawii (pl. ruwaat) al-Hadiith
## راوي (رواة) الحديث

Narrator, transmitter

The person who reports a prophetic tradition.

## raaziq (ar--) / ar-razzaaq
## الرّازق / الرّزّاق

The Best Provider

A Divine Attribute of Allah. The provider for every being in the universe, Whose bounties have no limits.

## rabb (pl. 'arbaab)
## رب (أرباب)

Lord, master / owner

In the Qur'an the word is found both in the singular and plural forms. It is used in the sense of deity or Allah as well as lord and master. This term is associated with "rabbaa/ tarbiyah" which mean bringing up, nourishing, educating…etc.



## rabbaaniyy
## ربّاني

God fearing, devout person.

## rabii' al-'aakhar
## ربيع الآخر

Rabi' the Second.

Another name for "rabii' ath-thaanii", the fourth month of the Islamic calendar.

## rabii' al-awwal ربيع الأول

Rabi' the First

The third month of the Islamic calendar. It was in this month that the Prophet Muhammad (PBUH) was born, most probably on the 12th day of that month in the year 570 AD.

## rabii' ath-thaanii ربيع الثاني

Rabi' the Second

The fourth month of the Islamic calendar.

## raDaa' رَضاع

Breast feeding

Breast feeding (especillay five or more times) makes the woman a 'foster mother' to the baby if it is not her own. This has legal ramifications in the area of marriage. The foster brothers and sisters in this sense cannot marry each other.

## raD'ah (pl. raD'aat)
## رضعة (رضعات)

Breast feeding once

Every time a woman breast feeds a baby this is called "raD'ah". The number of times (five or more) is very important in the case of the woman feeding another person's baby. (See "raDaa'").

## radd as-salaam
## ردّ السّلام

Return a greeting

See" radd at-taHiyyah ."In Islam returning a greeting is obligatory.

## radd at-taHiyyah
## ردّ التّحيّة

Returning the greeting

The Qur'an teaches Muslims that when they are greeted they should return the same or with better greeting) .See the Qur'an.(86 :4 ,

## radhiilah (pl. radhaa'il)
## رذيلة (رذائل)

Vice

sinful act.

## raDiya allaahu' anhu
## رضي الله عنه

May Allah be pleased with him

A prayer often said after mentioning the name of a companion of the Prophet Muhammad (PBUH). If it is a female then we say "'anhaa" instead of "'anhu".

## raf 'al-Haraj
## رفع الحرج

Removing hardship

Removing cause of hardship ,such as permission to break the fast if one is ill or is on travel.

## rafath رَفَث

Obscenity

The word has been translated into 'obscenity, lewdness and sex act' all of which are forbidden for the pilgrim during pilgrimage. (See the Qur'an, 2: 197.)

## rahbaaniyyah
## رهبانية

Monasticism

Devoting one's life to worshipping God. The term is often used with reference to Christianity (the Qur'an, 57: 27).

## rahbah رهبة

Awe

With reference to a Muslim's relation with Allah ,this term

means fear of disobedience to Allah.

**raHiim (ar--) الرّحيم**

The Most Merciful

A Divine Attribute of Allah. The One Who shows special mercy to the believers. (cf. "ar-raHmaan").

**raHim 1 (pl. arHaam)**

**رحم 1 (أرحام)**

Womb

**raHim 2 (pl. arHaam)**

**رحم 2 (أرحام)**

Blood relative

See" dhawuu ar-raHim."

**raHmaan (ar--) الرّحمن**

The All-Merciful ,Beneficent

A Divine Attribute of Allah .The One Whose mercy encompasses the whole universe ,including disbelievers.This name or attribute is never used except with Allah, unlike most of the other attributes that may be used with others.

**raHmah رحمة**

Mercy ,kindness

This word means not just mercy, but it means kindness ,tenderness, caring and the like as well.

**rahn (ruhuun)/ rihaan**

**رَهن (رُهون)/ رهان**

Pledge

Something given by a creditor to a debtor as a security for paying back a loan.

**ra'iyyah رعيّة**

Subjects

People under the charge of a certain person, be it a ruler, a father or a mother. (See "raa'ii").

**rajaa' رجاء**

hope, good expectation

Wishing or asking for or expecting something good.

**rajab رجب**

Rajab

The seventh month of the Islamic calendar. It was in this month that "al-israa' and mi'raaj" took place.

**raj'ah 1 رجعة**

Revoking the divorce

See "raj'iyy (Talaaq)".

**raj'ah 2 رجعة**

Return, change of mind

**raj'iyy (Talaaq)**

**رجعي (طلاق)**

Revocable (divorce)

First time and second time divorces are considered revocable in the sense that a divorced wife may go back to her ex-husband within the waiting period (three 'menstrual periods'). After that waiting period they may not go back unless they remarry. This ruling is contrasted with "Talaaq baa'in ('final or irrevocable divorce').

## rajiim (ar--) الرّجيم

The outcast

This term is used to describe Satan who is cursed and outcast from Divine mercy, due to his rebellion against Allah and His commands.

## rajm رجم

Stoning

Throwing stones at sth. or sb. But often it refers to stoning to death of the adulterer and adulteress.

## rajm bi-l-ghayb رجم بالغيب

Conjecture

Making a baseless statement or conclusion.

## rak'ah (pl. rak'aat) ركعةً (ركعات)

A bowing

Technically, this covers not just bowing, but a set of actions that are done in "Salaah": standing, bowing, two prostrations and the sitting between them. (See "rukuu'").

## ramaDaan رمضان

Ramadan

The ninth month of the Muslim calendar which is the month of fasting. This is the month in which the Qur'an was first revealed. (See the Qur'an, 2: 185)

## ramal (ar--) الرَّمَل

Jogging

Walking fairly swiftly in the first three rounds of circumambulation around the Ka'bah ,to be done by men only .This is observed only in the" Tawaaf" for "'umrah" or "Hajj."

## ramy رَمي

Throwing ,stoning

The term refers to throwing seven pebbles at the pillar of the' jamrah" in Mina as part of the pilgrimage rituals.

## raqabah رقبة

Person

This is often found in the context of liberating slaves .So we find the expression'" itq raqabah" or "fakku raqabah" (setting a slave free). Literally, it means a neck.

**raqiib (ar--) الرّقيب**

The Ever-Watching

A Divine Attribute of Allah. One Who is constantly Watchful of His creatures' actions.

**rashaad رَشاد**

Discretion, guidance

In the Qur'an, we have the expression "sabiil ar-rashaad" (See the Qur'an, 40:29)

**rashad رَشَد**

Right course

Correct or right course of action. (See the Qur'an 18: 10)

**rashiid (ar--) الرّشيد**

The Ever-Right

A Divine Attribute of Allah. The One Who never errs in His decisions or actions, and Who guides others.

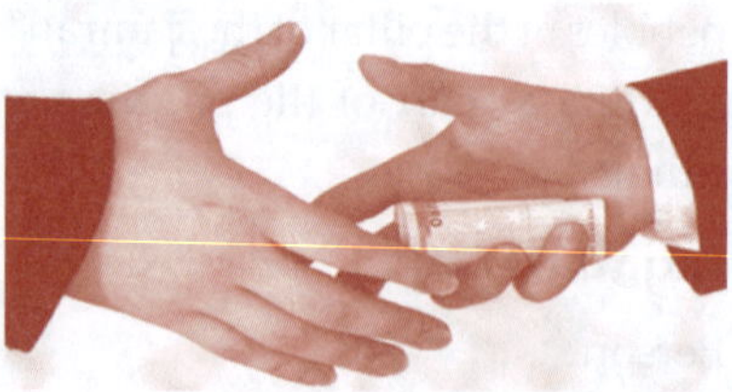

**rashwah رَشوة**

Bribery

Paying undeserved something to someone for favours or services. Bribery is strongly condemned in Islam. In fact, the Prophet (PBUH) is reported to have condemned the giver of the bribe, the receiver and the mediator.

**rasuul (pl. rusul) رسول (رسل)**

Messenger, apostle

In the religious context, this usually refers to a prophet sent by the Almighty Allah to a certain nation or to the whole world (as in the case of the Prophet Muhammad (PBUH).

**rattala (yurattil) رتل (يرتل)**

To read or recite carefully, usually with reference to the Qur'an.

See "tartiil."

**ra'uuf (ar--) الرّؤوف**

The Ever-Compassionate

A Divine Attribute of Allah. The One Who is Most Kind and Merciful.

**rawaa (yarwii) روى (يروي)**

Report ,narrate

The word is used in its general sense as well as technical sense, which means to report a Prophetic tradition.

## rawDah (ar--) ash-shariifah الرّوضة الشّريفة

The holy Rawdah

The name of the section in the Prophet Muhammad's Mosque which lies between the tomb of the Prophet and his pulpit. Reference is made in a tradition of the Prophet PBUH (that this part is a" rawDah) "garden (of the gardens of Paradise.

## ribaa رِبَا

Usury ,interest

The money one charges for giving someone a loan. Taking interest on loans, which is forbidden in Islam and is strongly condemned in the Qur'an where it is sharply contrasted with charity. (See the Qur'an, 2: 275-276).

## ribaaT رِباط

Guarding Muslim frontier

Guarding the borders of Muslim lands against possible attacks from the enemies .It is considered one of the highly praiseworthy forms of worship.

## ribawiyy رِبَوي

Usury related

A transaction that involves usury.

## riDaa رِضا

Contentment

Feeling satisfied with whatever one has or befalls him.

## ridaa' ('ardiyah) رِدَاء (أردية)

Upper torso cover

The sheet used by a male pilgrim (for example) to cover the upper part of his body, as opposed to the "izaar" for the lower part.

## riddah رِدّة

Apostasy

Abandoning one's faith. Islam forbids this for a Muslim; it is considered a capital offense.

## riDwaan 1 رِضوان

Pleasure, satisfaction

Very often, this term refers to Divine Pleasure. In other words, it refers to God's being pleased with someone, which should be the ultimate goal of a believer's actions and deeds.

## riDwaan 2 رِضوان

RiDwaan

Name of the angel in charge of guarding "jannah" (Paradise).

## rihaan رِهان

Security, pledge

Something a borrower, for example, leaves with the lender for security. This meaning should not be confused with the modern usage which is 'betting.'

## rijaal al-Hadiith رجال الحديث

Narrators of the hadeeth

The term refers to all the people involved in transmitting the Hadiith (prophetic tradition). Knowledge about them helps determine the degree of its authenticity.

## rijs رِجس

Abomination

Something most detested in the sight of Allah, which implies prohibition. (See the Qur'an, 5: 90).

## rikaaz ( pl. 'arkizah) ركاز (أركزة)

Buried treasure or minerals

Natural or buried treasures found in one's land ,including minerals and precious stones .There are certain regulations regarding the "zakaah" on these.

## rikhw رخو

Lenis/ soft

In Qur'anic phonetics, the term refers to the sounds which are produced without a complete obstruction of the air passage; in Modern phonetics the term 'continuant" may be used.

## risaalah (pl. risaalaat) رسالة (رسالات)

(Divine) message

The message given to God's messengers to convey to mankind. In this sense, it is synonymous to 'religion'.

## riwaayat al-Hadiith رواية الحديث

Narration of the hadeeth

Reporting prophetic traditions. The science of hadeeth authentication stipulates that a "hadeeth" would not be accepted unless we know the exact chain of transmitters up to the Prophet Muhammad (PBUH).

## riyaa' رِياء

Making show, sanctimony, sanctimoniousness

Doing something good to get attention and admiration of people, not to please God. This is considered a case of "shirk aSghar" (minor polytheism), because the doer of such an act is in a sense, associating others with God.

## rizq (pl. 'arzaaq) رِزق (أرزاق)

Provision, sustenance

Normally, the term is used in the context of Allah's provisions for His creation for their sustenance, since He is the true Provider.

## ru'yaa رؤيا

Dream, vision

Usually, a good dream, especially when contrasted with "Hulm" (dream).
For the sense of vision, see the Qur'an, 37: 60. For 'dream', see the Qur'an, 12: 43.

## ru'yaa SaaliHah رؤيا صالحة

Good dream

A dream whose meaning may come true.

## ru'yat al-hilaal رؤية الهلال

Sighting of new moon

Since the Islamic calendar is based on the lunar month, it is important to look for the new moon (crescent) to determine the beginning of the month.

## rubuubiyyah ربوبية

Lordship, Sovereignty

See "rabb". This term is sometimes contrasted with "uluuhiyyah" (Divinity, deity).

## rukhSah (pl. rukhaS) رخصة (رخص)

License ,permission

License to do something. For example, an ill person has the license to break the fast during Ramadan, and make up for the day(s) later.

## rukn (ar--) al-yamaanii الرّكن اليماني

The Yamaanii (Southern) Corner

The corner of the Ka'bah south of the Black Stone. The person doing "Tawaaf" starts here to recite the prayer which translates: "Our Lord, give us good in this world and good in the Hereafter and save us from Hell fire" until he reaches the Black Stone.

## rukn (pl. arkaan)(ركن (أركان)

Corner-stone, pillar

The supporting element of a structure, without which it would collapse. The term is used in many contexts to mean something absolutely essential, such as "arkaan al-islam", "arkaan al-iimaan", "arkaan aS-Salaah"… etc.

## rukuu' رُكوع

Bowing

Rukuu' in the "Salaah" (formal prayer) means: bowing with one's palms resting on the knees with the back as straight as possible. One's eyes should be kept on the spot where he puts his forehead during prostration.

## ruqyah (pl. ruqaa) رُقية (رُقى)

Islamic incantation

Verses from the Qur'an and/or prophetic prayers recited for the purpose of curing from various types of illnesses, psychological and physical, including driving away evil spirits from a person or place (exorcism).

Parts of the Qur'an that are especially known for this are: Chapter 1, the Verse of the Throne (2: 255) and Chapters 113 and 114.

## rushd رُشد

Discretion, maturity

This word is often found in the phrase "sinn ar-rushd" meaning the age of discrimination or legal responsibility.

## ruuH (ar--) al-amiin الرّوح الأمين

The Trustworthy Spirit

The term refers to Archangel Gabriel, who brought the Divine messages from Allah to His messengers.

## ruuH (pl. 'arwaaH) روح (أرواح)

Soul, spirit

The essence of life whose departure means death. According to Islamic teachings, the soul does not die, but it leaves the body, and it will come back to it upon Resurrection.

## ruuH al-qudus رُوح القدس

Holy Spirit

A reference to Archangel Gabriel.

## ruum (ar--) الرّوم

Romans, Byzantines

In Islamic history, the term is used to refer to the Romans, especially the people of Byzantine or Eastern Roman Empire.

# Ss

## sa'aa 1 (yas'aa)

## سعى1(يسعى)

To walk, move

to walk specially between Safa and Marwah.
See" sa'y".

## sa'aa 2 (yas'aa)

## سعى2(يسعى)

To work for ,pursue

We have this verb in expressions like "sa'aa 'alaa quuti 'iyaalih / rizqihi" (to work to earn a living'), or "sa'aa fii al-amr" (to pursue the matter).

## Saa' (pl. aSwaa')

## صاع (أصواع)

Sa'

An Islamic unit of dry measure. For wheat ,it is roughly equivalent to 2.172 kg.

## saa'ah (as--) السّاعة

The Hour

The Time of Resurrection.

## Saabi'ah (aS--) / aS-Saabi'uun

## الصّابئة / الصّابئون

Sabians ,Sabaeans

A group of people in the Fertile Crescent who are believed to believe in stars and to worship them, or they worship the angels. In the Qur'an, they are grouped along with Christians and Jews. (See the Qur'an, 5: 69).

## Saabir صابر

Patient ,perseverant

This terms refers to the person who shows patience and acceptance of misfortunes and / or perseveres in the doing of good deeds .See "Sabr".

## Saadiq صادق

Truthful

Someone who is telling the truth.

## SaaHib al-Huut صاحب الحوت

Man of the whale

The reference to Jonah. See "dhuu an-nuun".

## SaaHib (pl. aSHaab) an-niSaab

## صاحب (أصحاب) النّصاب

Holder of "niSaab"

Someone who has the specified amount of anything for the payment of" zakaah", such as 40 or more heads of sheep. See "niSaab."

## saaHir (pl. saHarah) ساحر (سحرة)

Sorcerer

Practitioner of black magic.See "siHr ."It is also used to mean 'charmer.'

## saa'il سائل

Beggar ,questioner

The term could mean either, depending on the context.

## Saa'im صائم

Fasting

See" Sawm."

## saa'imah (pl. sawaa'im) سائمة (سوائم)

Grazing cattle

In the calculation of" zakaah" (alms or poor tax) these are treated differently from cattle that are fed by the owner.

## saajid (pl. sujjad) ساجد (سُجّد)

Prostrating person

See "sujuud."

## sa'ala 1 (yas'al) سأل 1 (يسأل)

To question

Generally ,it means to ask .In a technical sense this means to ask in the form of interrogation ,for example in the grave or in the Hereafter.

## sa'ala 2 (yas'ala) an-naas سأل 2 (يسأل) الناس

To beg

This is considered by Islam a detestable act ,since it degrades the person who does it .In fact ,the Prophet) PBUH (warned those who beg needlessly.

## SaaliH صالح

Saleh

Name of a prophet who lived in North - Western Arabia, mentioned in many verses of the Qur'an. (See 27: 45-53). His people were called "thamuud".

## SaaliH (pl. SaaliHaat) صالح (صالحات)

Good deed

The word is short for" 'amal SaaliH" (a good deed). In Islam, any deed that conforms to the teachings of the religion and/ or benefits people is considered a 'good deed' for which a person will be rewarded by God. Good deeds are considered complementary to "iimaan" (belief/ faith), one is not acceptable without the other. In the Qur'an, rewards are promised to those "who believe and do good deeds". (See, e.g., the Qur'an, 2: 62; 16: 97; 25: 70.)

## SaaliH (pl. SaaliHuun) صالح (صالحون)

Good, righteous man

Very often, the term is used to refer to a pious person.

## saamiriyy (as--) السّامري

The Samaritan

In the Qur'an, the word is used to refer to the Israelite who misled the followers of Moses, during his absence, to worship the golden calf. (See the Qur'an 20: 85-91.)

## saarah سارة

Sara

The name of the wife of Prophet Abraham (PBUH) and mother of Isaac. She is not mentioned by name in the Qur'an. For the Divine promise of giving her a son despite her old age, see the Qur'an, 11: 69-73.

## sab'at 'aHruf سبعة أحرُف

Seven modes

Qur'anic study specialists say this expression, used by the Prophet (PBUH), refers to seven 'dialects', modes or variations in reading / reciting the Qur'an. Naturally, these variations apply to a limited number of words or groups of words in the Qur'an.

## sab' (as--) al-mathaanii السّبع المثاني

The seven oft-repeated

The reference is most probably to the Opening Chapter of the Qur'an which consists of seven verses, and it is recited at least 17 times in a Muslim's five daily prayers. Muslims also recite this chapter on many occasions for blessing.

## Saba'a (yaSba') صبأ (يصبَأ)

Renounce one's religion

This expression was frequently used by polytheists to refer to conversion to Islam, because they looked at it from the point of view of renouncing the religion of their forefathers.

## sabab (pl. asbaab) an-nuzuul سبب (أسباب) النّـزول

Occasion of the revelation

The occasion on which certain verses of the Qur'an were revealed. Knowledge of such occasions is necessary for the correct interpretation of such verses. Many work have been written on the subject in Islamic literature.

## sabbaHa (yusabbiH) سبّح (يسبّح)

To glorify (Allah)

To glofiy Allah in general, or to say: "subHaan-allaah" (Glorified be Allah)

## sabiil allaah سبيل الله

Way (cause) of Allah

Normally, we have this phrase as a part of the expression: "fii sabiili-llaah" (In the cause of Allah/ God).

## sabiilaan (as--) السّبيلان

The two outlets

This refers to the outlets of urine and stool (private parts). Anything that comes out of them, as well as touching them, makes one ritually impure. Ablution is necessary before one can perform "Salaah."

## Sabr صبر

Patience ,perseverance

The term is fairly comprehensive, implying forbearance, endurance and persistence. It is a highly recommended trait for a Muslim. (See, for instance, the Qur'an, Chapter 103 and 2: 155.)

## sabr wa taqsiim سبر وتقسيم

Isolating effective causes

In the Science of Principles of Islamic Law ,the term means scrutinizing and isolating effective causes.

## Sabuur (aS--) الصّبور

The Ever-Patient

A Divine Attribute of Allah .The One Who never gets impatient, even with the sinners.

## Sadaaq صَدَاق

Dower

The money or gift paid by the groom to his bride, normally specified in the marriage agreement. Often, people specify an instant amount ("muqaddam aS-Sadaaq") and a postponed amount ("mu'akhkhar al-Sadaaq").

## Sadaaq mu'ajjal صداق مؤجَّل

Deferred dower

The part of the dower agreed by the bride to be paid to her at a later date ,usually upon separation from her husband .Another term is" mu'akhkhar aS-Sadaaq."

## Sadaaq mu'ajjal صداق معجَّل

Immediate dower

The dower to be paid by the groom to his bride at the wedding time. Another term is" muqaddam aS-Sadaaq."

## Sadaqah jaariyah صدقة جارية

perpetual charity

Charity whose effect lasts forever (or a very long time), such as endowments and dissemination of useful knowledge.

## sadanat al-bayt / al-ka'bah سدنة البيت/ الكعبة

Keepers of the Ka'bah

People who are in charge of the Ka'bah and take care of it. Officially, there has been one family which has been keeping the key of the Ka'bah, since it was given to them by the Prophet (PBUH), more than 1400 years ago.

## Sadaqa (yaSduqu) (يصدُق) صدق

To be truthful

To be truthful here includes telling the truth (not lying) and being truthful in action; that is, one's actions reflect his words.

## Sadaqah (pl. Sadaqaat) صدقة (صدقات)

Charity

Charity or charitable act. According to Islam ,any good deed that helps someone is a charitable deed for which a Muslim will receive rewards from Allah .More specifically" ,Sadaqah "means giving money or the like to needy people.

## Sadaqat al-fiTr صدقة الفطر

fast -breaking charity

Sometimes ,it is called" zakaat al-fiTr". (See that term).

## sadd adh-dharaa'i' سدّ الذرائع

Prevention of means (to sins)

Closing the door against possibility of committing illegal things. Sometimes, a permissible act may be forbidden by the law, because it leads or may, most probably, lead to illegal actions.

## Sadr al-'islaam
## صدر الإسلام

Early Islamic era

Usually, it refers to the time of the Prophet Muhammad (PBUH).

## Safaa (aS--) wa al-marwah
## الصّفا والمروة

Safa and Marwah Mounts

The two rocky hills adjacent to the Hoy Mosque of Mecca, between which the pilgrim performs the "sa'y" (walking seven times, while reciting prayers). (See "sa'y").

## Safar صفَر

Safar

The second month in the Islamic calendar.

## safiih (pl. sufahaa')
## سفيه (سفهاء)

Imbecile ,foolish

Sometimes ,this word is used to mean' vulgar.'

## Safiyy allaah صفي الله

Allah's chosen

A person especially chosen by Allah to receive special favours, such as Prophet Muhammad (PBUH). One of the Prophet's names is "al-muSTafaa" (the chosen one).

## safk ad-dimaa' سفك الدّماء

blood shed, killing

Normally, this refers to senseless killing or mass murder.

## Saghirrah (pl. Saghaa'ir)
## صغيرة (صغائر)

Minor sin

Sins which are committed by a person, often inadvertently, and are not criminal in nature. There are no specified punishments for them. Unless they hurt others, then "istighfaar" (asking God's forgiveness) will be sufficient for removal from the record of bad deeds.

## SaHaabah (sg. SaHaabiyy)
## صحابة (صحابي)

Companions

Companions of the Prophet Muhammad (PBUH); i.e., Muslims who met him. Many struggled with him and defended him, and were responsible for carrying his message after his death. Therefore, they deserve a special consideration and respect.

## SaHaabiyy (pl. SaHaabah)
## صحابي (صحابة)

Companion

Companion of the Prophet Muhammad (PBUH). (See "SaHaabah"). Due to their special status, a Muslim is recommended to say "raDiya-llaahu 'anhu (RAA)" (May Allah be pleased with him) upon mentioning the name of any SaHaabiyy.

## saHarah (sg. saaHir) سحَرة (ساحِر)

Sorcerers, magicians

Practitioners of black magic. (See "siHr").

## SaHiifat al-a'maal صحيفة الأعمال

Record of deeds

The record kept for everyone wherein the recording angels write every deed and word one does or says anywhere and at any time. On the Day of Judgment this record will be produced for him.

SaHiiH (pl. SiHaaH)

## صحيح (صِحاح)

Authentic / sound book

A book of prophetic traditions compiled on the basis of very strict rules of sifting and authentication procedures, such as "SaHiiH al-bukhaarii."

## SaHiiH al-bukhaarii صحيح البخاري

Al-Bukhari Authentic Book

The book of prophetic traditions compiled by Imam al-Buhkari (810-870 G), according to his extremely stringent rules of sifting and authentication procedures. Naturally, what we have in his book, which consists of a few volumes, represents only a small portion of the hadeeths he had examined. This book is considered the most authentic compilation of hadeeth, due to the very meticulous ways of the compiler.

## SaHiiH muslim صحيح مسلم

Muslim Authentic Book

The book of prophetic traditions compiled by Imam Muslim (820-875 G), according to his strict rules of sifting and authentication procedures. Naturally, what we have in his book, which consists of a few volumes, represents only a small portion of the hadeeths he had examined.

## SaHiiHaan (aS--) الصّحيحان

The Two Authentic Books

The two most authentic compilations of prophetic traditions, one compiled by

Imam al-Bukhari ("SaHiiH al-bukhaarii") and the other by Imam Muslim ("SaHiiH muslim").

## sahm (pl.'ashum)
## سهم (أسهم)

Share

In the distribution of war booties, the term" sahm "is used to indicate the share of each fighter. The number of shares depends on whether the fighter is a member of the infantry or a rider.

## sahw سهو

Forgetfulness ,inattention

Basically ,the word means 'inattention 'or not paying attention to something .But it is also used to mean neglecting something inadvertently .If this happens during performing regular prayers ,then it is corrected by performing" sujuud as-sahw".

## Sa'iid Tayyib
## صعيد طيّب

Clean dust

The reference here is to the dust that one gets from touching the earth in a spot that has not been soiled by any "najaasah". It can be used for "tayammum" (dry, symbolic ablution).

## sajdah (pl. sajdaat)
## سجدة (سجدات)

Prostration once

See "sujuud".

## sajdat at-tilaawah
## سجدة التّلاوة

Recitation prostration

A prostration one makes upon reciting specific verses from the Qur'an, such as 96:19. There are a few places in the Qur'an where this prostration is recommended.

## sajada (yasjud)
## سجد (يسجد)

To prostrate

Technically, prostration (sujuud) in Islam means putting one's forehead and nose on the floor, supporting the body with the open palms, the knees and the toes, all of which should touch the floor.

## sakhaT-allaah سخط الله

Divine wrath

Anger of Allah, brought about

by disobeying His commands and/or causing destruction and harm to innocent creatures.

## sakiinah سكينة

Calmness, tranquility

The feeling of peace and tranquility or the observance of such an attitude.

## saktah (pl. saktaat) سكتة (سكتات)

Pause

In "tajwiid", this means pausing very briefly, without taking a breath. This is contrasted with "waqfah" which means a stop.

## SalaaH صلاح

Goodness

The word is sometimes used to mean piety

## Salaah (aS--) al-'ibraahiimiyyah الصّلاة الإبراهيمية

Abrahamic blessing prayers

The second part of "tashahhud" prayers, which begins: "allaahumma Salli 'alaa muHammadin wa'alaa 'aali muhHammadin kamaa Sallayta 'alaa 'ibraahiima wa'alaa 'aali "ibraahiima…" (O Allah, shower your blessings on Muhammad and the family of Muhammad as you did on Abraham and the family of Abraham…).

## Salaah (pl. Salawaat) صلاة (صلوات)

Formal prayer

The prayer that one performs, not just says ,like the regular five daily prayers ,which consists of standing ,bowing ,prostration and sitting ,in a particular manner and order ,while reciting certain verbal prayers .This is contrasted with" du'aa'" (supplication).

## Salaah (aS--) al-wusTaa الصّلاة الوسطى

The middle prayer

This refers to either dawn ("fajr") or afternoon ("'aSr") prayers. Both are emphasized for their special significance. Dawn is middle in the sense that it is preceded by sunset and late evening and followed by noon and afternoon. The afternoon is preceded by dawn and noon and followed by sunset and late evening prayers. ( See the Qur'an, 2: 238.)

## Salaah faa'itah صلاة فائتة

Missed prayer

The obligatory prayer not

performed in its regular time for some reason or another. It is considered like a debt, to be performed as soon as possible.

## Salaah maktuubah
## صلاة مكتوبة

Obligatory prayer

Any of the five daily prayers which must be observed by a Muslim.

## salaam سلام

Peace

A key word and concept in Islam, to which the word Islam and Muslim are lexically related. One of the Divine Attributes of Allah is "as-salaam", and one of the names of Paradise is "daar as-salaam". The word is also used in greeting, bidding farewell and in concluding the "Salaah" (formal prayer).

## salaam (as--) السّلام

The Supreme Peace

One of the Divine Attributes of Allah.

A Divine Attribute of Allah: the Only true Source of peace and tranquility.

## Salaat (aS--) 'alaa an-nabiyy
## الصّلاة على النبي

Prayer for blessings on the Prophet

See "Sallaa (yuSallii) 'ala an-nabiyy."

## Salaat al'-iidayn صلاة العيدين

Two Eid prayers

The two Eids of" al-fitr" and "al-aDHaa" have special services. The service consists of a two-"rak'ah prayer, with extra "takbiir" in the standing position, followed by the sermon. The service is recommended to be done in the open, if possible, as it was done by the Prophet (PBUH).

## Salaat al-fadhdh / al-fard
## صلاة الفَذّ / الفرد

Praying alone

Usually, this refers to performing alone the prayers which are normally held in congregation.

## Salaat al-farD صلاة الفرض

Obligatory prayer

Each of the five daily prayers.

## Salaat al-istikhaarah
## صلاة الاستخارة

Prayer for guidance

This consists of two "rak'ahs". After the "Salaah" a person says a prayer the gist of which says:

"O Allah, I seek Your guidance, because You know what I do not. If you know that X (deal or action) is good for me make it easy for me, but if it is bad for me turn it away from me and keep me away from it, and guide me to what is good for me." This Salaah is strongly recommended before doing something important, such as entering into a deal or marriage… etc., since it is a form of seeking Divine consultation.

## Salaat al-istisqaa'

صلاة الاستسقاء

Rain seeking prayer

A special service held to ask Allah for rain. It consists of a two-"rak'ah" prayer, a sermon and supplications for rain and.

## Salaat al-jamaa'ah

صلاة الجماعة

Congregational prayer

Performing (the obligatory prayer) in a group, with others. Sometimes, even two worshippers could be considered a group for this purpose. In the hadeeth we are told that praying in a group is 27 times better than praying alone.

## Salaat al-janaazah

صلاة الجنازة

Funeral prayer

The prayer for the deceased person is done in the following manner. The "imaam" stands with the corpse in front of him, and the other worshippers standing behind him. It consists of four "takbiirs", without bowing or prostration, with certain prayers said in between and one "tasliim".

## Salaat al-jumu'ah

صلاة الجمعة

Friday service

The Friday service consists of a two- part sermon, followed by two "rak'ahs."

## Salaat al-khawf

صلاة الخوف

Prayer of fear for fighters

Literally, this means the prayer of fear or danger. It means praying in the battlefield while the worshippers are in danger of being attacked by the enemy. There are certain procedures to be followed in such a case. (See the Qur'an, 4: 102).

## Salaat al-kusuuf wa al-khusuuf صلاة الكسوف والخسوف

Eclipse prayer

The prayer is performed upon the eclipse of the sun (kusuuf) or the moon (khusuuf). Special procedures are observed in this "Salaah".

## Salaat al-layl صلاة الليل

Night prayers

This usually refers to the supererogatory prayers one performs during the night .The best time is the last third of the night.

## Salaat al-mariiD صلاة المريض

The prayer of the ill

Depending on the nature of the illness ,certain types of licenses are given to the ill person in performing the" Salaah ,"such sitting or even lying on one's side or back instead of standing.

## Salaat al-musaafir صلاة المسافر

Traveler's prayer

A person on travel may shorten the four" rak'ahs "prayers to two "rak'ahs "and combine the noon and afternoon prayers together and the sunset and late evening prayers together.

## Salaat al-qiyaam صلاة القيام

Late night prayer

The optional prayers performed by some people late at night, preferably towards the last third portion of the night .Sometimes, the term is used to mean" Salaat at-taraawiiH."

## Salaat an-naafilah صلاة النافلة

Voluntary / supererogatory prayer

See" Salaat at-taTawwu."'

## Salaat as-sunnah صلاة السنّة

Sunnah prayer

The prayer observed by the Prophet Muhammad (PBUH), before and after the regular obligatory prayers. Sometimes, it is called "sunnah raatibah" (regular sunnah).

## Salaat at-tahajjud صلاة التّهجّد

Late night prayers

Prayers performed usually very late at night by a devout believer.

## Salaat at-taraawiih صلاة التّراويح

Taraaweeh prayer

The special prayers performed during Ramadan after the late evening prayer .It may consist of any number of two"-rak'ah" sets or units (often between 4 and 10).

## Salaat at-taTawwu' صلاة التطوُّع

Supererogatory prayer

Prayers performed by a Muslim above and beyond those required and/or specified by the religion. Another term is "naafilah" prayer.

## Salaat al-witr صلاة الوِتر

Witr prayer

The salah performed at the end of the night, usually consisting of one or three rak'as (an odd number); hence the name "witr".

## salaf (as--) aS-SaaliH السّلف الصّالح

The good predecessors

Often, this term is used to refer to the first three generations of Muslims, though it simply means the pious predecessors or earlier generations. The word "salaf" is contrasted with "khalaf" (successor(s) or later generation(s)).

## salas al-bawl سلس البول

Incontinence

Inability to control urination, especially the passing of drops of urine.

## Salawaat (aS--) al-khams الصّلوات الخمس

The five prayers

The regular daily prayers to be observed by a Muslim at their specified times (fajr, Zuhr, 'aSr, maghrib, 'ishaa').

## Salla-llaahu 'alayhi wa-sallam صلّى الله عليه وسلّم

Blessings and peace of Allah be upon him.

This is the expression a Muslim often says after mentioning the Prophet Muhammad or his name. Every time a Muslim says that he receives blessings from Allah too. (See the Qur'an, 33: 56.) Sometimes, this expression is shortened to 'alayhi-ssalaam" (Peace be upon him - PBUH).

## Sallaa (yuSallii) صلّى (يصلّي)

To pray

To perform formal prayers ("Salaah").

## Sallaa (yuSallii) 'alaa an-nabiyy
## صلّى (يصلّي) على النّبيّ

To pray for blessings on the Prophet

Saying something like "Salla-llaahu 'alayhi wa sallam" (Blessings and peace from Allah be upon him) or "allaahumma Salli 'ala muHammad" (O Allah, shower your blessings on Muhammad).

## sallama 1 (yusallim)
## سلّم 1 (يسلّم)

To greet

Literally, it means 'to say: "assalaamu 'alaykum", but it is often used simply to refer to greeting. See also "tasliim 1,2,3".

## sallama (yusallim) amrahu
## سلّم (يسلّم) أمره

To surrender oneself

To put oneself in the hands of someone. Very often, the expression is used in the context of leaving one's affairs to Allah ("li-llaah"), meaning resigning his will to Divine Will.

## sam' (as--) waT-Taa'ah
## السّمع والطّاعة

Hearing and obeying

Full obedience.

## samaaHat al-islaam
## سماحة الإسلام

Islamic tolerance

The spirit of tolerance that Islam requires its followers to observe in dealing with non-Muslims. (See, e.g., the Qur'an, 60: 8-9.) It is also used to refer to the easy, uncomplicated nature of Islam.

## Samad (aS--) 1 الصّمد

The Everlasting Refuge

A unique Divine Attribute of Allah. The One Whose protection all creatures seek, and is eternally besought of all. (See Chapter 112 of the Qur'an.)

## sami'a-llaahu li-man Hamidah
## سَمِعَ اللهُ لِمَن حمِده

Allah hears whoever thanks or praises Him

This is the expression a Muslim normally says upon raising his head from the bowing position in formal prayers.

## samii' (as--) السّميع

The All-Hearing

A Divine Attribute of Allah. The One

Who hears everything, however low or inaudible it might be.

## Sammaa 1 (yusammii)

## سمّى 1 (يسمّي)

To say: "bismillaah"

This is short for "sammaa bi-llaah" that is, to say: "In the Name of Allah…"

## Sammaa 2 (yusammii)
## سمّى 2 (يسمّي)

To name

To give someone or something a name.

## sanad al-Hadiith

## سند الحديث

Hadeeth chain of authority

Chain of transmitters or narrators of a prophetic tradition, which should normally go back to an eye witnessing companion of the Prophet (PBUH).

## Sanam (pl. aSnaam)
## صنَم (أصنام)

Idol

Idol used for worship by idolaters.

## saqar سقر

Hell

Another name for Hell-fire.

## sariyyah 1 (pl. saraayaa)

## سريّة 1 (سرايا)

Military expedition

In Islamic history, the term was used to refer to an expedition sent by the Prophet (PBUH); therefore, he was not part of it.

## sariyyah 2 ( pl.saraayaa)
## سريّة 2 (سرايا)

Concubine

A slave girl treated as a wife by her master. So the relationship is a legal one, because her children will be legitimate children.

## sarraa' (as--) waD-Darraa'

## السرّاء والضرّاء

Ease and difficulty

The expression "fi as-sarraa' waD-Darraa'" means 'under all circumstances'.

## satr al-'awrah سَتر العورة

Covering the private parts

Covering the parts that have to be covered by a Muslim man or woman in the presence of strangers or when performing the formal prayers. (See "'awrah").

## Sawm صوم

Fasting

In Islam, fasting means complete

abstention from food, drinks and sexual intercourse from pre-dawn time (about 2 hours before sunrise in normal zones) until sunset.

## Sawm at-taTawwu' صوم التّطوّع

Voluntary fasting

Fasting days other than those of Ramadhan on a voluntary basis. It is recommended to fast on certain days ,such as Monday and Thursay.

## sa'y سعـي

Walking

Walking between the Mounts of Safa and Marwah (seven times) as a part of 'umrah and pilgrimage rituals. Walking in each direction is counted one.

## Sayd al-baHr صَيد البحر

Catch of the sea

Any animal caught from water. The ruling is that fishing is permissible for a pilgrim in a state of" iHraam ,"unlike hunting.

## Sayd al-barr صيد البر

Hunting game

An animal caught by hunting .It is forbidden for a pilgrim in a state of" iHraam" to hunt animals. If he does, then he has to offer a similar animal for sacrifice in Mecca or feed some poor people or fast a few days. (See the Qur'an, 5: 95).

## sayf allaah سيف الله

The Sword of Allah

This is a title given to the military genius and companion of the Prophet Muhammad (PBUH), Khalid ibn al-Waleed who was responsible for many victories against the Byzantines and others. This title was given to him by the Prophet (PBUH).

## sayyi'ah (pl. sayyi'aat) سيّئة (سيّئات)

Sin, demerit

Sayyi'ah (opposite of "Hasanah") often means what one earns by doing something wrong (committing a sin). According to the hadeeth, if one does one thing wrong he will receive one 'demirit', but if he intends to do it and restrains himself he will be rewarded.

## shaafi'iyy شـافعي (شوافع)

Shafi'i

A follower of Imam ash-Shafi'iyy, the leader of one of the four major schools of Islamic law, which is common in South Arabia, Egypt and South East Asia.

## shaahid (pl. shuhuud) شـهود ( شاهد )

witness

Someone who sees or has seen something or testifies to it.

## sham (ash--) الشام

Sham

In Islamic history, the word refers to the area known today as Syria, Lebanon, Palestine and Jordan.

## shaari' (ash--) الشّارع

The Legislator

The legislator in Islam is Allah and, by implication, His messenger.

## Shaarib al-khamr شارب الخمر

Drinker of alcoholic beverage

It could also mean an alcoholic person. See "khamr" and "shurb al-khamr."

## sha'baan شـعبان

Sha'ban

The eighth month of the Islamic calendar ,which precedes Ramadan.

## shadiid شـديد

Fortis / strong

In Qur'anic phonetics, the term refers to the sounds which are produced with a complete obstruction of the air passage, called stops, such as /b/ and /d/.

## shaf ' شـفع

Shaf 'prayer

Technically ,this refers to the two rak'ahs one prays before the "witr" (odd number) prayer at night.

## shafaa'ah شـفاعة

Intercession

Interceding on behalf of somebody with someone in authority.

## shafaa'ah (ash--) al-kubraa الشّـفاعة الكبرى

The Greatest Intercession

The intercession that will be undertaken by the Prophet Muhammad (PBUH) on the Day of Resurrection on behalf of all mankind, when all the other prophets excuse themselves of doing it.

## shafaq شَفَق

Evening glow / twilight

The soft light (normally reddish) one sees in the sky after sunset. The time of "'ishaa'" prayer starts with the total disappearance of this evening twilight.

## shafawiyy شفوي

Labial

This means that the sound is produced with closure of the lips or the upper teeth touching the lower lip. Labial consonants in Arabic are: m, b, f.

## shafii' شفيع

Intercessor, intercessory

Someone who intercedes on behalf of others.

## shahaadah (ash--)

## الشّهادة

The Shahadah

The declaration that one bears witness that there is no deity except Allah (and that Muhammad {PBUH} is His messenger). Sometimes, it is called "kalimat ash-shahaadah" or "ash-shahaadataan" (the two testimonies').

## shahaadah شهادة

Testifying, testimony

Offering testimony to something.

## shahaadat az-zuur

## شهادة الزّور

False testimony, perjury

False testimony is considered one of the major sins; it violates the Qur'anic teachings on justice and fairness, which emphasize telling the truth even if it is against oneself and nearest of kin. (See the Qur'an, 4: 135) The Prophet (PBUH) strongly warned against it.

## shahaadataan (ash--)

## الشّهادتان

The two testimonies

Testifying that (1) there is no deity except Allah and (2) that Muhammad is the messenger of Allah.

## shahiid (ash--) الشّهيد

The Ever-Witnessing

A Divine Attribute of Allah. The One Who witnesses His creatures' actions and deeds.

## shahiid (pl. shuhadaa')

## شهيد (شهداء)

Martyr

Someone who dies for the Cause of Islam. The term is extended in the prophetic traditions to include victims of natural disasters and people who die while defending their honour or possessions. (For the status of the first category, see the Qur'an, 3: 169-171).

### shahr (ash--) al-Haraam (pl. al-ashhur al-Hurum) الشّهر الحرام (الأشهُر الحرُم)

The sacred month

The months during which Muslims were not supposed to initiate fighting: Dhul-Qi'dah, Dhul-Hijjah, Muharram and Rajab (11th, 12th, 1st and 7th months of the Islamic calendar).

### sha'iirah (pl. sha'aa'ir) شعيرة (شعائر)

Rite

A religious rite or ritual.

### shakuur (ash--) الشّكور

The Ever-Thankful

A Divine Attribute of Allah. The One Who accepts the minimum of good deeds from His servants and rewards them generously for these deeds.

### shar' (ash--) الشّرع

Shari'ah

The body of Islamic law. A more common term is "sharii'ah".

### shar'iyy شرعيّ

Legal

According to "sharii'ah" (Islamic law). In modern times, the word is used sometimes to mean 'legitemate'.

### shara'a (yashra') شرع (يشرع)

To legislate, ordain

To issue a command or make a law.

### sharii'ah (pl. sharaa'i') شريعة (شرائع)

Shari'ah

Body of the canonical law of Islam.

### shariik (pl. shurakaa') شريك (شركاء)

Partner

In the religious sense, someone or something, for example, worshipped with Allah. From this comes the word "shirk" (taking partners / polytheism). This is the sense we have in the expression "laa sharriika lah" (He (God) has no partner).

### sharr 1 (pl. shuruur) شرّ 1 (شرور)

Evil

Something bad and forbidden by the religion.

### sharr 2 شرّ

Worse

## sharT 1 (pl. shuruuT) شرط 1 (شروط)

Requirement, prerequisite

Something that is necessary, for example, for the validity of certain deeds.

## sharT 2 (pl. shuruuT) شرط 2 (شروط)

Condition, term

Something agreed upon in a contract.

## sharT 3 (pl. ashraaT) شرط 3 (أشراط)

Sign

This term is usually heard in the plural, such as in "ashraaT as-saa'ah" ('signs of the Hour/ Day of Judgement).

## shawwaal شوّال

Shawwal

The tenth month of the Islamic calendar. The first day of the month is "'iid al-fiTr" (The Feast of Breaking the Fast).

## shaykh (pl. shuyuukh / mashaayikh) شيخ (شيوخ/ مشايخ)

Sheikh

Religious scholar or teacher. Originally ,the word means an elderly man ,but in religious literature it is often used to refer to a religious scholar .In certain contexts it means' teacher ,'as opposed to disciple /student. There are other uses for the word as well in Modern Arabic.

## shayTaan (ash--) الشّيطان

Satan

The Evil One who was cursed by the Almighty Allah for his rebellion against Him ,and who has determined to lead astray everyone he can and to make people do evil things.

## shighaar (nikaaH ash--) الشِّغار (نكاح--)

Mutual marriage arrangement

See" nikaaH ashshighar."

## shii'iyy (pl. ash-shii'ah) شيعيّ (شيعة)

Shi'ite

A believer in the doctorine that the fourth Righteous Caliph ,Ali ibn Abi Talib ,was supposed to be the first Caliph) successor to the Prophet Muahmmad) PBUH,(( rather than Abu Bakr ,who was chosen by the Muslim Community at the time.

## shirk شرك

Taking partners ,polytheism

The act of worshipping someone or something besides God.

## shirk akbar شرك أكبر

Major polytheism

Worshipping others with God. This includes praying to' saints' and other dead men of piety ,with the belief that they may intercede for the worshipper .Islam does not recognize the principle of intermediaries between God and His servants .A Muslim can ,naturally ,ask a living pious person to pray for him / her.

## shirk al'-aadah شرك العادة

Polytheism of customs

The keeping up of un-Islamic superstitious customs ,such as belief in charms and bad omens.

## shirk al'-ibaadah

## شرك العبادة

polytheism in worship

Worshipping others besides Allah, such as praying to the graves or shrines of 'saints' or seeking help from the dead, regardless of their identity or position with Allah, including the Prophet Muhammad (PBUH).

## shirk al'-ilm شرك العلم

Polytheism of knowledge

The claim that some people, such as prophets, imams or holy men have knowledge of "ghayb" (the unseen) of their own. For even the prophets would not know anything of the unseen unless they are informed of it by Allah. For the Qur'an is very specific on the fact that "with Him are the keys of "al-ghayb" (the unseen). None but Him knows them..." (the Qur'an 6:59)

## shirk aSghar شرك أصغر

Minor polytheism

This means taking partners with Allah in an indirect way ,such as swearing to someone other than Allah or doing pious deeds to gain people's admiration, rather than for the sake of Allah alone" .Riyaa "'comes under this category.

## shirk at-taSarruf

## شرك التّصرّف

Polytheism of disposal

Ascribing power to others besides God or claiming that there are beings who share the power of the disposal of affairs with God.

## shirk khafiyy شرك خفي

Hidden polytheism

An act which involves taking partners with Allah ,without a Muslim realizing it ,such as swearing to others besides Allah or doing righteous deeds to be praised by people ,rather than seeking Divine pleasure.

## shu'ayb شعَيب

Shu'aib

A prophet of Allah mentioned in the Qur'an (See 11: 84-95).

## shubhah (pl. shubuhaat) شبهة (شبُهات)

Suspicion ,suspicious case

Sometimes,thetermisusedtomean allegation or misconception.

## shuf'ah شفعة

Preemption

The priority to purchase a property ,usually given to the neighbour.

## shurb al-khamr شُرب الخمر

drinking an alcoholic beverage

See" khamr ."Flogging is the usual penalty for drinking in Islam.

## shuuraa شورى

Consultation

Consultation is an important institution in Islamic government. (See the Qur'an, 42: 38).

## Siddiiq (aS--) الصدّيق

The trusting friend

The reference is to Abu-Bakr, the Prophet's closest friend, because he always showed unflinching trust in the Prophet (PBUH) and in his words.

## Sidq 1 صدق

Truth

As opposed to falsehood.

## Sidq 2 صدق

Truthfulness

Telling the truth.

## sidrat al-muntahaa سدرة المنتهى

Lote-tree of the Boundary

The tree next to the Divine Throne beyond which no angel could go. Reference to this tree is given in the Qur'an, Chapter 53: verses 14 and 15, in the context where the Qur'an speaks about the Ascension of the Prophet (PBUH) to heaven, known as "al-Mi'raaj".

## SifaaH سفّاح

fornication ,extra marital

A child whose father is unknown

is sometimes called "ibn sifaaH" (child born out of wedlock).

**Sifaat al-Huruuf صفات الحروف**

Characteristics of sounds

The features that characterize sounds ,such as voicing and nasalization.

**SiHaaH (aS--) as-sittah**

**الصّحاح السّتة**

The six authentic books

The term is used for the best known compilations of the "aHaadiith" (traditions) of the Prophet Muhammad (PBUH): al-Bukhari, Muslim, at-Tirmidhi, an-Nasaa'iy, ibn Maajah, abu Dawood, and ibn Hanbal.

**SiHaaq سِحَاق**

Lesbian sex act

Sexual act between females .This is strongly condemned in Islam, and it is considered a major sin.

**SiHHah صحة**

Authenticity ,soundness

In the science of hadeeth terminology this means whether a certain hadeeth is authentic or not.

**siHr سحر**

Sorcery ,witchcraft

Black magic in which the sorcerer usually resorts to help from evil jinn to do mischievous things to people and to perform various types of tricks and unusual feats. Sorcery is forbidden by Islam.

**siirah (as--) an-nabawiyyah**
**السّيرة النّبويّة**

Biography of the Prophet

Life story of the Prophet Muhammad (PBUH), which should not be confused with the "Hadiith" (prophetic traditions).

**Silat ar-raHim / al'-arHaam**
**صِلة الرّحِم / الأرحام**

Goodness to relatives

Being good to one's relations on both the father's and the mother's side .Literally" ,raHim "means the womb.

**sinn al-buluugh سِن البلوغ**

Age of puberty

See" buluugh."

**sinn ar-rushd سِن الرُّشد**

Age of maturation

The age at which one is considered mentally mature.

**sinn at-takliif**
**سِن التّكليف**

Age of accountability

The age at which a person

becomes legally and religiously accountable .Normally ,this is also" sinn al-buluugh" (age of puberty).

## sinn at-tamyiiz سِن التّمييز

Age of discrimination

Another term for age of maturation.

## siqaayah سقاية

Providing water

This used to refer especially to the practice of providing water to the pilgrims by the Meccans.

## SiraaT (aS--) al-mustaqiim الصّراط المستقيم

The Straight Path

The right way that leads to Divine Pleasure.

## SiraaT (aS--) الصّراط

The Narrow Bridge

The bridge over Hell-fire which everyone has to cross after the Judgment. Depending on one's beliefs and deeds, some cross it swiftly, others slowly. Still others do not make it, and they fall into the Fire.

## sirriyyah (Salaah --) سِرّيّة (صلاة...)

Secret prayer

The term refers to the two prayers performed during the day: Zuhr (noon) and 'aSr (late afternoon). The word 'secret' means that the worshipper recites the Qur'an in a manner not heard by others.

## siwaak سِـواك

Tooth brushing

Brushing the teeth, usually with a "miswaak", which is the Islamic forerunner of tooth brushes. (See "miswaak").

## Siyaam صيام

Fasting

See "Sawm"

## Siyaam ad-dahr صيام الدّهر

Continuous fast

Observing the fast every day of the year ;i.e ,.one fasts during the day and breaks the fast at night every day.

## Siyaam daawuud صيام داوود

David's fasting

The manner in which the Prophet Daawuud) David) (PBUH (used to fast :fasting alternate days all the time.

## Siyaanat al'-irD صيانة العِرض

Protecting one's honour

Protecting one's honour is equal to protecting one's own life; whoever kills an aggressor in a fight to protect his honour it is considered a case of self-defense.

## su'aal سُؤال

Questioning ,begging

Very often this connotes some form of interrogation .Begging is another meaning of the word.

## subHaan-allaah سُبحان الله

Glorified be Allah!

Roughly equivalent to "hallelujah / alleluia". Synonymous to this is "subHaana rabbii" (Glorified be my Lord!)

## subHaanahu wa ta'aalaa سُبحانه وتعالى

Glorified and exalted be He

An expression commonly used after the mention of the word Allah as a sign of reverence.

## subHaanak-allaahumma سُبحانك اللهم

Glorified are You my Lord

## subHah (pl. subaH) سُبحة (سُبَح)

Prayer beads

A string of beads ,normally of 33or 99 beads ,used by Muslims to count the number of certain prayers ,such as" subHaan-allaah", "al-Hamdu li-llaah" and "allaahu akbar". It is sunnah to say each 33 times, especially after regular "Salaah". Then say: "laa ilaaha ill-allaah" to make it 100.

## sufuur سُفُور

Unveiling

Usually, a female's unveiling especially her face and head or ignoring the rules of Islamic dress in general. This is usually contrasted with 'Hijaab.'

## suHt (pl. asHaat) سُحت (أسحات)

Illicit gain

Something that one gains through illegal means.

## SuHuf (sg. SaHiifah) صُحُف (صحيفة)

Holy Books or Writs ,records

In the Qur'an) Chapter(18-19 :87 this term refers to books revealed to messengers of Allah.

## suHuur سَحُور

Predawn meal

The meal a Muslim takes before dawn when he intends to fast that day .It is recommended that one delay it as much as possible .This would lighten the burden of the fast for him.

## sajjaadah (pl. sajaajiid) سـجّادة (سـجاجيد)

Prayer rug

A rug often used by Muslims to pray on, usually as a precaution that the spot of prayer is ritually clean ("Taahir"). Naturally, one could pray on anything, including bare floor or ground, as long as he knows it is ritually clean.

## sujuud سُـجود

Prostration

The act of prostrating. In Islam, this is done in the following manner: one kneels on his knees, puts his face on the floor (forehead and nose), while supporting his body on the hands which are placed almost parallel to the head, with the palms down. The elbows are raised from the floor.

## sujuud as-sahw سـجود السّـهو

Prostration for forgetting

Two prostrations made just before the end of the" Salaah "when one makes certain mistakes during his prayer.

## sujuud ash-shukr سـجود الشّـكر

Gratitude prostration

The prostration one makes upon receiving good news ,for example, to show gratitude to Allah.

## sukr سُـكْر

intoxication

The condition of being intoxicated, usually by drinking an alcoholic beverage.

## sulaymaan سُـليمان

Solomon

The Prophet Solomon (PBUH), who was also a king endowed by Allah with many special powers. (See, e.g., the Qur'an, 21: 81-82 and 27:16-44, where his story with the Queen of Sheba is told).

## SulH al-Hudaybiyyah صلح الحديبيّة

The Truce of Hudaybiyah

The agreement or pact (of

reconciliation) made between the Prophet (PBUH) and the Meccans at Hudaybiyah near Mecca in the sixth year of Hijra.

### sulTaan سُلطان

Authority

Authority or control over somebody .It is this sense that we often see this word in the Qur'an.

### sulTaan (pl. salaaTiin) سُلطان (سلاطين)

Sultan

Lexically, "sulTaan" means 'authority'. The word in the sense of 'ruler' is probably short for "SaaHib as-sulTaan" (the person who has the authority).

### Sunan سُنن

Hadeeth collections

The word sunan is the plural of "sunnah". It is used in that general sense. But technically, it has been used to refer to particular books or collections of Prophetic traditions compiled by certain scholars. Typicallly, the book is arranged according to the topics of "fiqh" : purification, prayer, fasting, transactions….

### sunan abii daawuud سُنن أبي داود

Abu Dawood Hadeeth Collection

The "Hadiith" collection compiled by Iamam Abu Dawood as-Sijistani (275 A.H.). See "sunan".

### sunan an-nasaa'iyy سُنن النّسائي

Al-Nasa'i Hadeeth Collection

The "Hadiith" collection compiled by Imam Abu Abdur-Rahman an-Nasa'i (303 A.H.).

### sunan at-tirmidhiyy سُنن التّرمذي

Tirmidhi Hadeeth Collection

The "Hadiith" collection compiled by Imam Abu 'Isa Muhammad at-Tirmidhi (279 A.H.).

### sunan ibn maajah سُنن ابن ماجة

Ibn Majah Collection of Hadeeth

The "Hadiith" collection

compiled by Imam Abu Abdillah Muhammad ibn Majah (273 A.H.).

## sunnah (as--) السُّنّة

Sunnah

Practice of the Prophet Muhammad (PBUH). Sometimes, the term is used to mean all his teachings. Alternative terms are "as-sunnah an-nabawiyyah".

## sunnah (pl. sunan) سُنّة (سُنن)

Way ,practice

Way or practice in general.

## sunnah fi'liyyah سُنّة فِعليّة

Practical tradition

This refers to the practices and deeds of the Prophet Muhammad (PBUH).

## sunnah mu'akkadah سُنّة مؤكّدة

Emphasized sunnah

A practice of the Prophet (PBUH) that was emphasized by him, through his meticulous observance of doing it.

## sunnah qawliyyah سنّة قوليّة

Verbal tradition

The refers to the sayings of the Prophet (PBUH).

## sunnah raatibah (pl. sunan rawaatib) سُنّة راتبة (سُنَن رَواتب)

Regular sunnah prayer

The sunnah prayer which is regularly observed before and/ or after the obligatory five daily prayers :two" rak'ahs "before "fajr ,"two or four before" Zuhr" and two after it ,four before'" aSr," two after" maghrib "and two after '"ishaa."'

## sunnah taqriiriyyah سُنّة تقريريّة

Reported tradition

This refers to the reports on the reactions of the Prophet (PBUH) to something said or done in his presence, such as indicating approval or disapproval.

## sunniyy سُنّيّ

Sunni

A member of the majority of Muslims who agree, among other things, that Abu Bakr, Omar, Othman (RAA) were as legitimate successors to the Prophet (PBUH) as Ali (RAA), and in that order, since they were all elected by the Muslim Community.

## surrah سُـرّة

Navel

The navel is considered the upper boundary of the' private parts.' For example ,for men' decency' requires covering the parts from the navel to the knees .This is the minimum for him to cover before praying ,for example.

## sutrat al-muSallii سُـترة المصلّي

worshipper's barrier

Anything that is made to stand in front of a worshipper so that people do no walk directly in front of him. It could be a wall, a pillar or simply a portable object of reasonable height (one foot high, for example).

## Suufiyy (pl. Suufiyyah) صوفي (صوفيّة)

Sufi

Originally ,a person who lives an ascetic life of devotions seeking spiritual purification .But often, this refers to a member of a Sufi order.

## Suufiyyah (aS--) الصّـوفيّة

Sufism

See" Suufiyy."

## Suur (aS--) الصّـور

The Trumpet

The Trumpet which is blown (for the second time) to announce the Resurrection. (See the Qur'an 6:73; 18:99; 20:102; ...).

## suurah (pl. suwar) سُـورة (سُـوَر)

Chapter

Chapter of the Qur'an ,which comprises 114 chapters .All the chapters of the Qur'an ,with the exception of ,9 begin with "basmalah."

# T t

## Taa'ah (pl. Taa'aat) طاعة (طاعات)

Good deed

Literally, this means 'obedience'. Here it refers to deeds that are done in obedience to Allah's commands.

## ta'abbudiyy تعبُّدي

Ritual, by Divine command

Something a Muslim does because he has been so commanded by his religion.

## taabi' at-taabi'iin تابع التّابعين

Follower of the Followers

This refers to the third generation of Muslims, the Companions of the Prophet Muhammad (PBUH) being the first generation.

## taabi'iyy تابعيّ

Second generation Muslim

This refers to a Muslim who came in contact with a companion of the Prophet Muhamad (PBUH), most probably being born after the death of the Prophet or near that time.

## taabuut (pl. tawaabiit) تابوت (توابيت)

Ark of the Covenant, coffin

The word originally means a coffin, but in the Qur'an the reference is to the Ark of the Covenant. (See the Qur'an 2:248.)

## ta'addud az-zawjaat تعدّد الزّوجات

Polygyny, multiplicity of wives

The practice of having more than one wife at the same time. Some people mistakingly use 'polygamy' which can mean having more than one wife or husband.

## Taafa (yaTuuf) طاف (يطوف)

Circumambulate

To go around the Ka'bah. Circumambulating the Ka'bah seven times is considered an act of worship, like the "Salaah" in the sense that one should be ritually pure.

## Taaghuut (pl Tawaaghiit) طاغوت (طواغيت)

False deity

Anyone who is worshipped besides God. A despotic tyrant is

also sometimes called Taaghuut.

## Taahir طاهر

Immaculate, ritually pure,

A person is ritually pure if he fulfills certain requirements, such as not having any urine, stool, or blood on his body or not being in a state that requires "ghusl", for example. The term applies to things as well, such as clothing or a place, which is a prerequisite for performing "Salaah" in or on them.

## taa'ib تائب

Repentant

A repenting person. See "tawbah" (repentance).

## ta'alaa-llaah تعالى الله

Allah be exalted!

A common expression Muslims use after the word Allah is "subHaanahu wa- ta'aalaa" ('May He be glorified and exalted') as a sign of reverence.

## Taalib (pl. Talaba) al-'ilm طالب (طلبة) العلم

Seeker of knowledge

Often, a student of religious knowledge.

## Taaluut طالوت

Saul

The king chosen by Allah for the Israelites to fight Goliath. (See the Qur'an 2: 241-251.)

## taarik aS-Salaah تارك الصّلاة

Neglector of prayer

Someone who does not perform the (five) daily prayers. Naturally, this violates one of the five cornerstones of Islam.

## ta'awwadha (yata'awwadh) تعوّذ (يتعوّذ)

seek refuge (with Allah)

See "ta'awwudh".

## ta'awwudh تعوُّذ

Seeking refuge

Generally, this means seeking refuge with God. A common prayer is "a'uudhu bi-llaahi min ash-shayTaan ar-rajim" ('I seek refuge with Allah from Satan the accursed one'.)

## tabaaraka-llaah تبارك الله

Hallowed / Blessed is God

This expression is often used to express admiration for something. In general use, it means something like 'God bless!'

## tabannaa (yatabnnaa) تبنّى (يتبنّى)

Adopt

See "al-tabannii."

## tabannii (al--) التبنّي

Adoption

Adopting someone to be one's child, to carry his name and be treated like a natural son or daughter is not permissible in Islam. (See the Qur'an 33:4-5). However, kindness to orphans and sponsoring them is strongly recommended.

## tabarrajat (tatabarraj) تبرّجت (تتبرّج)

Display finery or beauty

See "tabarruj".

## tabarruj تبرُّج

Display of finery or beauty

Technically, this means showing any part of the woman's body (except the face and hands) and her ornaments to 'strangers' (marriageable males) and wearing make up or perfumes in public.

## tabarruk تبرك

Seeking blessings

Doing something to gain blessings from someone or something.

## tabattala (yatabattalu) تبتّل (يتبتّل)

To be pious and chaste.

to retire from the world and devote one's life to the worship of God.

## tabattul 1 تَبَتُّل

Devotion

To devote one's time in celebrating the Name of God and in worshipping Him.

## tabattul 2 تَبَتُّل

Celibacy

Abstaining from marriage. Mary, mother of Jesus, is sometimes referred to as "al-batuul" ('the celibate').

## tabdhiir تبذير

extravagance

Squandering one's money or possessions is forbidden in Islam, because these gifts from Allah should be properly made use of for the benefit of the individual and society. (See the Qur'an 17:26-27)

## tabii' (pl. tibaa') تبيع (تباع)

one year calf

A male calf that has completed one year of age.

## tabliigh تبليغ

Conveying message

Another word for "balaagh",

though not specifically found in the Qur'an.

## taDarra'a (yataDarra') تضرّع (يتضرّع)

To supplicate in humility

To pray in a humble and earnest manner.

## taDarru' تضرُّع

Humble supplication

Praying in a humble and earnest manner.

## tadbiir ar-raqiiq تدبير الرقيق

Posthumous manumission

The decision to set a slave free upon master's death.

## tadhkiir تذكير

Reminding

To bring to attention certain facts or teachings.

## ta'diil تعديل

Testifying to character/ integrity

The term is used in the evaluation of narrators of "Hadiith" to mean testifying to the integrity of a narrator. It is the opposite of "jarH" ('exposing faults').

## ta'diyah تعدية

Extending

In the Science of Principles this means extending the effect of a ruling on a main issue to cover subsidiary ones.

## tadwiir تدوير

normal recitation

Reciting the Qur'an at average rate of speed, while observing all the rules of correct enunciation.

## tafaqquh fii ad-diin تفقّه في الدين

Learning the religion

The act of studying to learn and understand religious matters.

## tafkhiim تفخيم

Velarization

The raising of the back part of the tongue towards the roof of the mouth while pronouncing certain consonants like the Saad and Taa' (always) as well as the l and r (sometimes).

## tafriij al-kurubaat تفريج الكربات

Alleviation of distress

Helping one overcome hardships or solve his/her distressing problems.

## tafriiq تفريق

Legal separation

The act of separating a husband

Tt

and a wife and considering them divorced.

**tafriiT تفريط**

Negligence

Ignoring something or neglecting a duty.

**tafsiir تفسير**

Exegesis, interpretation

Explaining the meaning of Qur'anic text and / or commenting on it.

**tafwiiD تفويض**

Delegation of affair

Delegating power, for example, or leaving something in the hands of another. (For the second meaning, see the Qur'an, 40:44.)

**taghriib**
**تغريب**

Exile, banishment

Banishing someone who commits certain crimes to a distant land.

**Tahaarah طهارة**

Ritual purity or cleanliness

The state in which one can pray and touch the Qur'an. It is also used to refer to moral purity.

**tahajjud تهجُّد**

Late night prayer

This is short for "Salaat at-tahajjud" which is the optional prayer one performs in the depth of night.

**taHallul تحلُّل**

Freedom from iHraam

Doing something (like cutting the hair or shaving the head) at the end of Hajj or 'umrah to indicate finalization of the state of "iHraam". After that a person may do things which are forbidden for a person in a state of "iHraam'.

**taHannuth تحنُّث**

Devoting time to worship

A case of devoting oneself to worshipping God and seeking religious purification.

**taHiyyaat (at--)**
**التّحيّات**

Salutations prayer

The prayer which starts "al-taHiyyaatu li-llaahi ..." ('Salutations belong to God...') which a Muslim says in his Salaah in the sitting position after two or four "rak'as". (See "at-tashahhud".)

**taHliil تحليل**

Permitting, making lawful

Making or considering something

permissible or lawful, opposite of "taHriim" (make unlawful).

## tahliil تهليل

Saying "laa ilaaha illallaah" ')There is no deity except God.("

Associated words are: "tasbiiH," taHmiid," takbiir."

## taHmiid تحميد

saying "al-Hamdu li-llaah" ('Praise and thanks to God').

## taHqiiq تحقيق

Deliberate recitation

In the science of Quraanic phonetics, this means a fairly slow and deliberate recitation of the Qur'an, observing all the rules of correct enunciation. Usually, this is done in teaching situations. (See also "tilaawah)".

## taHqiiq al-manaaT تحقيق المناط

Verifying underlying cause

In the Science of Principles, investigating possible causes in order to verify their existence.

## taHriif تحريف

Distortion of meaning

Misinterpretation of a text or word.

## taHriim تحريم

forbidding

Making or considering something unlawful.

## taHriim bi-lmuSaharah تحريم بالمصاهرة

Ban due to marriage

Ban on marrying certain in-laws, such as mother and daughter in-law or two sisters at the same time. (See the Qur'an 4: 23.)

## taHriim bi-nnasab تحريم بالنّسب

Ban due to lineage

The ban on marrying certain blood relatives, such as sisters and their daughters and aunts… (See the Qur'an 4: 23.)

## taHriim bi-rraDaa' تحريم بالرّضاع

Ban due to suckling

This term is used in the context of deciding marriageable persons in Islamic law. According to Islamic law, a Muslim cannot marry someone who shared suckling from the same woman at least 5 times. (See the Qur'an 4: 23.)

## taHriir raqabah تحرير رقبة

Manumission of a slave

Setting a slave free is one of the highly recommended acts of devotion.

## Tahuur طَهور

Ritually purifying

Clean water is normally ritually purifying. Other liquids, like juices for example, may be clean and pure in themselves, but they are not ritually purifying; they cannot be used for ablution, for example.

## tajarrud تجَرُّد

Divesting oneself

Divesting oneself physically in the sense of removing his ordinary clothes, for example, and spiritually in the sense of disregarding worldly gains and affairs.

## tajawwuz fii as-Salaah تجَوُّز في الصلاة

Hurrying in prayer

This means that a person recites and performs the minimum requirements of proper Salaah, without violating the condition of properiety, or reading short chapters of the Qur'an, usually for an urgent reason.

## tajdiid تجديد

Revival

Literally, the word means renewing. However, it is used to mean to bring back the correct understanding of the religion and purifying it from misconceptions and wrong practices that have crept into it.

## tajmiir تجمير

Aromatizing a shroud

Using insence or the like to give a shroud of a dead person good smell.

## tajwiid تجويد

Perfecting

This word comes from "jawwad" which means to make "jayyid" (good). As a term it has been used to refer to the meticulous enunciation of Qur'anic words or recitation of the Qur'an. It also refers to the science which deals with the rules and methods to be observed in its recitation (Qur'anic phonetics).

## takabbur تكبُّر

Arrogance, conceit

Haughtiness and considering oneself above others and better than them, a quality strongly condemned by Islam.

## takbiir تكبير

Saying "allaahu akbar"

Saying what is equivalent to "Allah is Greater or the Greatest.'

## takbiirat al-iHraam تكبيرة الإحرام

Initial takbiir

Saying" allaahu akbar "at the beginning of the" Salaah ,"raising the palms just in front of the shoulder ,with the palms facing forward .This is a signal that one has entered into a special spiritual state.

## takfiin تكفين

Enshrouding the corps

Wrapping the corps of a dead person in clean sheets of cloth after washing the body .It is also recommended to scent the body and the shroud with perfume.

## takhaaruj تخارج

Buying out

A group of partners or heirs buying out a share of one of them for a compensation.

## takhliil تخليل

Passing the fingures through

In the context of ablution ,this means passing wet fingers through the beard and between the toes to make sure that water reaches the different parts.

## takhriij al-Hadiith تخريج الحديث

Tracing sources of Hadiith

A process in which a scholar traces the Hadiith back to its sources in order to evaluate its authenticity.

## takhriij al-manaaT تخريج المناط

Specifying underlying cause

A scholar's attempt to show a possible underlying cause ,not explicitly stated.

## takhyiir تخيير

Givng right of choice

In the case of conflicting courses of action one may be given the right to choose the one he prefers.

## takliif تكليف

Charging with responsibility

Often we find this word in a phrase like" sinn at-takliif" meaning the age of accountability, puberty.

## takriim al-insaan تكريم الإنسان

Honoring man

In the Qur'an, reference is made to this special favour from God bestowed on human beings (17:70). This necessarily entails respecting human rights.

## takyiif 1 تكييف

Qualifying

In theology, this refers to qualifying an attribute or act of God by indicating its "howness", which is considered a blasphemy.

## takyiif 2 تكييف

Verification

In the Principles of Islamic law, this means verifying the origins of an issue to indicate its limits.

## Talaaq طلاق

divorce

Divorce in Islam is considered a necessary evil or a last resort, when the husband and wife try everything, including arbitration, to get along. The divorce is done by the man declaring his wife divorced. There is a chance of reconciliation after each of the first and second times, without any formal procedures, provided that it is done within three menstrual periods of the wife after the divorce. The wife should stay in the home during this period, which makes it conducive to a quiet reconciliation.

## Talaaq al-bid'ah طلاق البدعة

Improper divorce

Divorce that is done in violation of "sunnah", such as divorcing the wife more than once within one cycle of her menstruation. See "Talaaq as-sunnah."

## Talaaq as-sunnah طلاق السّنّة

Proper divorce

Divorcing the wife in accordance with the teachings of the Prophet (PBUH): (1) It should be during a menstruation cycle (between two periods) while she is free from bleeding and provided he did not have sex with her during that period. (2) No more than one divorce during any cycle.

## Talaaq baa'in طلاق بائن

Final divorce

The divorce after which a woman may not go back to her former husband, except with a new contract or unless she marries another man, consummates her marriage, then gets separated by divorce or death from the second husband. (See "baynuunah kubraa" and "baynuunah Sughraa").

## Talaaq raj'iyy طلاق رجعيّ

Revocable divorce

The case in which a man and his divorced wife may return to each other without remarrying (a new marriage contract). This happens after the "first divorce" or "second divorce" before the passage of the waiting period, known as "'idddah").

## talbiyah تلبية

Saying" ,labbayk allaahumma labbayk"

Saying the prayer that a piligrim should keep saying all the time: "labbayk allaahumma labbayk..." ('I am obeying Your command my Lord...')

## ta'liil تعليل

Ratiocination ,justification

Giving causes and justifications for a certain action or ruling.

## ta'liiq تعليق

Making dependent

Making something conditional on another.

## talmuud تلمود

Talmud

The primary source of Jewish law.

## Talqah (pl. Talqaat) طلقة (طلقات)

Divorce once

A Muslim is allowed divorce three times. After either of the first two times the wife and husband can go back to each other within a three (menstrual) periods. (See "Talqah raj'iyyah" and "Talaaq baa'in").

## Talqah thaalithah طلقة ثالثة

Third divorce

This is the third time a man divorces his wife ,which is considered final. They may not return to each other except after her marrying another man ,consummating the marriage, then getting separated from the second husband by divorce or death .Naturally ,a new marriage contract is required.

## Talqah thaaniyah طلقة ثانية

Second divorce

Divorcing the wife for the second time, which means that the man takes back his wife after divorcing her the first time during the waiting period ("'iddah"), then divorces her again. It is considered "revocable divorce".

### Talqah' uulaa طلقة أولى

First divorce

Divorcing the wife for the first time ,which is considered a revocable divorce.

### talqiin al-mayyit تلقين الميّت

Prompting the dying person

The word" mayyit" could mean either one who is dying or is dead. When we see a Muslim dying we should prompt him/ her to say the "shahaadah" ("I bear witness that there is no deity except Allah and that Muhamad is the messenger of Allah").

### tamiimah (pl. tamaa'im) تميمة (تمائم)

Talisman, amulet

Something one keeps and usually wears for protection against evil spirits for example. Islam forbids this, because true protection is provided by Allah Alone. One may read verses of the Qur'an (e.g., Chapter 1, 2:255; Chapters 113&114) for that purpose.

### tamjiid تمجيد

Glorification

Though the word means glorification in general, it is often used in the context of glorifying Allah and praising Him.

### Tamth (aT--) الطّمث

Menstruation

Regular monthly vaginal bleeding.

### tamthiil تمثيل

Comparing, likening

In theology, this means comparing the acts and attributes of God with those of humans, which is considered a blasphemy, since the Qur'an tells us that "There is nothing like unto Him."

### tanwiin تنوين

Nunation

The pronunciation of an n after the last vowel in an idefinite noun in Arabic, such as kitaab(un) 'a book'. In Arabic this is indicated by doubling the short vowel diacritic mark (e.g.. كتاباً ).

### tanziih تنـزيه

De-anthropomorphism

This means that we should not ascribe any human qualification to the Divine attributes of God, because "There is nothing like unto Him." (The Qur'an, 42:11 and Chapter 112).

Tt

## taqarrub ilaa allaah تقرُّب إلى الله

Seeking Divine Pleasure

Doing something good in order to please Allah and be closer to Him.

## taqiyyah (at--) التقِيّة

Concealing identity

A Shi'ite principle of behaving in a manner acceptable to others in order to conceal one's true identity.

## taqliid (at--) التّقليد

Imitation, emulation

In religious terms, this means following the views and /or practices of a certain imam or school of thought.

## taqSiir ash-sha'r تقصير الشعر

Shortening the hair

Cutting some hair from various parts of the head for men and cutting about 2 centimeters from a woman's hair at the end of "'umrah" or main rituals of "Hajj."

## taqwaa تقوى

God-fearing

The Arabic term covers many concepts that include God-fearing, righteousness and piety .In the Qur'an ,the adjective derived from this word ,muttaquun/ muttaqiin, is found much more frequently. (See, e.g., Chapter 2: 2-5.) Sometimes, we may find the word "birr" used as a synonym. (See the Qur'an, 2: 177.)

## taraawiiH تراويح

Taraweeh prayers

See "Salaat at-taraawiiH".

## taraHHum ترحُّم

praying for mercy for s.b.

Often, this can be in the form of "May Allah have mercy on X."

## Tariiqah Suufiyyah طريقة صوفيّة

Sufi order

An order is very often named after its leader, such as Naqshabandiyyah, Tiijaaniyyah… etc.

## tanaajush تناجُش

deceitful bargaining/ offering

In a commercial transaction, making a false bid to make others pay a higher price.

## tan'iim (at--) التنعيم

Taneem

The place on the border of Mecca

where people in Mecca intending to make Hajj or 'umra go to wear the iHraam (or make their intention of the rite).

## taqriir (muwaafaqah) تقرير (موافقة)

Approval

In the definition of the term "Hadiith" this word is used to mean tacit approval of the Prophet (PBUH) of an action seen or known by him.

## tarajiiHaa al-matn ترجيحات المتن

Weighing/ comparing text

In the Science of Principles, evaluating texts in terms of language and form and possible justifications…etc. for the purpose of giving one more weight over another.

## ta'riiD تعريض

Hinting

Making an offer, e.g., indirectly, such as in the case of indicating one's desire to marry a widow during her 'waiting period'. (See the Qur'an, 2: 235.)

## tarjiiH ترجيح

showing superiority

Showing the strength of an argument as opposed to a weaker one.

## tarjiiHaat as-sanad ترجيحات السند

Weighing/ comparing narrators

Carrying out a process of evaluation of narrators of a "Hadiith" in terms of piety, memory, reputation, direct contact with predecessor…etc .for the purpose of giving more weight to a "Hadiith" over (an)other one(s).

## tarjii'1 ترجيع

(Saying :innaa lillaahi wa innaa ilayhi raaji'uun)

Saying the expression which means 'To Allah we surely belong, and to Him we shall return,' usually, upon receiving bad news or meeting an unfortunate incident.

## tarjii' 2 ترجيع

Repetition

Repetition of the words of the adhaan ('the call to prayer') after the muezzin.

## tark as-Salaah ترك الصّلاة

Neglecting formal prayers

Not performing the obligatory five daily prayers. This act is considered an act of disbelief by the Prophet (PBUH).

## tarqiiq ترقيق

Unvelarization

Pronouncing a consonant, especially the r and l, without raising the back of the tongue. It is the opposite of "tafkhiim" ('velarization').

## tartiil ترتيل

Careful recitation, reading

Usually, this refers to reciting or reading the Qur'an in a slow and deliberate manner, observing all the rules of correct enunciation ("tajwiid") while contemplating the meanings of the verses.

## taSaddaqa (yataSaddaq) تصدّق (يتصدّق)

Give out charity

See "taSadduq."

## taSadduq تصدُّق

Giving charity

Doing a charitable deed can be through giving out something, for example ,or offering help to someone who needs it.

## taSawwafa (yataSawwaf) تصوّف (يتصوّف)

Become a sufi

See" taSawwuf."

## taSawwuf تصوُّف

Becoming sufi ,Sufism

In general ,this means living a simple life of devotions .But Sufism has taken many forms, some of which are considered objectionable by the orthodox Muslims.

## tasbiiH تسبيح

Glorification

Glorification of Allah. The usual expression is "subHaan-allaah" ('Glorified be Allah').

## tashahhud 1 تشهُّد

Saying the" shahaadah"

Saying, "ashahadu an-laa ilaaha ill-allaah" ('I bear witness that there is no deity except Allah'). One may add, "wa ashhadu anna muHammadan rasuul-ullah" ("and I bear witness that Muahmmad is the messenger of Allah').

## tashahhud 2 تشهُّد

Sitting prayers

The prayers one says in the sitting position during the Salaah (formal prayers). (See "at-taHIyyaat".)

## tashbiih تشبيه

Anthropomorphism

In theology this means attributing human qualities to God,or comparing Divine attributes and actions to human ones, which is a grave blasphemy. (See "tanziih".)

## tashmiit al'-aaTis تشميت العاطس

Responding to the sneezer

Saying "yarHamkum-allaah" ('May Allah have mercy on you') when a person sneezes and says: "al-Hamdu li-llaah" ('Thank Allah').

## tashrii' تشريع

Legislation

Making laws. A related word is "sharii'ah" ('Islamic Law').

## tashriik تشريك

sharing of inheritance

## tashyii 'al-janaazah تشييع الجنازة

Accompanying the funeral

Walking along or behind the bier and helping in carrying it .All these are strongly recommended acts for a Muslim to do for fellow Muslims.

## tashyii 'al-mayyit تشييع الميّت

Escorting the deceased

Walking along or behind the bier and helping in carrying it. (See "tashyii' al-janaazah".)

## tasliim 1 تسليم

Greeting

Saying, "assalaamu 'alaykum" ('Peace be with you') or something to that effect.

## tasliim 2 تسليم

Surrendering

Surrendering something or someone (including oneself) to somebody.

## tasliim 3 تسليم

Ending the "Salaah" by turning one's face to the right and saying: "assalaamu 'alaykum" ('Peace be with you') and turning the face to the left and saying the same.

## tasmiyah 1 تسمية

Saying "bismi-llaah", naming

Saying the expression which means ' In the Name of Allah'.

## tasmiyah 2 تسمية

Naming

Giving someone or something a name.

## tasriiH تسريح

Letting go

This word is used in the Qur'an in the context of treating a non-finally divorced wife, where the husband is instructed either to let go amicably or keep her and treat her well. (The Qur'an, 2:229)

## taswiyat al-Saff تسوية الصّف

Straightening the line

In congregational worship this means making the lines/ rows straight, usually by making sure the feet and the shoulders of the worshippers are next to each other.

## taTahhur تطهُّر

Purification

Purifying oneself by removing impurities and making ablution or washing the body.

## taTawwa'a (yataTawwa') تطوّع (يتطوّع)

To volunteer

## taTawwu' تطوُّع

Volunteering

Doing a voluntary act of worship, such as optional prayers or fasting.

## taTayyub تطيُّب

wearing perfume

Prophet Muhammad used to like perfumes, and he encouraged his followers to wear them, especially before going to the mosque.

## taTayyur تطيُّر

believing in bad omens

A Muslim is encouraged to have faith in God and believe in good omens ("al-fa'l al-Hasan"); i.e., be optimistic. He should not believe in bad omens or behave according to them. Another word is "Tiyarah."

## ta'Tiil تعطيل

Negation of attributes

In theology ,this refers to the claim that we should negate all attributes from our concept of God.

## ta'wiidhah (pl. ta'aawiidh) تعويذة (تعاويذ)

Talisman ,incantation

Something worn or recited over someone for protection against evil. In Islam one should seek only Divine help, not of amulets and charms, which have no power to help or protect anyone. (See "tamiimah".)

## ta'wiil al-qur'aan تأويل القرآن

Interpretation of the Qur'an

Technically ,this often refers to unconventional interpretation of the Qur'an ,as opposed to" tafsiir al-qur'aan."

## Ta'wiil / ta'biir al-ru'yaa

## تأويل / تعبير الرؤيا

Interpretation of dreams

This is one of sciences Muslims pioneered in .Usually ,a Muslim scholar would resort to the Qur'an ,hadeeth ,conventions and other sources in interpreting the dreams.

## Tawaaf

## طواف

Circumambulation

Going around the Ka'bah seven times ,starting with the' black stone 'and ending there" .Tawaaf" is a highly recommended act of worship .Like" Salaah "one should not do it unless he is ritually pure.

## Tawaaf al-ifaaDah

## طواف الإفاضة

IfaaDah circumambulation

The" Tawaaf" a pilgrim performs on the tenth day of the month of pilgrimage. It is an essential part of "Hajj". Another name for this is "Tawaaf az-ziyaarah."

## Tawaaf al-quduum

## طواف القُدوم

Circumambulation of arrival

The" Tawaaf "the pilgrim performs upon arrival at Mecca.

## Tawaaf al-wadaa'

## طواف الوَداع

Farewell Circumambulation

The" Tawaaf "the pilgrim performs before leaving Mecca.

## Tawaaf az-ziyaarah

## طواف الزّيارة

Ziyaarah circumambulation

The" Tawaaf "a pilgrim performs normally on the tenth day of the month of pilgrimage.It is an essential part of" Hajj ."Another name for this is" Tawaaf al-ifaaDah."

## tatabbu 'ar-rukhaS

## تتبُّع الرُّخَص

Looking for licenses

Basically ,this means looking for the easy views in different schools of thought to follow them ,without investigation of proof.

**tawaatur تواتُر**

Continuous succession

For a Hadiith ,this means a continuous chain and multiplicity of narrators ,making the text more reliable.

**tawaDDa'a (yatawaDDa') توضّـأ (يتوضّـأ)**

Make ablution

See" wuDuu."'

**tawakkala (yatwakkal) 'ala-llaah توكّل (يتوكّل) على الله**

To trust in God

To have faith in God and put one's trust in Him.

**tawakkaltu' ala-llaah توكّلت على الله**

I trust in Allah

I am putting my faith in Allah and depending on Him. Sometimes, this expression and its alternative "tawakkalnaa'ala-llaah" ('We trust in God') is said upon concluding a deal or making an agreement.

**tawakkul توكُّل**

Trusting and depending

Normally ,this refers to putting one's trust in Allah ,and stop worrying.

**tawallii al-qaDaa' تولّي القضاء**

Becoming a judge

To have the job of a judge.

**tawarruk تورُّك**

Sitting on buttock

Sitting in the" Salaah" with left buttock touching the floor, while the right buttock rests on the right foot whose toes touch the floor.

**tawassul توسُّل**

Entreaty, fervent plea

Normally, this is used with reference to praying to God, which should be direct, not through anyone.

**tawbah توبة**

Repentance

See "tawbah naSuuH".

**tawbah naSuuH توبة نصوح**

Sincere repentance

There are three conditions for sincere repentance: (1)stop doing the wrong act, (2) regret having done it and seeking Divine forgiveness and (3) resolving not to repeat the wrong doing.

## tawfiiq توفيق

Reconciliation

In the Science of Principles, this means the attempt to reconcile conflicting views or evidence.

## tawHiid توحيد

Monotheism, Islamic theology

The belief in the absolute oneness of Allah (God) and behaving accordingly in one's supplications and worship. Sometimes, the study of theological issues in Islam is called "tawHiid" or "'ilm al-tawHiid" ('science of monotheism')

## tawHiid al-asmaa' waS-Sifaat

## توحيد الأسماء والصفات

Monotheism of names and attributes

The term is used with reference to Divine Names and Attributes where one has to believe in their absolute uniqueness.

## tawHiid al-'ibaadah

## توحيد العبادة

Monotheism in worship

Devoting and directing worship to God alone, without intermediaries or partners.

## tawHiid ar-rubuubiyyah

## توحيد الربوبية

Monotheism of lordship

Belief that there is only One Lord and Sustainer of the whole creation.

## tawHiid al-'uluuhiyyah

## توحيد الألوهيّة

Monotheism of deity

The belief that there is only One God Who is Unique. He has no partners, no wife nor children, and none is equal to Him. (See the Qur'an, Chapter 112.)

## tawqiifiyy

## توقيفي

Decided by the religion

Something that is not subject to debate and argument, because it has been decided by the religion in a command by God or instructions from His messenger.

## tawraah توراة

Torah

The Book that was revealed to Prophet Moses. Some scholars say that it is the Mosaic Law or the Pentateuch.

## tawwaab (at--) التوّاب

The Ever Relenting

An Attribute of Allah. The One Who constantly accepts the repentance of His servants.

## tayaamun تيامُن

Going rightward

Starting something with the right hand side (such as washing the right arm first or entering a mosque with the right foot first) or moving in that direction.

## tayammum تيمُّم

Wiping with dust

The symbolic act of wiping the face and the hands with light dust instead of ablution, in the absence of water or due to inability to do ablution.

## taraaHum تراحم

Compassion, mutual kindness

A quality required to be observed by believers in dealing with each other, so that they may become like a single body.

## tayammun تيمُّن

Seeking blessings

Considering something a source of blessings.

## tays-at al-musta'aar التيس المستعار

Temporary husband

The terms literally means a 'borrowed he-goat .'It refers to a man who marries a finally divorced woman ,consummates the marriage and divorces her ,for the sole purpose of legalizing her return to her former husband.

## taysiir تيسير

Facilitation

Making things easier ,by suggesting an easy ,but lawful, way of doing something.

## ta'Ziim al-Hurumaat تعظيم الحرمات

Honoring prohibitions / sanctities

Observing prohibitions and respecting sanctified objects.

## ta'ziir تعزير

Discretionary punishment

Punishment the nature of which is not specified in Islamic law; therefore ,it is left to the discretion of the judge or ruler.

## ta'ziyah تعزية

Offering condolences

Usually ,this is used in terms of offering condolences for someone who had death in the family.

## tazkiyah 1 تزكية

Testifying to goodness

Testifying to the good character of a person ,especially a witness.

## tazkiyah 2 تزكية

Purifying

Sometimes we find this word in discussing the' zakaah' as an act of purifying one's possessions from wrongful gains, for example.

## tazkiyat an-nafs تزكية النفس

Self-righteousness

Praising oneself in terms of piety and God fearing. A Muslim is instructed not to do so. (See the Qur'an 53:32.)

## thabt (pl. thubuut) ثبت (ثُبوت)

Of reliable memory

In the context of evaluating the narrators of the Hadeeth ,a person with a remarkably retentive memory.

## thaniyyat al-wadaa' ثنية الوداع

Thaniyyat al-wadaa'

The name of a place in Medina where, it is reported, the citizens of the town received the Prophet Muhammad (PBUH) upon his immigration from Mecca to Yathrib (the old name of Medina). It is mentioned in the famous chant "Tala'a al-badru 'alaynaa..." ('The moon has shined upon us...') with which people received their noble guest.

## thaqalaan (ath--) الثّقلان

Humans and jinnis

The term refers to the two main categories of accountable beings, the visible humans and the invisible beings known as jinn.

## thawaab ثواب

Reward

The opposite of "'iqaab" ('punishment').

## thayyib ثيّب

Not virgin

A man or woman that was previously married. In some aspects of Islamic law he /she is treated differently from a virgin.

## thiqah (pl. thiqaat) ثِقة (ثِقات)

Trustworthy

With reference to a Hadeeth narrator, this means that he is trustworthy, due to his impeccable character.

## thubuut al-shahr ثبوت الشهر

Confirmation of the month

The official announcement regarding the beginning of the lunar month, such as Ramadhan.

## Tiib (pl. Tuyuub) طيب (طيوب)

Perfume

Perfumes were among the favourite things to the Prophet (PBUH).

## tilaawah تلاوة

Recitation, reading

Usually, this refers to the careful recitation or reading of the Qur'an.

## Tiyarah طِيَرة

belief in bad omens

Islam is against believing in bad omens, because a Muslim should have faith in God.

## Tuhr طُهر

Freedom from menses

The time when a female is not menstruating.

## Tuma'niinah 1 طمأنينة

Peace and serenity

The feeling of peace and serenity.

## Tuma'niinah2 طمأنينة 2

Deliberateness

With reference to performing "Salaah" this means to do it carefully and slowly, not in a hurried manner.

## Tuubaa li... طوبى لـ...

May Allah grant Paradise to

An expression of encouragement for people to do or undergo something. It is a form of prayer for them to earn Paradise if they do or undergo what is specified.

## Tuur (jabal aT--) الطّور (جبل ---)

Mount Sinai

The mountain in Sinai which is mentioned in the Qur'an in the context of the story of Moses. (See the Qur'an, 23:20, e.g.)

## Tuur siinaa' /siiniin طور سيناء / سينين

Mount Sinai

Nowadays, it is called "jabal at-Tuur" in the Peninsula known as Sinai Desert to the North East of Egypt. It was around here that Moses received the Ten Commandments.

Uu

# Uu

## 'ubuudiyyah عبوديّة

servitude ,slavery

In religious terms ,this is usually used to refer to the relationship of man to God .He is a slave and servant of His Lord Who is the Master of the Universe .This includes worshipping Him and obeying every command of His.

## uDHiyah (pl. 'aDaaHii) أضحية (أضاحي)

Animal offering ,sacrifice

The animal offered for sacrifice especially during pilgrimage. This could be a goat (not less than one year old), a sheep (at least six months), a cow / ox , or a camel (both not less than two years old). A goat or sheep is offered for one pilgrim while a cow / ox and camel may be offered for seven people. For non-pilgrims, these animals are offered one per family, not individual..

## 'udhr (pl. a'dhaar) عُذر (أعذار)

Excuse

Reason for not doing or observing a required act. Often, we hear the expression "'udhr shar'iyy" (legitimate excuse).

## uHSina (yuHSanu) أُحصِن (يُحصن)

Got married

The verb in the passive form is used in the Qur'an to refer to marriage. (See the Qur'an, 4: 25.)

## 'uhuud wa mawaathiiq عهود ومواثيق

Covenants and treaties

Confirmed arrangements and agreements ,often put in writing.

## ukhrawiyy أُخروي

Related to the Hereafter

Any matter related to ''aakhirah" (life Hereafter).

## ukht min ar-raDaa'ah أُخت من الرّضاعة

Foster-sister

We also read" ukht bir-riDaa'ah". She is a female person who shared the suckling milk with another person of a different mother and father. According to Islamic law she is considered like a natural sister from the point of view of marriage.

## uluu al-'azm أولو العزم

Men of resolution

This term is used in the Qur'an to refer to certain messengers of Allah. According to some scholars, these are: Noah, Abraham, Moses and Jesus. (See the Qur'an, 46: 35.) But the term basically means people who are resolute, persistent and patient in carrying out their mission.

## uluu al-albaab أولو الألباب

Men of understanding

Another translation of this term is 'men possessed of minds'. (See the Qur'an, 3: 190ff.)

## uluu al-amr أولو الأمر

Authorities

People in charge of community affairs.

## uluu al-arHaam أولو الأرحام

Relatives

Blood relatives of various degrees.

## uluuhiyyah ألوهيّة

Divinity, Godhead

Being a deity or God.

## umm al-kitaab 1 أم الكتاب

The Opening Chapter

One of the meanings of this term is the Opening Chapter of the Qur'an, being the most important.

## umm al-kitaab 2 أم الكتاب

Foundation of the book

For this meaning, see the Qur'an, 3: 7.

Uu

## umm (pl. 'ummahaat) almu'miniin
## أم (أمهات) المؤمنين

Mother of the believers

This term refers to any of the wives of the Prophet (PBUH). (See the Qur'an, 33: 6). They should be shown due respect, and a Muslim was not allowed to marry a former wife of the Prophet Muhammad (PBUH). The term is based on the Qur'anic declaration in Chapter 33, verse 6. One of the special rulings regarding them is that no one can marry them after the death of the Prophet (PBUH).

## umm al-quraa أم القرى

Mother of towns (Mecca)

One of the names used for Mecca al-Mukarramah.

## umm al-walad أم الولد

Mother's child

In legal terms, this refers to a bondswoman who gives birth to a child from her master. She automatically becomes free upon the master's death.

## ummah (pl. umam)
## أمّة (أمم)

Nation, community

## ummiyy أميّ

Illiterate

Though the general meaning of the word is someone who cannot read or write. It is found in the Qur'an to mean both illiterate and non-Jew (gentile). See, e.g., the Qur'an, 7: 157; 2: 78; 3: 20.)

## 'umrah عمرة

Lesser pilgrimage

Lesser pilgrimage means wearing the pilgrim's garb, making the "Tawaaf" around the Ka'bah and "sa'y" between Safa and Marwah any time of the year.

## umuur (sg. 'amr)
## أمور (أمر)

Affairs, issues

Very often this word is found in the plural form to mean matters of all sorts.

## 'unnah عنّة

Impotence

The male's inability to perform sexual intercourse. The wife has the right to seek divorce on this ground.

## 'uqdat an-nikaaH
## عقدة النكاح

Marriage contract

## 'uquuq al-waalidayn
## عقوق الوالدين

Disobedience to parents

Showing disrespect to parents and disobeying their commands, or mistreating them, which a major sin, being an act of disobedience to Divine commandments (the Qur'an, 17: 23).

## 'urf (pl. 'a'raaf)
## عُرف (أعراف)

Convention

Common practice by people in a certain community. In Islamic law, we often find reference to these practices in the absence of clear legislation regarding certain practices or worldly duties. Naturally, these should not conflict with any injunctions of the religion.

## 'uruud at-tijaarah
## عروض التجارة

Commodities

Things prepared for trade. There are special rules regarding the alms paid on them.

## 'uSaah (sg. 'aaSii)
## عصاة (عاصٍ)

Sinners, rebellious people

See "'aaS(in)."

## 'uSuul (sg. 'aSl) 1 أصول (أصل)

Principles

See" aSl ('uSuul) 1."

## uSuul ('aSl)2 أصول (أصل)

Lineage

See" aSl ('uSuul) 2 ".

## uSuul al-fiqh أصول الفقه

Principles of jurisprudence

Literally, the term means 'origins of fiqh' (jurisprudence). It has been defined as the "science of Islamic jurisprudence", which deals with the methodology of deriving laws from the sources of Islam and of establishing their juristic or constitutional validity.

## uSuul al-Hadiith
## أصول الحديث

Principles of the hadeeth

This is short for "'ilm ..." It deals with the principles of hadeeth (traditions of the Prophet [PBUH]) authentication, such as methods of text verification and the critical evaluation of the narrators.

## uSuul at-tafsiir

## أصول التفسير

Science of Qur'anic exegesis

This is short for "'ilm ..." which is the science that deals with the issues and rules to be observed in interpreting the Qur'an, such as full knowledge of the Qur'an and the Prophet's traditions, the Arabic language, history of the revelation of different verses…etc.

## uswah Hasanah

## أسوة حسنَة

Exemplar model

The Prophet Muhammad (PBUH) is supposed to be the exemplar model for all Muslims. They should emulate his conduct. (See the Qur'an, 33: 21).

## uuqiyyah أوقيّة

Ounce

There are two types of 'ounce' in traditional Islamic terms: one for silver (119.4 grams) and another for other types of materials (127 grams). Both should not be confused with the modern use of ounce (28.349 grams).

## 'uzayr عـزَير

Ezra

The Qur'an points out that some Jews claimed that Ezra was a son of Allah. (9:30).

## 'uzuubah عزوبة

Celibacy

Celibacy is not recommended by Islam, since it is considered against human nature.

## 'uzzaa (al--) العُزّى

The'Uzza

One of the female deities worshipped by the pagan Arabs.

# Ww



## waaHid (al--) الواحد

The One

A Divine Attribute of Allah. The One Who is Absolute in oneness and uniqueness and has no partners.

## waa'iZ (pl. wu''aaZ) واعظ (وعاظ)

preacher

Someone who gives sermons or preaches to others.

## waajib 1 واجب

Obligatory

Required by the religion.

## waajib 2 (pl. waajibaat) واجب 2 (واجبات)

Duty, obligation

Something made obligatory by the religion.

## waajib al-wujuud واجب الوجود

Inevitably existing

The term is used to refer to Allah Whose existence is inevitable.

## waajid (al--) الواجد

The Finder

A Divine Attribute of Allah. The One from Whom nothing is hidden or lost.

## waal(in) (pl. wulaah) وال (ولاة)

Governor

A governor appointed by a caliph or king to rule a certain part of the country.

## waalii (al--) الوالي

The Patron

A Divine Attribute of Allah. The Bestower of bounties and protector from evils.

## waalii (pl. wulaah) والي (ولاة)

Governor

A governor of a region appointed by the Caliph.

## waaqa'a (yuwaaqi') واقع (يواقع)

to copulate

To have sexual intercourse with someone.

## waarith (al--) الوارث

The Inheritor

A Divine Attribute of Allah. The True Inheritor of things, because He is the only Eternal Being.

## waarith (pl. warathah) وارث (ورثة)

Heir

Someone who inherits. The distribution of the inheritance in Islam is clearly specified in the Qur'an; it is not a matter of conventions or the will of the deceased. (See, e.g., Chapter Four of the Qur'an, verses 11-12 and 176. There is a special science for this, called "'ilm al-faraa'iD".

## waasi'(al--) الواسع

The All-Embracing

A Divine Attribute of Allah. The One Whose knowledge and mercy embrace everyone and everything.

## wa'd وعد

Promise

Promise to do something good for someone.

## waD' (fil-Hadiith) وضع (في الحديث)

Fabrication of Hadiith

In Hadiith studies the term means inventing a Hadiith and ascribing it to the Prophet Muhammad (PBUH).

## wadii'ah وديعة

Object in trust

Something left with a person for safe keeping.

## wafaa' وفاء

Fulfillment, loyalty

Fulfilling one's promise, or showing loyalty to someone.

## wafaa' ad-dayn وفاء الدين

Paying a debt

Paying back the money one borrowed from somebody.

## wafaa' bin-nadhr وفاء بالنذر

Fulfilling a vow

Doing the act one vows to do, such as fasting or giving out charity. However, if one vows to do something wrong he should not do it, and atone for it instead. (See "kaffaarah").

## wahhaab (al--) الوهّاب

The Highest Bestower

A Divine Attribute of Allah .The One Who gives with no bounds, and expects no reward from anyone.

## wahhaabiyy (pl. wahhaabiyyah) وهّابي (وهّابية)

Wahhabi

A follower of Sheikh Muhammad ibn Abdul-Wahhab of Najd ,who was a Muslim revivalist that emphasized in his teachings the importance of fighting all sorts of "shirk" (polytheistic practices), such as worshipping saints and building mosques over their tombs.

## wahhaabiyyah (al--) الوهّابية

Wahhabism

Teachings of Sheikh Muhammad ibn Abdul-Wahhab, a strict Islamic revivalist, which emphasized the return to the pristine teachings of the religion and fighting all sorts of polytheistic practices and superstitions.

## wa'iid وعيد

Warning

Warning or threat to do something bad to someone.

## wajh allaah 1 وجه الله

Pleasure of Allah

We find this phrase in expressions like "li-wajhi-llaah" (for the sake of Allah) and "ibtighaa' wajhi-llaah" (seeking the pleasure of Allah).

## wajh allaah 2 وجه الله

the Face of God

The direction which Allah has accepted for you. (See the Qur'an, 2: 115).

## wakaalah وكالة

Proxy, power of attorney

Appointing someone to act on one's behalf, giving him the power of attorney.

## wakiil (al--) الوكيل

The Ever-Trustee

A Divine Attribute of Allah. The One Whom we should always trust, and Who takes care of us.

## wakiil (pl. wukalaa') وكيل (وكلاء)

Proxy, agent

Someone who has legal authority to represent someone else. Sometimes, we have "al-wakiil ash-shar'iyy" (legal representative') to emphasize this aspect of legality.

## walaa' (al--) الولاء

loyalty, show of solidarity

The term is sometimes used in the sense of a Muslim's show of solidarity in his relationship with other Muslims, considering them as brothers and friends, different from non-Muslims.

## waliimah (pl. walaa'im) وليمة (ولائم)

Wedding banquet / party

It is recommended for a Muslim to

have a wedding party as a means of announcing the marriage. Invited people are urged to attend it.

Ww

## waliyy (al--) الولي

The Ever-Patronizing

A Divine Attribute of Allah. The One Who patronizes His loyal servants and protects them.

## Waliyy 1 (pl. awliyaa') ولي 1 (أولياء)

Holy man, man of God

This is the Islamic equivalent to a 'saint'. A "waliyy" is a man of high integrity and is devoted to worshipping Allah. Sometimes, a man of God may be given special unusual abilities, called "karaamaat". (See "karaamah"). The expression "awliyaa' allaah" is found in the Qur'an, 10: 62.

## waliyy 2 (pl. awliyaa') ولي 2 (أولياء)

Ally

Someone we trust and rely upon for support. (See, e.g., the Qur'an, 60: 1.)

## waliyy (pl. 'waliyaa') al-'amr ولي (أولياء) الأمر

Guardian, person in charge

This term means both the person in charge of the community as well as a guardian of a person.

## waqf (pl. 'awqaaf) وقف (أوقاف)

Endowment

Allocating part of one's possession for a certain good purpose; it should not be sold or disposed of except under the conditions stipulated by the endowing person, or with the aim of perpetuating it.

## waqfah (pl. waqfaat) وقفة (وقفات)

in Qur'anic phonetics, a pause or stop while reciting the Qur'an.

## waqfah (al--) الوقفة

Stay

See "al-wuquuf bi-'arafah". Some people loosely use the term to refer to the day that immediately precedes the "'iid", whether it is the "'iid al-aDHaa" or "'iid al-fiTr."

## wara وَرَع '

Meticulous godliness/

conscientiousness

Avoiding acts that one does not feel comfortable with for fear of committing a sin.

**wasiilah وسيلة**

Approach to God

Whatever means or acts that bring one closer to God. (See, e.g., the Qur'an, 5:35)

**waSiyy وصي**

trustee

Someone entrusted with taking care of the affairs of someone else, usually a minor or lacking legal capacity.

**waSiyyah (pl. waSaayaa)**

**وصية (وصايا)**

Will / testament

A legal document left by a person giving instructions regarding his property. In Islam, beneficiaries should not be legal heirs, whose shares in the inheritance are specified by the Qur'an. (See the Qur'an, 4: 7, 10-13 and 176).

**waswasah (pl. wasaawis)**

**وسوسة (وساوس)**

Evil suggestion / whisper

Often this term refers to the bad suggestions made by Satan to mislead people into doing forbidden things .It is also used to mean constant doubting.

**waT' وطء**

Copulation

Having sexual intercourse.

**wathan (pl. awthaan)**
**وثن (أوثان)**

Idol

A statue or icon polytheists pray to or worship.

**wathaniyy وثني**

Idol worshipper / pagan

A person who worships idols.

**wathaniyyah وثنية**

Idolatry / paganism

The practice of worshipping idols, statues ,icons and the like.

**wayHak وَيحَكَ !**

WayHak

An exclamation expressing mild blame.

**waylak وَيلَكَ**

Woe to you!

An exclamation expressing condemnation and warning.

**wa'Z وعظ**

Preaching

Offering advice and giving warning to others for doing wrong things.

Ww

## Wilaayah 1 ولاية

Guardianship

The power and/or responsibility to supervise the affairs of someone else .See" waliyy."1

## Wilaayah 2 ولاية

Governership

The post of waalii ('governor').

## wiSaal وِصال

Continuation

To continue the fast for more than one way.

## wiSaayah وصاية

Trusteeship

See "waSiyy".

## wisq (pl. awsuq) وسق (أوساق)

Wisq

A unit of measurement of quantity used for food. It is equivalent to 60 "Saa's". (See "Saa'").

## witr وتر

Odd in number

Of odd number, usually one or three. The term "al-witr" may be short for "Salaat al-witr."

## wuDuu' وضوء

Ablution

Washing the hands ,rinsing the mouth ,sniffing water and rinsing the nostrils ,washing the face, washing the arms up to the elbow, wiping the head with wet hands and washing the feet .All of these, with the exception of wiping the head ,are done three times ,starting with the right hand side first.

## wujuub وجوب

obligation

Being required by the religion ;to ignore it is a sin.

## wuquuf وقوف

Standing

Standing position in formal prayers during which one would normally read at least" suurat al-faatiHah" (Opening Chapter of the Qur'an).

## wuquuf (al--) bi'arafah الوقوف بعرفة

Stay at Arafah

Staying at the plain of 'Arafah on the ninth day of the month of pilgrimage (Dhul-Hijjah) is considered the most important single rite of "Hajj". A pilgrim should stay there until sunset, then he moves to "Muzdalifah."

# Yy

## yadan bi-yad يدا بيد

Instantaneous exchange

In Islamic law certain commodities should be exchanged immediately for the transaction to be valid.

## yaghuuth يغوث

Yaghooth

The name of a deity worshipped by the people of Prophet Noah. (See the Qur'an 71:23)

## yahuud (sg. yahuudiyy) يهود (يهوديّ)

Jews

See" yahuudiyy."

## yahuudiyy (pl. yahuud) يهوديّ (يهود)

Jew

A member of the Jewish faith. According to Islam, Jews are members of the 'people of the Scripture'. A distinction should be made between Jews and Israelites (descendants of Jacob), since not all followers of the Jewish faith are Israelites.

## (--al) yahuudiyyah اليهوديّة

Judaism

The religion originally taught by the Prophet Moses ,but greatly tampered with after him . Its holy scripture is" at-tawraah ."But it is said that actually it is the Talmud that is considered the primary source of Jewish law.

## yaHyaa يحيى

John

A prophet of Allah, son of Zachariah born to him miraculously, since his father was very old and his mother was barren. (See the Qur'an, 19: 2-15).

## ya'juuj wa ma'juuj يأجوج ومأجوج

Gog magog

A nation of a highly destructive force. (See the Qur'an, 18: 94).

## yalamlam يلملم

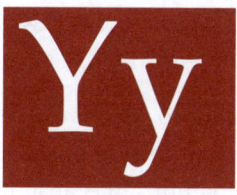

Yalamlam

The name of a port in Yemen where all prospective pilgrims from Yemen or those passing by it should start their status of "iHraam."

Y y

## yamiin1 يمين

Right hand side

A Muslim should start all important and good things with the right hand side or do them with the right hand ,such as greeting ,eating and drinking with the right hand ,or with the right foot first ,such as entering a mosque .Believers are called "aSHaab al-yamiin" (people of the right hand), because they are handed their records of deeds in their right hands on the Day of Judgment.

## yamiin 2 (pl. aymaan) 2 يمين (أيمان)

Oath

In Islam an oath should be in Allah's name only; i.e., one should not swear except to God.

## yamiin al-laghw يمين اللغو

Unintentional oath

An oath said in passing without the intention of swearing to Allah, such as saying, "wa-llaah"… just to emphasize an invitation to something, for example. No expiation is required if this type of oath is not fulfilled.

## yamiin ghamuus يمين غموس

False oath

An oath made to deceive the hearer and convince him of a lie. It is called "ghamuus" because it causes the person who makes it to be 'dipped' in Hell-Fire.

## yaqiin (al--) اليقين

Certitude

Absolute certainty. In the Qur'an, sometimes we find the phrase "Haqq al-yaqiin" (real certainty).

## ya'quub يعقوب

Jacob

The Prophet Jacob whose name was also "israa'iil" (servant of Allah / Israel). He is the son of Isaac and grandson of the Prophet Abraham. Early Jews are often called "banii israa'iil " ('children of Israel'- Israelites-') in the Qur'an. Naturally, not all Jews of the present time, most of whom are Khazar converts, are Israelites. (See "israa'iil" for a comment on this point.)

## yathrib يثرِب

Medina

The old name for the city later called "al-madiinah" the city of the Prophet (PBUH)).

## yatiim/ah (pl. aytaam) يتيم (أيتام)

Orphan

A child who has lost its father especially. The Qur'an and the sunnah strongly recommend kindness and fair treatment of orphans, even sponsoring their upbringing. (See, e.g., the Qur'an, 4: 8-10.)

## ya'uuq يعوق

Ya'ooq

The name of a deity worshipped by the people of Prophet Noah. (See the Qur'an 71:23)

## yawm (pl. ayyaam) يوم (أيام)

Day

In Islamic texts, this word is frequently used in the sense of day as opposed to night. (See "yawm wa laylah").

## yawm ad-diin يوم الدّين

The Day of Judgement

The Day on which people will be resurrected and judged according to their deeds in the present life. (See, for example, the Qur'an, 82).

## yawm (al--) al-'aakhir اليوم الآخر

The Last Day

The Day of Judgement.

## yawm al-ba'th يوم البَعث

Day of Resurrection

The day on which all creatures are resurrected and made to account for their actions in this world. See "al-qiyaamah" (the Resurrection).

## yawm al-faSl يوم الفصل

Day of Judgment

The Day of Judgment on which the doers of good are separated from the wrong doers.

## yawm al-Hashr يوم الحَشر

The Day of Gathering

The day when the whole creation will be resurrected and gathered together for the Judgement. (See "al-qiyaamah").

## yawm al-Hisaab يوم الحساب

The Day of Reckoning

The Day when everyone will see records of all his deeds, and will be asked to account for them. (See, for example, the Qur'an, 38: 49-64).

## yawm al-jam' يوم الجمع

Day of Gathering

The Day of Resurrection when all creatures are gathered for the Judgment.

Y y

## yawm an-naHr يوم النّحر

Day of Sacrifice

The tenth day of "Dhul-Hijjah" (month of pilgrimage), on which a Muslim starts offering his sacrifice. One may slaughter the sacrifice on this and the following three days. Originally, "naHr" means slaughtering a camel.

## yawm al-qiyaamah يوم القيامة

Day of Resurrection

See "al-qiyaamah".

## yawm at-tarwiyah يوم التّروية

Eighth of Dhul-Hijjah

The eighth day of the month of pilgrimage when pilgrims go to Mina.

## yawm al-waqfah يوم الوقفة

Day of Stay in Arafah

The ninth day of Dhul-Hijjah (month of pilgrimage) on which pilgrims stay in the plain of 'Arafah until sunset, then move to Muzdalifah.

## yawm wa laylah يوم وليلة

One day and night

Twenty-four hours. Yawm is used here to mean daylight, as opposed to night. The other more specific word for day (as opposed to night) is "nahaar" which means the time between dawn and sunset.

## yuHtaDar يحتضر

To approach death

To be on deathbed. It is sunnah that when a Muslim is in such a condition we should prompt him to say the "shahaadah" so that it would be his last words.

## yuunus يونس

Jonah

A prophet of Allah who was swallowed by a whale and returned to land safely by Allah's Will. He is also referred to in the Qur'an as "dhu-nnuun" (man of the fish / whale). (See the Qur'an, 37: 139-147 and 21: 87-88, where you find his famous prayer of distress).

## yuusuf يوسف

Joseph

The Prophet Joseph, son of the Prophet Jacob, exemplar for his beauty, chastity and his knowledge of interpreting dreams. (See the Qur'an, Chapter of Joseph (12) for his story).

# Zz

## Zaahara (yuZaahir) ظاهر (يظاهر)

To declare zhihar

See "Zihaar."

## zaahid زاهد

Ascetic

A person who lives an ascetic way of life. (See "zuhd"). To such a person life in this world is a journey to the everlasting life of the Hereafter; the lighter the load, the easier and safer the trip is.

## Zaahir (aZ –) الظّاهِر

The Obvious

A Divine Attribute of Allah .The One Who is Most Obvious through His creation and deeds ,because they are all absolute proofs and signs of His existence.

## Zaahir al-madhhab ظاهر المذهب

Apparent ruling of a madhhab

What is understood from a certain school of thought.

## Zaahiriyyah (aZ-) ظاهرية (ال-)

Literalism /literalists

Followers of the school of thought that sticks to the literal sense of Islamic law and teachings.

## Zaalim ظالم

Aggressor

## zaaniy/ah (pl. zunaah) زاني/ة (زناة)

Fornicator ,adulterer

A person who commits an illicit sexual relation, male or female whether married or not married. (See "zinaa" for comments.)

## zaawiyah زاوية

Mosque-school

Literally, the word means a corner or nook. In some Muslim countries, there were some small mosques built near or over the tomb of a 'saint' and used for teaching, with a housing facility attached to it. Often, they were maintained by sufi orders.

## zabaaniyat jahannam زبانية جهنّم

Guards of Hell

Angels in charge of carrying out the punishment of the sinners and disbelievers in Hell.

### zabuur (az--) الزّبور

Psalms

The scripture that was revealed to the Prophet Daawuud (David).

### zakaa (yazkuu) زكا (يزكو)

To be pure

This is the intransitive form of "zakkaa," to which the term "zakaah" is etymologically related.

### zakaah زكاة

Alms, poor dues/ tax

The obligatory poor dues that a Muslim should pay to certain categories of people in the community, including the poor, the needy, the way-farer… Paying the "zakaah" is one of the five pillars of Islam. For money, 2.5% of the savings are paid after the passage of one year.

### zakaat al-fiTr زكاة الفطر

Breaking the fast poor due

The charity that one should give to the poor before one attends the "'iid" service at the end of Ramadan. It consists of about 2 kilograms of wheat, rice, other grains, or "iqT" (dried yogurt curds) for each member of the household.

### zakaat al-maal زكاة المال

Alms on wealth

In simple terms, this means the alms one should pay on the savings one has for one year, if it exceeds the "niSaab". It is two and a half percent of those savings.

### zakariyyaa زكريّا

Zachariah

The name of a prophet, father of the Prophet YaHyaa (John) and guardian of Mary. See reference to them in the Qur'an, 3: 37-41 and 19: 2-15).

### zakkaa 1 (yuzakkii) زكى 1 (يزكّي)

Give alms / pay zakat

To pay the obligatory poor dues known as alms or "zakaah."

### zakkaa 2 (yuzakkii) زكى 2 (يزكّي)

Vouch for someone

To bear witness that someone is good or to praise him .This also applies to oneself ;hence ,we have "zakkaa nafsahu" meaning that he claimed to be good or better than others. (See the Qur'an, 53: 32).

**zamzam زمزم**

Zamzam

The blessed well of Zamzam in the Holy Mosque of Mecca. Tradition has it that the spring of water first came out at the feet of Ishmael when he was a baby, left with his mother Hager, by his father Abraham in the area known today as Mecca. The Prophet Abraham (PBUH) was carrying out Divine orders. He prayed for that barren valley to be a blessed one. While Hager was frantically looking for something for her baby water sprang from beneath his feet. This is the origin of the Well of Zamzam whose water is considered blessed by all Muslims. Its water has been running from the pre-Islamic era.

**zandaqah زندقة**

heresy

Holding religious views contradictory to the teachings of Islam.

**zindiiq**

**زنديق (زنادقة)**

Heretic

A person who believes in and/or calls to ideas and beliefs that are contrary to Islamic teachings.

**Zann (pl. Zunuun)**

**ظن (ظُنون)**

Speculation, conjecture

Islam encourages its followers not to make hasty judgments on basis of conjecture. (See the Qur'an, 17: 36 and 49: 12.) In the Principles of Islamic Law, scholars suggest different types and degrees of "Zann".

**Zanniyy ظنّي**

Speculative, doubtful

In the Science of Principles this means a possible meaning, though another meaning may be inferred.

**zaquum زقوم**

Zaqquum tree

A most hateful type of tree in Hell offered as food for the unbelievers and sinners. (See, e.g., the Qur'an 37: 62-65; 44: 43-46.)

Zz

## zawaaj زواج

Marriage

Marriage is a strongly recommended "sunnah" for both the protection of individuals from illicit sexual relations and propagation.

## zawaaj al-mut'ah زواج المتعة

Temporary marriage

Literally, this means 'marriage for pleasure'. It is a marriage in which the duration is stipulated in the marriage contract. Prophet (PBUH) declared the illegality of such marriage.

## zawaaj / nikaaH ash-shighaar زواج / نكاح الشغار

Exchange marriage

An arrangement in which a guardian of a female agrees to marry off his trustee to another person in exchange for the other guardian of a female to give his trustee to him in marriage, without either paying the necessary "Sadaaq" (dower). This is forbidden in Islam, because it deprives the brides of their rights to the dower and freedom of choice.

## zawaal ash-shams زوال الشمس

High noon

The time when the sun crosses the local meridian. It is forbidden for a Muslim to pray at this time. The real time of noon prayer ("Salaat az-Zuhr") starts after this.

## zawj (pl. 'azwaaj)1 زوج (أزواج)

Spouse

In the Qur'an this word is used for both male and female spouse. Later, people used the word "zawjah" (wife) to distinguish female from male spouse. This word is used in later Arabic to mean a pair, which is in the Qur'an is "zawjaan".

## zawj (pl. 'azwaaj)2 2 زوج (أزواج)

Member of pair, mate

In Qur'anic usage, this refers to one member of a pair; hence "zawjaan" (2 zawjs) means a pair. (See, e.g., the Qur'an, 11: 40.)

## zawjaan زوجان

Pair

In Qur'anic Arabic the word means a pair, not two pairs as

many people may understand. (See "zawj".)

## zaydiyyah زيدية

Zaydi (Shi'ites) sect

A Shi'ite sub-sect. Those who claim to follow Zaid the son of Ali ibn al-Hussain instead of the other son Ja'far aS-Saadiq (called "Ja'fariyyah"). This sect is especially dominant in Yemen.

## Zihaar ظهار

Zihar

An old Arab practice, similar to divorce, in which a man says to his wife, "You are like my mother's back to me." (See reference to this in the Qur'an, 58: 1-4).

## Zinaa زنى / زنا

Fornication, adultery

In Islamic terms, any sexual act between a male and female outside wedlock is called "zinaa". It is considered one of the major sins (kabiirah), the punishment for which depends on the persons involved, whether they have been previously married ("thayyib") or not ("bikr").

## zuhd زهد

Asceticism

Living the simplest way of life with the barest of necessities.

## Zuhr (aZ--) الظهر

Noon

Noon prayer time starts a few minutes after mid-day.

## Zulm ظلم

Injustice, aggression

Injustice and unfair dealing is forbidden in Islam, even when a Muslim is dealing with non-Muslims or enemies. This is the opposite of "'adl" (justice and fairness).

## zuur زور

Falsehood

The word is often found in association with "qawl" ('saying') or "shahaadah" ('testifying'), meaning perjury or false testimony, both of which are strongly condemned by Islam.

# APPENDIX

## SURAS (CHAPTERS) OF THE QUR'AN

# Aa

### 'aadiyaat (suurat al-- )

**سورة العاديات**

Chapter of the Galloping Horses

This is Chapter 100 of the Qur'an, taking its title from the word in the first verse. The word has been interpreted to refer to horses running in battle fields. A vivid picture of these horses is given in the next four verses. This is followed by a statement about some characteristics of unbelievers, who are warned of their fate upon Resurrection.

### 'aala 'imraan (suurat --)

**سورة آل عمران**

Chapter of the Family of 'Imran

The third chapter of the Qur'an, taking its name from the story of the family of 'Imran, including the mother of "maryam" (Mary) and "Zakariyyaa" and "YaHyaa", Mary and her son Jesus (PBUH). This is one of the two chapters of the Qur'an where the story of Jesus is given in some detail. (See verses 42- 63).

In verse 61 we have the reference to the "mubaahah". In verse 110 the reasons for good Muslims being the best of nations are given, and in verses 169-171 we read about the special life of martyrs who are killed in the Cause of God. Among the frequently recited verses in this Chapter are the ones that begin with, "Behold! In the creation of the heavens and the earth and the alternation of night and day there are Signs for men of understanding..." and give instances of the characteristics of these men and their prayers. (verses 190-200). A part of a verse commonly cited to call Muslims to solidarity and unity is: "And hold fast, all together, by the Rope [or Covenant] of Allah, and be not divided" (verse 103).

### 'abasa (suurat -- ) سورة عبس

Chapter of 'He frowned'

This is Chapter 80 of the Qur'an, taking its title from the verb at the beginning of the Chapter. The reference is to the incident when the Prophet (PBUH) was eagerly preaching Islam to some pagans when he was interrupted by one of his poor followers, a blind man. Obviously he was annoyed (frowned) and kept on preaching. Though the man did not see the frown, God wanted to teach His own Messenger. Thus the early parts of the Chapter were revealed, reminding the Prophet (PBUH) that the Qur'an is a reminder for those willing to accept it, and that it has a special status (verses 1-16). In the next part of the Chapter man is reminded of his creation and the Divine bounties provided for him (17-32). Then we are reminded of the Day of Judgment when everybody cannot but think of his own salvation. A contrast is made between the fate of the believers and that of the unbelievers (33-42).

### aHqaaf (suurat al- ) سورة الأحقاف

Chapter of Winding Sand- tracts

This is Chapter 46 of the Qur'an, taking it name from the word found in verse 21 with reference to the people of the Prophet Huud, his preaching to them, their rejection of the Faith and their miserable fate (verses 21-25). One of the verses often quoted is the one where God enjoins on man kindness to parents, especially one's mother who "in pain bore him, and in pain gave him birth..." (verse 15). In this Chapter we also find one of the references in the Qur'an to a company of the "Jinn's" listening to the Qur'an [recited by the Prophet (PBUH)], their acceptance of Islam and preaching it to their people (29-32).

### aHzaab (suurat al- ) سورة الأحزاب

Chapter of the Confederates

This is Chapter 33, taking its title from the word "aHzaab" (confederates' or 'group of clans') mentioned in verse 20. In this Chapter we read about one of the most difficult battles of early Islam, when many polytheist clans came together to attack Medina, the Town of the Prophet. They were helped by some treacherous

Jewish and hypocrite residents of the Town who had a defense treaty with Prophet Muhammad (PBUH). Through Divine support the Muslims came out victorious, and proper punishment was inflected on the traitors (verses 9-21). In this Chapter we read the Islamic injunction against adoption (since it leads to violation of birth rights and prohibition of lawful acts). (See verses 4 and 5). The special status of the wives of Prophet Muhammad, being 'mothers of the believers', is mentioned, including the verse which dictated that Muslims should not ask them for anything 'except from behind a "Hijaab" ('screen'). (See, e.g.., verses 28-34 and 53-55.) Among the often quoted verses in this Chapter are the verses that emphasize the finality of prophecy with Muhammad, declaring him to be the Seal of the Prophets (verse 40) and verse 56 where God instructs Muslims to pray for blessings on the Prophet and to salute him with all respect. Another set of verses frequently recited by Muslims are verses 70 to 72, where reference is made to the special responsibility of man versus the other creation.

## a'laa (suurat al-- )

### سورة الأعلى

Chapter of the Most High

This is Chapter 87 of the Qur'an, taking its name from the word in verse one. Some of the favours of Allah are mentioned, followed by the Divine declaration, "We shall teach you to recite [the Qur'an], so that you may not forget except as God wills..."(verses 6-7). Muhammad (PBUH) is commanded to "give admonition in case the admonition profits [the hearer]. He will heed who fears [God]" But the unfortunate will not benefit from it. The prosperous is one who purifies himself, remembers the name of His Lord and prays (verses 9-15). A universal statement about the nature of man and the real fact is given in verses 16 and 17: "Yet, you give preference to the present life, while the Hereafter is better and more lasting." This Chapter was often recited by Prophet Muhammad (PBUH) in the first standing position of the Friday prayer.

## an'aam (suurat al- )

### سورة الأنعام

Chapter of the Cattle

This is the sixth chapter in the Qur'an, taking its name from the word "al-an'aam" (cattle) mentioned a few times (e.g., verses, 136, 138, 139 and 142). In this Chapter we also read a set of commandments, regarding things a Muslim should and should not do (verses 151-153). Among the often quoted verses are the verses that give a comprehensive meaning of Islam: "Say: 'Truly, my prayer, and my service of sacrifice, my life and my death are (all) for God, the Cherisher of the worlds. No partner has He: This I am commanded, and I am the first of those who submit to His Will.'" (162-3)

In this Chapter we also have the verses known as "aayaat al-futuuH" (verse 59 ff.).

## anbiyaa' (suurat al- )

**سـورة الأنبياء**

Chapter of the Prophets

This is Chapter 21 of the Qur'an, taking its title from the stories of the different prophets and messengers of God and their peoples as well as about the constant conflict between good and evil and between monotheism and polytheism. Of special significance is the story of Prophet Abraham, his smashing of his people's idols, their throwing him into a big fire and God's protection from it. "They said, 'Burn him…' We said: 'O Fire! Be you cool, and a (means of) safety and peace for Abraham!" (51-73) References are made to most other prophets and people of God, including Noah, Ishmael, Isaac, David, Solomon, Job, Idrees, Zakariyyah, John, Mary. The relevant verses are concluded by the Divine statement: "Verily, this Community of yours is a single Community, and I am your Lord and Cherisher. Therefore, serve and worship Me (an no other)." (92). An often quoted verse, which declares the universality of the message of Muhammad (PBUH), and that Muhammad is a source of Mercy for the whole universe, is: "We sent you not [O Muhammad], but as a Mercy for all creatures." (107)

## anfaal (suurat al- )

**سـورة الأنفال**

Chapter of the Spoils of War

This is chapter 8 of the Qur'an. It takes its name from the word "anfaal" (spoils of war) which is found in the first verse of the Chapter. The word is not found in any other chapter. In this Chapter and the next one (Chapter 9) we find many of the rulings related to etiquettes of fighting enemies of the Faith and other issues of relevance, among many other matters. Reference to the first major battle in Islam ("Badr") is found in verses 5 to 14 and 42-44. A part of a verse commonly cited to warn Muslims against dissention and disunity is: "and contend not with each other lest you lose heart and your power depart" (46).

## 'ankabuut (suurat al- )

### سورة العنكبوت

Chapter of the Spider

This is Chapter 29 of the Qur'an, taking its title from the parable of the spider's flimsy web to which is compared the protection unbelievers seek from partners they worship other than God, "The parable of those who take protectors other than God is that of the spider, which builds (for itself) a house; but truly the flimsiest of houses is the spider's house; if only they knew." (verse 41). Two frequently quoted verses are the following: "Recite what is sent of the Book by inspiration to thee, and establish Salaah (re.g.ular prayer); for Salaah restrains from shameful and evil deeds; and the Remembrance of God is the greatest (thing in life)..." (verse 45, often recited at the conclusion of the Friday sermon). The other is, "And dispute you not with the People of the Book except in the best way, unless it be with those of them who do wrong. But say, ' We believe in the Revelation which has come down to us and in that which came down to you; our God and your God is One; and it is to Him we submit (in Islam)." (verse 46, which lays down the principles of Muslim dialogue with Christians and Jews.)

## a'raaf (suurat al- )

### سورة الأعراف

Chapter of the Heights

This is the seventh chapter of the Qur'an, taking its name from the word "a'raaf" uniquely mentioned in the Qur'an in verses 46 and 48of this Chapter. Among the verses often quoted from this Chapter is the verse that emphasizes the universality of the message of Muhammad (PBUH): "Say: 'O mankind, I am sent unto you all, as the Messenger of God to Whom belongs the dominion of the heavens and the earth... So believe in God and His Messenger, the unlettered Prophet, who believes in God and His Words, and follow him that you may be guided." (158)

### 'aSr (suurat al-- )

### سورة العصر

Chapter of Time

This is Chapter 103 of the Qur'an, taking its name from the word in the first verse, which refers both to Time in general or the time after noon. In this Chapter, God the Almighty very emphatically declares that "Man is in loss." He can only be saved by the following three things: (1) Having Faith, (2) doing righteous deeds and (3) mutual enjoining of Truth and of Patience and Constancy. The comprehensive nature of this Chapter made a great scholar of Islam, Imam ash-Shaafi'ii, say that this Chapter stands for the whole Qur'an.

# Bb

### balad (suurat al-- )

### سورة البلد

Chapter of the City

This is Chapter 90 of the Qur'an, taking its name from the word, which refers to Makkah, in the first verse. We read about the fact that Man has been created into toil and struggle. Yet, some think that they have power over all things, forgetting that whatever they have of abilities have been provided by God. "But he has made not haste on the path that is steep." The climbing of this steep path to His Lord requires good deeds , such as liberating slaves, feeding the orphan with claims of relationship or the indigent poor, being among those who believe and enjoin patience and constancy and enjoin deeds of compassion and kindness. Such will be the people of the Right Hand. As for the unbelievers, they will be the people of the Left Hand, imprisoned in Hell.

### baqarah (suurat al- )

### سورة البقرة

Chapter of the Cow

The second chapter of the Qur'an. It is the longest chapter, consisting of 286 verses. It also includes the longest verse in the Qur'an, being one page long. It is verse 282, known as "the verse of debt or lending money" (ad-dayn). The name of this suurah comes from the story of the cow of the Children of Israel (verses 67 to 71).

Due to its length (being a little less than one tenth of the Qur'an), this Chapter covers many spiritual and wordly affairs, starting with the classification of people with regards to belief in God and their characteristics (verses 2-20), Ramadhan and fasting ( verses180- 187), maritial relations and divorce (verses 221-242), freedom of belief ( verse 256) charity and its rewards (verses 261-274) as well some aspects of financial transations, including, usuary, borrowing and witnesses thereof (verses 275 -276 and 282-283).

In this Chapter there are three verses of special significance: the greatest verse in the Qur'an, the Verse of the Throne (255) whose recitation is recommended for great rewards and 'Divine protection', and "khawaatiim suurat al-baqarah" (the concluding verses, 285-286) which were strongly recommended by the Prophet Muhammad (PBUH) to be recited in the evening. In fact, the Verse of the Throne was recommended by the Prophet (PBUH) to be recited after the five daily prayers and before going to bed. Reciting the whole Chapter in a house drives away Satan from it, according to a saying by Prophet Muhammad (PBUH).

This Chapter and the following one (Chapter 3) have a special status according to a Prophetic tradition, where the Prophet Muhammad (PBUH) says that the whole Qur'an, led by these two chapters, will come on the Day of Judgement to the defense of those who learn it act upon it.

## bayyinah (suurat al-- )

سورة البيّنة

Chapter of the Clear Evidence

This is the 98th Chapter of the Qur'an, taking its title from the last word in verse one. This Chapter states the fact that many Christian, Jews (People of the Book) and polytheists would not quit their old beliefs until they received "the Clear Evidence, a Messenger from God reciting scriptures kept pure and holy wherein are writings straight and correct"; i.e., the Holy Qur'an. "Those People of the Book were only divided after receiving the Clear Evidence, [though] they were only commanded to worship God, offering Him sincere devotion, being True [in faith]; to establish regular prayer; and to pay the zakat ('poor dues')/ and that is the Religion Right and Straight." (verses 1-5) The last three verses contrast the fate of believers and unbelievers in the Hereafter

## buruuj (suurat al-- )

### سورة البروج

Chapter of the Constellations

This is Chapter 84 of the Qur'an, taking its name from the last word in verse one. In the first part of this Chapter we are told the story of the "people of the pit [of fire]" who were tortured for no reason other than their belief in "God, the Exalted in Power, Worthy of all Praise". A strong warning is made to "Those who persecute the Believers, men and women, and do not repent will have the punishment of Hell and they will have punishment of the Burning Fire." (verses 4-10) In contrast is the great success prosperity of the believers who do righteous deeds (11). Verses 12-16 give mention to some Attributes of God Who can do whatever He intends. We are told God is Well Aware of what Unbelievers have done and that this Glorious Qur'an is inscribed in "a Tablet Preserved" (17-22).

# Dd

## dhaariyaat (suurat adh--)

### سورة الذاريات

Chapter of Scattering Winds

This is Chapter 51 of the Qur'an, taking its name from the word that occurs in the first verse. The Chapter has thus been summarized, "The winds may blow and scatter, lift and rush, or divide in all directions; but the Truth and Promise of God are sure and stable, whereof you may find Signs both around and within you (verses 1-23)." and "Past events and what you see before you point to the unfailing consequences of all you do: God, of His Grace, sends you a Reminder; the loss is your own if you reject and deny (verses 24-60)." Among the verses often quoted is, "I have not created Jinns and men except to serve/ worship Me." (56) This verse explains the reason for the creation of man, to serve God.

### dukhaan (suurat ad-)

### سورة الدخان

Chapter of Smoke (or Mist)

This is Chapter 44 of the Qur'an, taking its title from the word that occurs in verse 10, "Then watch you for the Day that the sky will bring forth a kind of smoke (or mist) plainly visible." In it we find the usual in fate of the arrogant unbeliers and the God fearing believers in the Hereafter (verses 40- 59).

This Chapter is strongly recommended to be recited in the evening before Friday.

### DuHaa (suurat aD-- )

### سورة الضحى

Chapter of the Forenoon

This is Chapter 93 of the Qur'an, taking its title from the word in the first verse. In this Chapter, God the Almighty asserts to the Prophet Muhammad (PBUH) that the lull in Revelation [in the early days of the Prophet's mission] was not a sign of God's forsaking him (as claimed by the polytheists). He tells him that the Hereafter is better than the present, and gives him good tidings of well-pleasing things to come. The Prophet (PBUH) is reminded of the many favours bestowed upon him, and he is instructed to "treat not the orphan with harshness, nor repulse the beggar" and to "rehearse and proclaim" the Bounties of His Lord.

## Ff

### faatiHah (suurat al- )

### سورة الفاتحة

Opening Chapter

This is the name of the first Chapter of the Qur'an which consists of seven verses, including the "basmalah". The Chapter starts with praising and thanking God "Lord and Cherisher of the worlds, the Most Beneficent, the Most Merciful, Master of the Day of Judgment", followed by professing worshipping Him Alone and seeking help from Him Alone, then asking His guidance to the Straight Path.

This Chapter has has been described by Prophet Muhammad (PBUH) as the "greatest chapter in the Qur'an". It is the most recited chapter of the Qur'an, since a

Muslim has to recite it in every standing position in the formal prayers (Salaat) - a minimum of 17 times per day- and it is often recited by Muslims on various occasions for blessings.

## faaTir (suurat --)

### سورة فاطر

Chapter of the
Originator of Creation

This is Chapter 35 of the Qur'an, taking its title from the word in the first verse. A running theme of this Chapter is the mysteries of creation and great blessings people enjoy in this world, with emphasis on God being the Originator of all. A sentence most frequently quoted from verse 28 is, "Those truly fear God, among His servants, are the ones who have knowledge," which is cited as evidence that according to Islam true learning and knowledge are supports of Faith or Belief in God, rather than being in conflict with it.

## fajr (suurat al-- )

### سورة الفجر

Chapter of Dawn

This is Chapter 89 of the Qur'an, taking its title from the word in verse one. In this Chapter we are reminded of the miserable fate of some powerful rejecters of the Faith. (verses 6-14) This is followed by statements about the nature of the ungrateful Man (15-20). In the next verses we read about some of the events on the Day of Judgment as well as the fate of the unbelievers and believers. The unbelievers will regret not having done good deeds. But to the soul of the believer, it will be said: "O soul in complete peace! Come back to your Lord, well-pleased and well-pleasing [unto your Lord]. Join, then, my devotees, and enter My Garden (Paradise)." (21-30).

## falaq (suurat al-- )

### سورة الفلق

Chapter of the Dawn

This is Chapter 113 of the Qur'an, taking its title from the word in the first verse. In this Chapter the Prophet (PBUH) is commanded by God the Almighty to seek Divine assistance and refuge from all created things, darkness, sorcerers and the evil eye. Since in this and the next Chapter (114) Muslims are instructed to seek refuge in God from all sorts of evils, they are referred to as "al-mu'awwdhataan"('the two refuge chapters'). The recitation of both was strongly recommended by Prophet Muhammad (PBUH) for treatment of and protection from all evils and evil beings.

### fatH (suurat al--)

### سورة الفتح

Chapter of Victory

This is Chapter 48, taking its name from the word that occurs twice (in verbal and nominal forms) in verse 1, "Verily, We have granted you a manifest Victory." The reference here is to "SulH al-Hudaybiyyah" ('the Treaty of Hudaybiyyah') which was concluded between Prophet Muhammad (PBUH) and the Meccan tribe of Quraish. Though the terms of the treaty looked more favourable to the Meccans, in realty it was a clear victory for Islam and Muslims, because the period of truce agreed to in this Treaty led to the conversion of masses of Arabs to Islam from all over Arabia. The Meccans' violation of the Treaty later led to the victorious capture of their city by the Prophet (PBUH); thus, cleaning the City from all traces of polytheism and idol worship. (See verses 1-27.) The last verse is often cited as evidence that hating the Prophet's Companions and saying bad things about them is a sign of disbelief (verse 29).

### fiil (suurat al-- ) سورة الفيل

Chapter of the Elephant

This is Chapter 105 of the Qur'an, taking its title from the word in the first verse. The Elephant refers to that of Abrahah al-Ashram, the Abyssinyan governor of Yemen who, intoxicated with power and fired by religious fanaticism, led a big expedition against Makkah with the intention of destroying the Ka'abah. But, as Abdul-Muttalib the grandfather of Prophet Muhammad had said, "The House (the Ka'bah) has a Lord and Master Who protects it". God did protect the Sacred House, and He miraculously destroyed the attacking forces. A vivid picture is delineated for that unusual form of punishment. Non-Muslim forces never dared to attempt such an attack since. It is interesting to note that 'Year of the Elephant' (as called by Arabs- ca. 570 G) was the same year in which Prophet Muhammad (PBUH) was born.

### furqaan (suurat al- )

### سورة الفرقان

Chapter of the Criterion

This is Chapter 25 of the Qur'an,

taking its title from the word "furqaan" ('criterion') in the first verse of the Chapter. The reference is clearly to the Holy Qur'an which is the Criterion by which we can judge what is good and evil and between right and wrong. Many parts of this Chapter deal with the contrast between these and their consequences. Among the verses often recited are 63 to 77, where some of the characteristics of "'ibaad-urraHmaan" ('the servants of God, the Most Gracious') are mentioned.

### fuSSilat (suurat --)

**سورة فصّلت**

Chapter of Detailed Verses

This is Chapter 41 of the Qur'an, taking its title from a word in verse 3. Among the verses often quoted is the one that explains why unbelievers give deaf ears to the Qur'an and try to tamper with it, "The unbelievers say: "Listen not to this Qur'an, but talk at random in the midst of its (reading), that you may gain the upper hand." (verse 26). Another often quoted verse is the one that says: "Nor can Goodness and Evil be equal. Repel (Evil) with what is better. Then will he between whom and you was hatred become as it were your friend and intimate!" (verse 34). A third often quoted verse is: "Who is better in speech than one who called (men) to God, works righteousness, and says, 'I am of those who bow in Islam"? (verse 33). In fact, many Muslims memorize and often recite the group of verses that include both; i.e., verses 30-35. Verse 53 is also often cited to declare the fact that future discoveries regarding the creation of man and the universe will confirm the existence of God and His powers.

## Gg

### ghaafir (suurat --)

**سورة غافِر**

Chapter of the Forgiver

This is Chapter 40 of the Qur'an, taking its title from the word at the beginning of verse 3. An alternative title of the Chapter is "al-mu'min" ('the Believer'). Contrasting the fate of believers with that of unbelievers is a major theme in this Chapter. A verse often quoted as evidence of eternal Divine support of believers is: "We will, without doubt, help Our messengers and those who believe, (both) in this world's life and on the Day when Witness will stand forth [i.e. Day of Judgment]" (verse 51).

## ghaashiyah (suurat al-- )
## سورة الغاشية

Chapter of the Overwhelming Event

This is Chapter 88 of the Qur'an, taking its title from the word in the first verse and refers to the Day of Judgment. A contrastive picture is given for the conditions of the believers and unbelievers on that Day (verses 2-16). Man is reminded of the miraculous creation of camels, the sky, mountains and earth in verses 17-20. Then, the Prophet (PBUH) is instructed, "Therefore do remind, for you are but one who reminds. You are not one who has control over them [people]..." (21-22) It is to God that they will return, and He is the One to call them to account (25-26). These verses are often quoted to prove Islam's emphasis on freedom of belief.

This Chapter was often recited by Prophet Muhammad (PBUH) in the second standing position of the Friday prayer.

# Hh

## Haaqqah (suurat al-- )
## سورة الحاقّة

Chapter of the Inevitable Reality

This is Chapter 69 of the Qur'an, taking its title from the opening verse and verses two and three, which are followed by the elucidation of this Reality: Truth must prevail and falsehood and its followers will perish. After citing examples ( verses 4-12), the Qur'an talks about the Inevitable Event (the Day of Judgment) and what follows of bliss for the believer "who receives his Record in his right hand' and miseries to be suffered by the unbeliever who receives his Record in his left hand"(verses 13-37). These are concluded by the affirmation of the Truth of the Message of Muhammad (PBUH) who dares not "invent any sayings in Our [God's] name" and the dire consequences if he did ( verses 38-52).

## Hadiid (suurat al-- )

## سورة الحديد

Chapter of Iron

This is Chapter 57 of the Qur'an, taking its title from the word that occurs in verse 25, where we read, "and We sent down Iron in which is great might, as well as many benefits for mankind...". The Chapter has been summarized in the following words: "God's Power and Knowledge extend to all things: follow His Light direct, without doubt or fear or half-heartedness, but humility, generous charity, and faith, and not in a life of isolation from the world." Among the parts of verses often quoted are: "Has not the time come for the Believers that their hearts in all humility should engage in the remembrance of God and of the Truth which has been revealed (to them)...?" (verse 16), and, "Be you foremost (in seeking) forgiveness from your Lord, and a Garden (of Bliss), the width whereof is as the width of Heaven and earth, prepared for those who believe in God and His messenger..."(verse 21).

As a footnote, some Muslim scientist point to the fact the Qur'an says that iron was sent down, which means it has an unearthly orign, which is an example of the miraculous aspects of the Qur'an.

## Hajj (suurat al- )

## سورة الحج

Chapter of Pilgrimage

This is Chapter 22 of the Qur'an, taking its title from the verses that tell us about God's command to Prophet Abraham to call people to pilgrimage to the Ka'bah in Mecca, giving mention to spiritual and worldly gains thereof (verses 26-33). Among the verses frequently quoted to prove the miraculous nature of the Qur'an, regarding information on development of human embryo is verse 5. In this Chapter we read the verses that gave permission to Muslims (after more than 13 years of patient endurance of injustice to them) to fight to defend themselves and for the protection of their Faith and various houses of worship of God (mosques, churches, synagogues) (verses 39-40).

## Hashr (suurat al-- )

## سورة الحشر

Chapter of Mustering

This is Chapter 59 of the Qur'an, taking its title from the word in verse two. In this Chapter we are told of the case of the Jewish tribe whose intrigues and treachery during the perilous days of a battle between the Muslims in Medina and invading forces of polytheists (verses 2-8). The Divine Judgment was their banishment from the town against which they plotted with its enemies, despite the fact they had a mutual protection treaty with the Prophet Muhammad (PBUH). In contrast were the Medinites who warmly welcomed the immigrant Meccans and gave them preference even over themselves (verse 9). Among the frequently recited verses from this Chapter are verses 18--24, especially the last three which give mention to about one fifth of the 99 Names/ Attributes of God in Islam, concluding with, "To Him belong the Most Beautiful Names. Whatever is in the heavens and on earth does declare His Praises and Glory, and He is the Exalted in Might, the Ever Wise." (24)

## Hijr (suurat al- )

## سورة الحجر

Chapter of al-Hijr (rocky tract)

This is Chapter 15 of the Qur'an, taking its name from the word mentioned only in verse 80 of this Chapter in the whole Qur'an. Like many other chapters, stories of various prophets of God are told. In this Chapter we read about the angels visiting of Prophet Abraham and giving him the glad tidings of a son to be born to him at that old age. They also told him of the fate of the people of Lot and his wife (verses 51-75). Among the often quoted verses from this Chapter is the one where God the Almighty declares His promise to preserve the Qur'an for eternity, "We have, no doubt, sent down the Message [i.e., the Qur'an]; and We will assuredly guard it (from corruption)." (9).

## Hujuraat (suurat al--)

## سورة الحجرات

Chapter of the Inner Apartments

This is Chapter 49, taking its title from the word in verse 4 which refers to the private rooms where the Prophet Muhammad (PBUH) and wives lived, next to his mosque at Medina. Many important rules of social behaviour are given in this Chapter, including the proper way of addressing the Prophet of God, verification of news brought by unreliable sources, making peace between fighting believers, respecting others, and shunning backbiting and spying...etc. In this Chapter we also read the verse frequently cited to prove the Islamic emphasis on the oneness of origin of mankind and that God fearing is the only criterion of superiority among men, rather than race, colour or language (verse 13).

## humazah (suurat al-- )

**سورة الهُمَزة**

Chapter of the Back-Biter

This is Chapter 104 of the Qur'an, taking its title from the word in the first verse which refers to the person involved in character assassination. A strong warning is made to everyone engaged in back-biting and taunting the Prophet (PBUH) and his followers. The type of grievous chastisement is detailed in verses 4-9.

## huud (suurat --)

**سورة هود**

Chapter of Hood

This is Chapter 11 of the Qur'an, taking its title from the name of Prophet "huud" and his people (verses 50 through 60). The story of Noah, his people and the Ark is also delineated in this Chapter (verses 25-49). Stories of some other prophets are also given. The detailed case of Prophet Shu'ayb of Madyan, his people's notorious misconduct in business transactions, and their doom are mentioned (verses 84-95).

# Ii

## ibraahiim (suurat --)

**سورة إبراهيم**

Chapter of Abraham

This is Chapter 14 of the Qur'an, taking its title from the name of Prophet Abraham to whom reference is made, along with his prayer to God to bless the land of Mecca where he left his son Ishmael and wife Hagar verses (35 to 41). Among the often quoted verses are the ones that refer to the effect of the 'good word' and of the 'bad word', "See you not how God sets forth a parable? A goodly Word is like a goodly tree, whose root is firmly fixed, and its branches (reach) to the heavens. It brings forth its fruit all times, by the leave of its Lord..."(25-27).

## ikhlaaS (suurat al-- )

**سورة الإخلاص**

Chapter of Sincerity and Purity

This is Chapter 112 of the Qur'an, taking its title, uniquely probably, from the theme of the Chapter (rather than a word from it), which is the purity of Faith and sincerity in the Belief in God. This Chapter precisely and in very few words gives the full, true concept of God in Islam: He is One, to Him Alone all turn for help while He is Self-Sufficient. He did not give birth to any, nor was He born. None is equal or similar to Him. (verses 1-4) (The last verse finds support in another verse in Chapter 42, "There is nothing whatever like unto Him, and He is the One Who hears and sees." (verse 11)) Each one of these characteristics of God may be used as a criterion of the correctness of any religion's concept of God, and in its contradiction we find the fault with any religion. Due to its importance, Prophet Muhammad (PBUH) is reported to have said," By God in Whose hand my life is it is equivalent to one third of the Qur'an".

## infiTaar (suurat al-- )

سورة الانفطار

Chapter of the Cleaving Asunder

This is Chapter 82 of the Qur'an, taking its title from the verb "infaTarat" ('is cleft asunder') in verse one. Like many early Revelations of the Qur'an, this Chapter gives a vivid picture of some the events that precede or occur on the Day of Judgment. Man is then, asked, "Who has deceived you about your Lord, the Most Generous?" (verses 1-6) Some of the favours of this Generous Lord are mentioned. Those who reject the Faith are reminded that the deeds of people are recorded by honourable angels. These records will be the basis of their Judgment on the Day "when no soul can be of any help to any other soul, and when God reign Supreme." (verses 7-19)

## 'insaan (suurat al-- )

سورة الإنسان

Chapter of Man

This is Chapter 76 of the Qur'an, taking its title from the word that occurs in both verses one and two. The fact that man was created by God and that He gave him hearing and sight as well as showing him "the Way whether he be grateful or ungrateful" is clearly stated (verses 1-3). After telling the future of the Rejecters of the Faith in verse 4, examples of the behaviour of the God fearing people and their rewards in the Hereafter are mentioned, concluding with, "Verily, this is a reward for you, and your endeavour is accepted and recognized." (verses 4-22). In the next section, the Qur'an addresses the Prophet (PBUH) reminding him of the favour of revealing the Qur'an a guidance for and reminder for him and others and instructing him to remember His Lord day and night and prostrate himself to Him "and glorify Him a long night through." (verses 23-31). This Chapter was often recited by Prophet Muhammad (PBUH) in the second "rak'ah" of the Friday Dawn Prayer.

## inshiqaaq (suurat al-- )

**سورة الانشقاق**

Chapter of the Rending Asunder

This is Chapter 84 of the Qur'an, taking its title from the verb "inshaqqat" ('is rendered asunder') in the first verse. After five verses of mention of some fantastic events that occur on the Day of Judgment, Man is addressed thus: "Verily you are ever toiling on towards your Lord, painfully toiling, but you shall meet Him" on the that Day. Verses 7 to15 give us a contrasting picture of a believer who "receives His Record in his right hand" and the unbeliever "who is given his Record behind his back" and their lot in the Hereafter. After a set of assertive verses, Man is told, "You shall surely travel from stage to stage. Why is it then that they believe not?" Rejecters of the Faith are warned that God is Aware of what they are hiding" and they will be severely punished (verses 16-24). Excepted from the grievous punishment will be those who believe and do righteous deeds (25).

iqra' (suurat -- )

**سورة العلق**

Chapter of the Clinging Clot

This is Chapter 96 of the Qur'an and the first in Revelation. It takes its name from the word in verse two, which has been variously translated. Another name of this Chapter is "suurat iqra'", based on the first word in the Chapter. Iqra' has been translated as 'read' or 'recite'. According to Prophetic traditions, Archangel Gabriel came to Muhammad at the Cave of Hiraa' in Makkah, and aksed him to read from a text shown to him. Muhammad (PBUH) said, "But I am illiterate!" He was strongly embraced by Gabriel asking to read, to which he gave the same response. After the third time, Gabriel recited the rest of the Revelation to Muhammad, telling him that he was chosen a Messenger of God. According to Muslim scholars, the facts of the beginning of the Revelation of the Qur'an, the repetition of the command to read and the Qur'anic declaration in verses 4 and 5 that God has taught (Man) with the pen things of which he has no knowledge, all of these point out the importance of learning for believers. In the rest of the Chapter, a strong warning is sounded to those who reject the Faith and prevent people from worshipping God.

### israa' (suurat al- )

### سورة الإسراء

Chapter of the Night Journey

This is Chapter 17 of the Qur'an, taking its title from the reference to the miraculous night journey of the Prophet (PBUH) from Mecca to Jerusalem (verse 1). Another title given to this Chapter is "banii 'israa'iil" (Children of Israel), since the early parts of the Chapter foretell the fate of the Israelites brought about by their behaviour in the holy land, concluding with the warning: "It may be that your Lord may (yet) show Mercy unto you; but if you revert (to yours sins) We shall revert (to Our punishment). And We have made Hell a prison for those who reject (all Faith)." (See verses 4-8.) The Chapter is also known for a set of about 11 Divine commandments, starting with the decree to worship none but God and being kind to parents and ending with exhortation to humility (verses 23-39).

# Jj

### jaathiyah (suurat al- )

### سورة الجاثية

Chapter of the Genuflecting

This is Chapter 45 of the Qur'an, taking its name from the word found in verse 28, "And you will see every nation kneeling / genuflecting [in humility and awe of their Lord the Supreme Judge]. Every nation will be called to its Record: 'This Day shall you be recompensed for all that you did!" Naturally, the reference is to the Day of Judgment.

## jinn (suurat al--)

**سورة الجن**

Chapter of the Jinn

This is Chapter 72 of the Qur'an, taking its title from the word that occurs in the first verse. The word jinn refers to a class of beings invisible to people. Often the words "'ins" and "jinn" are used to cover all beings accountable to God for their deeds. The teachings of Islam apply to both, as we can see from verse 56 of Chapter 52. The difference in origin is given in the following:" He [God] created man from clay like [that of] pottery. And He created jinn from a smokeless flame of fire." (Chapter 55: 14-15) In this Chapter we have the second reference to a company of the Jinn listening to Prophet Muhammad's recitation of the Qur'an and accepting Islam. They declared, "And as for us, since we have listened to the Guidance, we have accepted it... Amongst us are some that submit their wills (to God) [i.e., Muslims] and some that swerve from justice" (verses 13-14). The other reference to Prophet Muhammad's encounter with the Jinn is found in the Qur'an (46: 29-32).

## jumu'ah (suurat al-- )

**سورة الجمعة**

Chapter of Friday/ Congregation

This is Chapter 62 of the Qur'an, taking its title from the word in verse 9, where Muslims are commanded to leave off business and "hasten to the remembrance of God", upon hearing the call to the Friday prayer. The Chapter has been summarized in the following: "The Revelation has come among unlearned men, to teach purity and wisdom not only to them but to others, including those who may have an older Message but do not understand it. Meet solemnly for the Assembly/ Congregational (Friday) Prayer, and let not worldly interests deflect you therefrom."

# Kk

## kaafiruun (suurat al-- )

**سورة الكافرون**

Chapter of the Unbelievers

This is Chapter 109 of the Qur'an, taking its title from the last word in verse one. The word "kaafir" (plural, kaafiruun/iin or kuffaar) refers to anyone who disbelieves in God and His Message sent in its final version through Prophet Muhammad (PBUH), whether he is a follower of another Prophet of God, like Moses or Jesus, an atheist or a worshipper of gods other than Allah (the One True God). To all of these people the Prophet (hence, every follower of his) was instructed to declare, "To you be your Way and to me mine." (verse 6) This particular verse has been taken by Muslim scholars as an additional evidence of freedom of belief as preached by Islam. Other instances are found in Chapter 2, verses 256 and 272, and Chapter 81, verse 21.

## kahf (suurat al- )

**سورة الكهف**

Chapter of the Cave

This is Chater 18 of the Qur'an, taking its title from the story of the 'people of the cave' (young men who sought refuge in a cave to avoid persecution because of their beliefs, and their miraculous sleep for 309 years) (verses 9-22). It is strongly recommended to recite this Chapter every Friday. Memorizing and reciting ten verses from the beginning or end of the Chapter protect one from the False Messiah, according to Prophet Muhammad (PBUH).

## kawthar (suurat al-- )

**سورة الكوثر**

Chapter of al-Kawthar

This is Chapter 108 of the Qur'an, taking its title from the word in verse one. Kawthar has been variously interpreted as "abundance" and the name of a special river in Paradise. The Prophet (PBUH) is reminded of the special favour bestowed on him by His Lord, the Kawthar. Therefore, he should turn unto Him (Alone) in prayer and sacrifice. A warning is made to those who hate and defame him (Prophet Muhamad (PBUH).

# Ll

## layl (suurat al-- )

**سورة الليل**

Chapter of the Night

This is Chapter 92 of the Qur'an, taking its title from the word in the first verse. In this Chapter we are emphatically told that people strive for different ends. Those who are charitable and do good deeds God will "make smooth for them the path to Ease" while the miserly and wrong-doers theirs is "the path to Misery". We further read that God takes upon Himself to guide, "And verily unto Us [belong] the End and the Beginning of. Therefore do I warn you of a Fire blazing fiercely" which is the abode of the unfortunate unbeliever and from which is saved the pious "who pays the poor due and seeks self purification" for the sake of God Alone.

## luqmaan (suurat __)

## سورة لقمان

Chapter of Luqman

This is Chapter 31 of the Qur'an, taking its title from the name of a holy and wise man, Luqmaan whose name is mentioned in verses 12 and 13. Many teachings of universal wisdom are given by Luqmaan to his son ( verses 13-19). Among the often quoted verses are the verses that teach kindness to parents even if they are unbelievers who strive to mislead us in faith, but without obeying them in that (14-15).

# Mm

## ma'aarij (suurat al-- )

## سورة المعارج

Chapter of the Ways of Ascent

This is Chapter 70 of the Qur'an, taking its name from the word that occurs in verse three. In it we read about some of the events of the Day of Judgment, when the sinner/ criminal wishes if he could redeem himself with his children, wife, brother, tribe and everyone on earth (verses 6-14). A description is given of Hell-fire, the nature of man, the character of the saved ones and their reward in the Hereafter (verses 15-35). A final comment on the faltering unbelievers is found in the last few verses (36-44).

## maa'idah (suurat al- )

## سورة المائدة

The Chapter of Table Spread

This is the fifth chapter in the Qur'an, taking its name from the story of Jesus and his disciples and the table of food they asked for (verses 110-120, especially 112-115). Among the special issues in this Chapter are the animals whose flesh should not be eaten by a Muslim (verse 3). In verse 3 we also read one of the very important Divine declarations regarding the completion of His message to mankind: "This day I have perfected your religion for you, completed my favour upon, and have chosen for you Islam as a religion." In this Chapter we also find the ruling of objective justice and fair dealing with others, including enemies (verse 11).

The closing verses of this Chapter report on Jesus (PBUH) and his denial of calling people to take him and his mother as deities besides God, on the Day of Judgement (the Qur'an, 5: 116-117).

An interesting verse regarding the relationship between Muslims and Chrisitan and Jews is found in verse 5.

## maa'uun (suurat al-- )

### سورة الماعون

Chapter of the Neighbourly Needs

This is Chapter 107 of the Qur'an, taking its name from the word in the last verse. The word "maa'uun" literally means a vessel, like pots and plates, and tools, like axes, etc. which people in Arabia usually borrowed from others (neighbours, for instance). In this Chapter it seems to refer to simple favours. We can see the emphasis in this Chapter on religion in its practical sense of helping the orphan and the indigent and observing the religious duty of formal prayers as well as shunning the practice of hypocritical charity and making show, in addition to helping others with their daily needs.

## maryam (suurat __)

### سورة مريم

Chapter of Mary

This is Chapter 19 of the Qur'an, taking its title from the story of Mary and her son Jesus. It begins with the story of Zakariyya and the son born to him at old age, YaHyaa (John), followed by the story of Mary and her life of chastity and devotions and the miraculous birth of Jesus. The miracle of speaking in his cradle is mentioned, and so is the denial of his deity ("He said: 'I am indeed a servant of God; He has given revelation and made me a prophet." (30). See verses 2-35. Other prophets (Abraham, Ishmael, Idrees…) and some of their characteristics are also mentioned in the Chapter.

### muddaththir (suurat al-- )
### سورة المدّثّر

Chapter of the One Shrouded

This is Chapter 74 of the Qur'an, taking its title from the word in the first verse, with reference to Prophet Muhammad (PBUH) who, we are told, was so scared at the sight of Gabriel (in his true form) at the beginning of the Revelation of the Qur'an that he rushed home shivering and asked his wife Khadija (RA) to enshroud him. At the beginning of the Chapter we read God's commanding His Messenger to arise and deliver his message, to magnify his Lord, to purify his clothes, to shun all abomination, not consider any favour by him great and expect more (from others) and be patient and constant for the sake of His Lord (verses 1-7). Warnings are sounded to the unbelievers, with a special mention of the case of one of them (8-31). Then, the Qur'an emphatically returns to the fact that "Every soul will be [held] in pledge for its deeds," contrasting the fate of the believers and the evil doers in the Hereafter.

### muHammad (suurat --)
### سورة محمد

Chapter of Muhammad

This is Chapter 47 of the Qur'an, taking its title from the reference to the Prophet Muhammad (PBUH) by name in verse 2. One of the commentators pointed out that the "present suurah deals with the necessity of defense against external foes by courage and strenuous fighting, and [the Chapter] dates from the first year of the Hijra, when the Muslims were under threat of extinction by invasion from Makkah."

### mujaadalah (suurat --al- )
### سورة المجادلة

Chapter of Dispute

This is Chapter 58 of the Qur'an, taking its name from the content of the first verse, "God has indeed heard the statement of the woman who disputes with you concerning her husband and complains to God…" Some call it the Chapter of "the Woman Who Pleads/ Disputes", on the basis of another way of reading the title word. The Chapter has been summed up in the following: "All false pretences, especially those that degrade a woman's position, are condemned, --as well as (whispered) private conferences and intrigues with falsehood, mischief, and sedition." The early parts of this Chapter are cited as evidence of the 'democratic' spirit a Muslim ruler should show in conducting the affairs of the state.

## mulk (suurat al-- )

## سورة المُلك

Chapter of Dominion

This is Chapter 67 and beginning of Part 29 of the Qur'an, taking its title from the word that occurs in the first verse, "Blessed be He in Whose hands is Dominion, and He over all things has Full Power." This Chapter, which consists of 30 verses, is strongly recommended by the Prophet Muhammad (PBUH) to be recited at the beginning and end of the day. He is reported to have said that it intercedes (with God) for forgiveness for its reader.

## mu'minuun (suurat al- )

## سورة المؤمنون

Chapter of the Believers

This is Chapter 23 of the Qur'an, taking its title from characteristics of the 'successful believers', contained in verses 1 through 11 and elsewhere in the Chapter. Stages of human development are summed in verses 12 to 15. Unity of the mission of all messengers of God is referred to in verses 51 and 52.

## mumtaHanah (suurat al-- )

## سورة المتحَنَة

Chapter of the Tested Woman

This is Chapter 60 of the Qur'an, taking its title from the reference to the believing women who migrated from Mecca to Medina to join the Community of Islam and their examination to "ascertain that they are serious believers…" since there are obligations to be fulfilled by the Community towards them (verse 10). In this Chapter we read two important rules of relationship between Muslims and non-Muslims: (1) Muslims should not take the enemies of God and theirs as friends (verse 1, 9 and 13). (2) If the non-Muslims do not commit acts of aggression against

Muslims, then Muslims are not forbidden from "dealing kindly and justly with them" (verse 8) (See also Chapter 5, verse 5). In this Chapter we also read another principle regarding the position of women in Islam: the fact that they had the right and duty of "taking an oath of allegiance" to the Leader of the Community (verse 12). An important ruling is given in verse 10 regarding the prohibition of a Muslim woman marrying a non-Muslim man and a Muslim man being married to an unbelieving woman. (For exceptions to this rule, see Chapter 5, verse 5.)

## munaafiquun (suurat al-- )

**سورة المنافقون**

Chapter of the Hypocrites

This is Chapter 63 of the Qur'an, taking its name from the word in verse one, where instructions are given to the Prophet (PBUH) regarding the hypocrites at his time, with a mention of some of their traits and manners, in this and the following seven verses (1-8). The next 3 verses of the Chapter warn Believers of being detracted by their possessions and children from the remembrance of God and spending for His Cause (9-11).

## mursalaat (suurat al-- )

**سورة المرسلات**

Chapter of those Sent Forth

This is Chapter 77 of the Qur'an, taking its name from the word in the first verse. The reference is to the winds sent forth, for the benefit of man, with many functions, including the air's function of carrying sound waves by means of which the "Remembrance" is spread about (verses 1-6). Various ways of reminding are the theme of this Chapter, such as reminders about the Day of Judgment, the fate of previous nations, the creation of man, Divine bounties, and the fate of the Believers and of the Unbelievers in the Hereafter. It is only befitting that the refrain "Woe, that Day, to the Rejecters/ Deniers [of Truth]" is repeated throughout the Chapter.

## muTaffifiin (suurat al-- )

**سورة المطففين**

Chapter of the Defrauders

This is Chapter 83 of the Qur'an, taking its title from the second word in verse one. These defrauders take their right in full measure, but they cheat others of their rights. They are reminded of the Day of Judgment when people stand before the Lord of the Worlds with the records of their misdeeds. A contrast of the record of the wicked (verse 7) and that of the Righteous (verse 18) and their fates in the Hereafter is given, in addition to examples of the misbehaviour of the wicked towards the Righteous in this life. In the concluding verses, we read: "But on this Day the Believers will laugh at the Unbelievers... Have not the Unbelievers been paid back for what they had done ?" (verse 34-36)

### muzzammil (suurat al--)

### سورة المُزّمّل

Chapter of the One Enwrapped

This is Chapter 73 of the Qur'an, taking its title from the word in the first verse, which refers to Prophet Muhammad (PBUH). It is one of the early Suras of the Qur'an revealed to him. We are told that when the Prophet (PBUH) first saw Gabriel at the beginning of his mission he was so scared that he rushed home shivering and asked his wife to wrap him. Therefore, he was addressed as "the one wrapped" at the beginning of this Chapter. The next Chapter (74) refers to the same event. In this Chapter, the Prophet (PBUH) is told, "Soon shall We send down to you a weighty Word" (verse 5). Apparently, to prepare himself for this weighty responsibility the Prophet (PBUH) is instructed to stand [in prayer] by night. In the concluding verse of the Chapter we find, "Read you, therefore, as much of the Qur'an as may be easy (for you), and establish regular prayer and pay the poor dues... And whatever good you send forth for yourselves, you shall find it with God; it will be more charitable and magnificent in reward. And ask God for forgiveness; surely, God is Ever-Forgiving, Most Merciful." (verse 20)

# Nn

### naas (suurat an-- )

### سورة الناس

Chapter of Mankind

This is Chapter 114 and the last Chapter of the Qur'an, taking its title from the word that occurs three times in the Chapter. In it the Prophet (PBUH) and his followers are instructed to seek refuge in God, Lord and God of mankind, from the mischief of "the Whisperer [of evil] who withdraws [after his whisper]". The reference is to Satan and his beguiles. No wonder the whole final chapter is devoted to seeking refuge from the Satan the Whisperer, since all evil intentions, sayings and actions are the result of his "whisper". He had threatened to mislead people (See the Qur'an, 4:118-119) and to "make [evil] attractive to them on earth and I will put them in the wrong, except Your [God's] chosen servants among them. (the Qur'an, 15: 39-40) and "lead them all astray except Your servants among them who are sincere and purified" ( the Qur'an, 38: 82-83). All this is done by the Evil One, Satan, in retaliation for his being kicked out of Heaven on account of Adam. (See, e.g.., Chapter 38, verses 71-83.) In this Chapter and the preceding one Muslims are instructed to seek refuge in God from all sorts of evil and evil beings. They are referred to as "al-mu'awwidhataan" for this reason. The recitation of both was strongly recommended by Prophet Muhammad (PBUH) both for treatment of (as "ruqyah") and protection ("taHSiin") from various forms of evil and the Devil himself.

## naazi'aat (suurat an-- )
## سورة النازعات

Chapter of the Pluckers

This is Chapter 79 of the Qur'an, taking its title from the word in the first verse. The reference of the word "naazi'aat" is a controversial one, which is reflected in the various translations of the verse: stars and planets, archers, or angels who tear out or pluck (the souls of the wicked). Many interpreters seem to favour the latter. The early verses are preliminary oaths to emphasize the greatest event of the Day of Judgment and the state of people on such Day which is constantly denied by the unbelievers, exemplified by the Pharaoh who not only rejected the Faith but even claimed godhood only to be punished by severe punishment both in this life and the Hereafter. To make the idea of the overwhelming Event people are reminded of the many miracles in the creation of man, the skies, night and day, earth and its waters and the mountains. Again we are taken back to the Day of Judgment "The Day when Man shall remember what he had striven for" and rewards and punishments for the believers and the unbelievers.

## naba' (suurat an-- )

## سورة النبأ

Chapter of the Tidings

This is Chapter 87 and the beginning of the last (30th) part of the Qur'an, taking its title from the word in the second verse, referring to the certain coming of the Hour of Judgment. Examples of God's bounties in the world around us are mentioned (verses 6-16) followed by the assertion of the coming of "the Day of the Verdict" and the concurrent and following events thereof, especially the punishment of the Rejecters of the Faith and the rewards of the Believers, concluding with "This is the True Day. Therefore, whoso will, let him take a return to His Lord! Surely, We have warned you of a chastisement near-- the Day when man will see the deeds he had sent forth, and the Unbeliever will say, 'Woe unto me! Would that I were [mere] dust!'" (17-40).

## naHl (suurat an- )

## سورة النحل

Chapter of the Bee

This is Chapter 16 of the Qur'an, taking its title from the reference to the bee, the miracle of its creation and the healing effect of its honey (verses 68-69). Other forms of God's favours to man are also mentioned in this Chapter. Among the often quoted verses from this Chapter are the ones that instruct Muslims in the proper ways of preaching the Word of God, "Invite (all) to the Way of your Lord with wisdom and beautiful preaching; and argue with them in ways that are best" (125). Another verse often heard at the conclusion of the Friday sermon is "Surely God commands justice, the doing of good, and giving to kith and kin, and He forbids all indecent deeds, wrong doing and aggression…" (90).

## najm (suurat an-- )

## سورة النجم

Chapter of the Star

This is Chapter 53 of the Qur'an, taking its name from the word in the first verse. In this Chapter we find the reference to Prophet Muhammad's miraculous Ascension ("mi'raaj") to the heavens where he met previous prophets and had a glimpse of Paradise and its future dwellers and Hell and its future dwellers.

In this journey to the heavens the Prophet (PBUH) communicated directly with God the Almighty (verses 1-18). Two often quoted verses from this Chapter are: "Nor does he [Muhammad] say anything of his own desire or whims. It is no less than inspiration sent down to him" to emphasize the point that anything said or done by Prophet Muhammad (PBUH) was in accordance with Divine inspiration or instruction. (See verses 3-4.)

## naml (suurat an- )

## سورة النمل

Chapter of the Ants

This is Chapter 27 of the Qur'an, taking its title from the stories of the miraculous ability of Prophet Solomon to understand the language of animals, including ants (18). Particular to this Chapter is the mention of many special favours bestowed by God on Prophet Solomon, including the gift of communicating with birds, especially the hoopoe who brought him information about the Queen of Sheba. The communications between her and Solomon, their meeting and her acceptance of Islam, preached by Solomon, are recounted in this particular Chapter (15-41). Stories of other prophets and their peoples are found as well.

## naSr (suurat an-- )

## سورة النصر

Chapter of Support

This is Chapter 110 of the Qur'an, taking its title from the word in the first verse, meaning support or aid offered to someone who needs it. This Chapter talks about Divine support and the real Victory God has given His Messenger Muhammad (PBUH), when multitudes of people, with the Grace of God, voluntarily and peacefully joined the fold of Islam after the Conquest of Makkah. To express his gratitude to God, the Prophet (PBUH) was instructed, "Celebrate the Praises of you Lord, and pray for His forgiveness, for He is Ever-Relenting [in forgiveness]."

## nisaa' (suurat an- )

## سورة النساء

Chapter of the Women

This is the fourth chapter of the Qur'an. It takes its name from the major theme of the chapter, women related issues. Among the issues specially treated in this chapter are polygamy or multiplicity of wives (verse 3) and laws of inheritance, (especially, verses 11-13, 19 and 176) and females one cannot marry (22-24).

## nuuH (suurat -- )

**سورة نوح**

Chapter of Noah

This is Chapter 71 of the Qur'an, taking its title from the name of Prophet Noah whose name is mentioned in verses 1, 21and 26) since the whole Chapter is about him and his people and the grave consequence of their disbelief in him and rejection of his teachings. This consequence is: "Because of their sins they were drowned [in the Flood] and were made to enter the Fire…" (verse 26). A further detailed recount of Noah, his people and the Ark are found in another Chapter (See the Qur'an, 11: 25-48.)

## nuur (suurat an- )

**سورة النور**

Chapter of Light

This is Chapter 24 of the Qur'an, taking its title from verse 35, "God is the Light of the heavens and the earth…" Among the special topics in this Chapter are the issues related to rules of conduct in the relationship between men and women, such as illicit sex, its punishment and punishment for slander, and acts that help avoiding them, such as verification of accusation of fornication, lowering one's gaze, concealing female ornaments from strangers, asking permission before entering abodes that do not belong to us… etc. In this Chapter we also read the refutation of the malicious slander spread by hypocrites at the time of the Prophet (PBUH) against his pure and chaste wife 'Aayshah and Divine exoneration of her as well as instructions and warning to Muslims in this matter, "God admonishes you that you may never repeat such, if you are (true) Beleivers..." (verses 11-19).

# Qq

## qaaf (suurat --)

**سورة ق**

Chapter of qaaf

This is Chapter 50 of the Qur'an, taking its name from the first letter-word in verse 1. This letter whose name is pronounced here is the 21st letter of the Arabic alphabet. It is worth noting that this letter/ sound is the most frequent letter/ sound in this Chapter or any other of the Qur'an. The Chapter is thus summed up, "Skeptics can look up to the heavens above and to Nature around them, as well as to the fate of sin in the history of the past: will they doubt God's Revelation when the veil is lifted? (verses 1-29)". A vivid picture of some of the events of the Day of Judgment is depicted in verses 30-45. The all-encompassing knowledge of God and His extreme closeness to man are mentioned in verse 16. In this Chapter we also read about the two angels who record everything a person says or does (verses 17-18).

## qaari'ah (suurat al-- )

### سورة القارعة

Chapter of the Striking Calamity

This is Chapter 101 of the Qur'an, taking its title from the first word-verse, repeated twice in verses 2 and 3, and refers to the Day Judgment. In this Chapter we can visualize some of the fantastic events on that Day (verses 4-5). Then we read about the two main categories of people: believers (people with heavy balance of good deeds) and rejecters of the Faith (whose balance is light). The fate of each is succinctly described in the following verses (6-11).

## qadr (suurat al-- )

### سورة القدر

Chapter of the High Status

This is Chapter of 97 of the Qur'an, taking its name from the word in the first verse. The word "qadr" has been variously translated as 'power, decree and value'. The Arabic word basically means status, value and significance. To these one may add "high" or "great" in this context. Another common meaning is 'quantity' (like miqdaar). Many translators confuse the word with "qadar" which means 'destiny, decree, as well as quantity'. The night referred to in this Chapter is the special night in which the first Revelation of the Qur'an occurred, according to some Qur'anic commentators. Therefore it has been given a special value by God, making it worth more than one thousand months. This means worship and devotions during this one night are worth in rewards more than 86 years of worship and devotions. There is almost a consensus among scholars that this night falls during the Month of Ramadhan, most probably in the nights of the odd days of the last ten of the month. Popularly, the night of the 27th day of Ramadhan is taken to be 'the Night of Qadr or High Status'.

## qalam (suurat al-- )

## سورة القَلَم

Chapter of the Pen

This is Chapter 68 of the Qur'an, taking its title from the word that occurs in verse one. In this Chapter we can see that despite the fact that Prophet Muhammad was the sanest, wisest and best mannered man, the enemies of truth who would not understand his message called him mad or possessed (verses 2 and 51). The contents of the Chapter have been summed up in the following: "Let the good carry on their work, in spite of the abuse of the companions of Evil. Let all remember God, before Whom all men are on trial (verses 1-33). True Judgment comes from God, and not from the false standards of men (34-52)." A frequently quoted verse is one has been variously translated as "And surely you [Muhammad] have sublime morals," "And indeed, you are of a great moral chacter" and "And indeed, you are of a magnificent character." (verse 4) The Arabic word "khuluq" covers a wide range of English words: character, morality, moral values, behaviour and conduct. According to this verse, Muhammad (PBUH) has the best of all. In fact, he was reported to have summed up his mission by saying, "I have been sent but to complete the best of 'akhlaaq [plural of khuluq]". It is interesting to note that the letter "nuun" ('n') is most frequently found in this particular Chapter, with which it starts.

## qamar (suurat al-- )

## سورة القمر

Chapter of the Moon

This is Chapter 54 of the Qur'an, taking its name from the word mentioned in the first verse of the Chapter. This Chapter has been summed up in the following: "The Hour of Judgment is close by, but men forget or reject the Message, as did the people of Noah, of

'Aad, of Thamuud, or Lot, and of Pharaoh. Is there any that will receive admonition?" In verse 1 we read about the miraculous phenomenon of the moon being cleft asunder under the sight of the Prophet (PBUH), his Companions and some unbelievers. In fact, we are told that recent scientific investigations support the occurrence of this phenomenon.

## qaSaS (suurat al- )

## سورة القصص

Chapter of the Narration

This is Chapter 28 of the Qur'an, taking its title from the stories of different prophets of God, especially the detailed one about Prophet Moses and his people. We find a brief life history of this great Prophet, starting from his infancy, including his flight from Egypt, marriage in Madyan, return via the Holy Valley in Sinai and appointment as a Messenger of God, encounter with Pharaoh, miraculous , safe exit of him and his followers from Egypt, and the drowning Pharaoh and his soldiers (verses 3-46). A story unique to this Chapter is that of Qaruun (Korah), his insolence and arrogance and the Divine punishment of having him and his house swallowed by the earth (verses 76-82). As usual, all these stories are told with lessons to be learnt from them by believers.

## qiyaamah (suurat al-- )

## سورة القيامة

Chapter of the Resurrection

This is Chapter 75 of the Qur'an, taking its title from the word in the first verse. Some of the events of the Day of Resurrection are mentioned in the Chapter, including things that happen to the sun and the moon, the Judgment and the fate of the believers and unbelievers. In the concluding verses, we read: "Does Man think that he will be left without purpose?", reminding people of their creation from a drop of sperm, then asking a rhetorical question: "Has not He [the same God], the Power to to give life to the dead!" (verses 36-40)

## quraysh (suurat -- )

## سورة قريش

Chapter of Quraysh

This is Chapter 106 of the Qur'an, taking its title from the word in the first verse. Quraysh is the name of the Meccan tribe of the Prophet Muhammad (PBUH). Here they are reminded of the blessings of their prosperous trade North (in the summer) and Southward (in the winter) and are urged to worship their Lord "Who provides them with food against hunger, and with security against fear [of danger]".

# Rr

## ra'd (suurat ar- )

## سورة الرعد

Chapter of Thunder

This is Chapter 13 of the Qur'an, taking its title from the word given mention in verse 13, "Thunder repeats His praises..." Many of the favours of God to mankind are mentioned in this Chapter. One of the often quoted verses from this Chapter is the following which declares that true peace of heart and mind comes from the remembrance of God: "Those who believe, and whose hearts find satisfaction and assurance in the remembrance of God. For without doubt in the remembrance of God do hearts find satisfaction and assurance (or peace)." (verse 28)

## raHmaan (suurat ar-- )

## سورة الرحمن

Chapter of the Most Gracious

This is Chapter 55 of the Qur'an, taking its name from the first word-verse in the Chapter. This chapter enumerates many of the bounties and favours God has bestowed on His servants, beginning with his creation and teaching him speech and concluding with various rewards and pleasures awaiting believers in Paradise. It is only befitting that this Chapter has the refrain repeated throughout, "Then which of the favours of your Lord will you (both) deny? The two categories of creatures addressed are humans and the Jinn (invisible beings).

This Chapter is sometimes called the "Jewel of the Qur'an".

## ruum (suurat ar- )

## سورة الروم

Chapter of the Romans

This is Chapter 30 of the Qur'an, taking its title from the report of the defeat of the Romans (at the hands of the Persians), when Jerusalem was lost by them in 614-15 C.E.

and the prophecy of their victory within ten years ( verses 2-4). Among the verses often recited at marriage ceremonies is the verse which reads, "And among His Signs is that He created for you mates from among yourselves, that you may find comfort in them, and He has put love and mercy between your (hearts)..." (verse 21). Marriage is cited here as one of many Signs (or favours) from God (verses 20-25).

The prophecy mentioned in verses 2-4 and its realization is mentioned by scholars as another proof of the Divine nature of the Qur'an.

# Ss

## Saad (suurat --)

### سورة ص

Chapter of Saad

This is Chapter 38 of the Qur'an, taking its title from the name of the fourteenth letter of the Arabic alphabet with which the Chapter begins. Though the Chapter relates the stories of various prophets, Prophets David and Solomon's stories stand clear. The stories begin with God's instruction to Muhammad (PBUH), "Have patience at what they [the unbelievers] say, and remember Our Servant David, the man of strength: for he ever turned (in repentance to God). The special gifts bestowed by God on Prophet Solomon are also mentioned (verses 30-39). We are also reminded of Satan's rebellion against God and his threat to keep leading people astray until the Day of Judgment and the fate of those who obey and follow him (verses 71-85). The story of Prophet Job and his exemplary patience and acceptance of Divine Will is mentioned in this verses 41-44 of this Chapter.

## Saaffaat (suurat aS- )

### سورة الصافات

Chapter of Those Ranged in Ranks

This is Chapter 37 of the Qur'an, taking its name from the word in the first verse. The constant contrast between believers and unbelievers and the fate of each is a major running theme of this Chapter. Unique to this Chapter is the story of the vision seen by Prophet Abraham to sacrifice his only son (Ishmael) and their ready acceptance of the Divine command. "So, when they had both submitted (to God), and he had laid him prostrate on his forehead, We called out to him, 'O Abraham! You have already fulfilled the dream!' --thus indeed do We reward those who do right. For this was a clear trial. And We ransomed him (Ishmael) with a momentous sacrifice."(verses 101-107). One of God's rewards was to give Abraham another sone, Isaac. (See verses 109-112.)

### saba' (suurat -- )

### سورة سبأ

Chapter of Saba'

This is Chapter 34 of the Qur'an, taking its name from the people of the city of Saba' (or Sheba) in Yemen (verse 15) who were prosperous and enjoyed good life, their land being well irrigated by the Ma'rib dam. But they turned away from God and were punished with scarce harvest and many hardships (verses 15-19). This is mentioned as a lesson for believers of all times.

### Saff (suurat aS-- )

### سورة الصف

Chapter of the Ranks

This is Chapter 61 of the Qur'an, taking it name from verse 4," Truly God loves those who fight in His Cause in battle ranks, as if they were a solid cemented structure". In this Chapter we read about the prophecy of Jesus (PBUH) of the coming of Prophet Muhammad after him, "and giving glad tidings of a messenger to come after me, whose name shall be Ahmad [the praised one]" (verse 6). Among the often quoted verses is verse 6: "Their intention is to extinguish God's Light [Islam] with their mouths, but God will complete His Light, even though the unbelievers may detest [it]" (verse 8).

### sajdah (suurat as- )

### سورة السجدة

Chapter of Prostration

This is Chapter 32 of the Qur'an, taking its title from the verse which reads, "Only those believe in Our Signs, who, when they are recited to them fall down in prostration (or adoration) and celebrate the praises of their Lord, nor are they (ever) puffed up with pride." (verse 15). This Chapter was often recited by Prophet Muhammad (PBUH) in the first "rak'ah" of "fajr" (dawn) prayer on Friday.

### shams (suurat ash-- )

سورة الشمس

Chapter of the Sun

This is Chapter 91of the Qur'an, taking its title from the word in the first verse. After reference to various natural phenomena created by the Almighty God, Man is reminded that his soul has been inspired to be bad or good. The good will prosper, but those who corrupt their souls will be losers, such as Thamood (the people of the Prophet Saleh) who disobeyed their prophet and were severely punished accordingly.

### sharH (suurat ashl-- )

سورة الشرح

Chapter of the Solace

This is Chapter 94 of the Qur'an, taking its name from the first verse where the verb "nashraH" ('We provided solace') is used. In fact, the verb has many meanings, including the one given here, but they all refer to the blessing of giving joy and solace to the heart (chest in the verse) of the Prophet (PBUH) by the Almighty God. Other favours are mentioned as well. Then, a universal comforting fact is given," Verily, with every difficulty, there is relief" repeated twice. Therefore, the Prophet is commanded, "When you are free [from worldly tasks] exert yourself in prayers and to your Lord direct [your] longing." Among the often quoted verses for obtaining solace at times of difficultly are verses 5 and 6 which emphatically say that with adversity comes ease.

### shu'araa' (suurat ash- )

سورة الشعراء

Chapter of the Poets

This is Chapter 26 of the Qur'an, taking its title from verse 224 and the following verses. Among the stories of the Prophets of God, one of the most prominent in this Chapter is that of Moses, his encounters with Pharaoh and his challenge of the Egyptian sorcerers, resulting in their conversion to the religion of the Islam preached by Moses. The safe crossing of the Israelites of the sea, pursued by Pharaoh and his soldiers, and the drowning of the unbelievers are mentioned (10-68). This is followed by the arguments between Prophet Abraham and his people regarding his belief in the One God and their worship of idols (69-89). Other Prophets whose stories with their peoples are mentioned in this Chapter include Noah,Huud, SaaliH, Luut and Shu'aib.

## shuuraa (suurat ash-)

سورة الشورى

Chapter of Consultation

This is Chapter 42 of the Qur'an, taking its name from the reference to consultation being one of the characteristics of believers, "Those who respond to their Lord, and establish regular prayer; who (conduct) their affairs by mutual consultation.." (verse 38) In fact, this verse and verse 159 in Chapter 3 are considered the main bases for the principle of consultation in government in Islam. Other characteristics mentioned in this part of the Chapter are found in verses 36-41. The last two of these verses teach forgiveness, though allowing fair punishment. Of the frequently quoted verses in this Chapter is the one that refers to the unity of God's message to mankind throughout the ages (verse 13).

# Tt

## Taahaa (suurat -- )

سورة طه

Chapter of Ta-ha

This is Chapter 20 of the Qur'an, taking its title from the first verse, Taa-haa, which is believed by some to be a name of Prophet Muhammad (PBUH), who is reminded that the Qur'an has been revealed to him, not as a source of difficulty, but rather a guidance and a reminder for those who fear God. A detailed story of Prophet Moses, starting with his return with his wife from Madyan, the encounter with the holy fire and God's speaking to him and appointing him a prophet and messenger. Moses is reminded by God of the favours He had received earlier in his life, and he is ordered, with the help of his brother Aaron, to preach the Faith to Pharaoh. Other parts of the story of Moses and his followers and their worship of the golden calf are also given in some detail. (See verses 9-97.)

Two of the often quoted verses are the one that says: "And enjoin prayer upon your family and be steadfast therein..." (verse 132) and the other that says: "And whoever truns away from My (God's) remembrance - indeed he will have a life of hardship, and We will raise him on the Day of Judgement blind." (verse 124)

## Taariq (suurat aT-- )

## سورة الطارق

Chapter of the Night Visitor

This is Chapter 86 of the Qur'an, taking its title from the word which occurs in the first and second verses and refers to the "Star of piercing brightness" (verses 1-3). After these opening verses, we are told: "There is no soul but has a guardian over it." (verse 4) Man is reminded of his creation and God's Ability to resurrect him.

## tabbat (suurat -- )

## سورة تبت

Chapter of 'It Perished'

This is Chapter 111 of the Qur'an, taking its title from the verb in the first verse. The word "tabba" means both losing and perishing. The reference is to the Prophet's uncle, neck named Abu Lahab ('father or man of the Flame'), who cursed the Prophet (PBUH) for calling the Meccans to an urgent assembly only to warn them of Hell-Fire and to preach the Word of God to them. His wife was also a source of harassment to the Messenger of God. Their miserable fate is mentioned in the Chapter.

## taghaabun (suurat at-- )

## سورة التغابُن

Chapter of Mutual Loss and Gain

This is Chapter 64 of the Qur'an, taking its title from word in verse nine where the Day of Judgment is called "yawm at-taghabun" ('Day of Mutual Loss and Gain'). The word "taghaabun" literally means 'mutual cheating or feeling of being cheated'. The summary of this Chapter reads: "Both the Unbelievers and the Believers were created by the One True God, Who created all and knows all: why should Unbelief and Evil exult in worldly gain when their loss will be manifest in the Hereafter as will as the gain of the Believers." One of the practical and realistic principles of Islam is given in the first part of verse 16, "So fear God as much as you can", which confirms another Divine declaration, "On no soul does God place a burden greater than it can bear." (Chapter 2, verse 286)

### taHriim (suurat at-- )

### سورة التحريم

Chapter of Prohibition

This is Chapter 66 of the Qur'an, taking its from the verb "tuHarrim" ('make forbidden') mentioned in verse one, where the Prophet (PBUH) is reminded by God not to forbid, for the sake of his wives, for himself something that is permitted to him by God. His wives are reprimanded for conspiring against him (verses 1-5). An often quoted verse is "O you who believe! Save yourselves and your families from a Fire whose fuel is men and stone..." This asserts man's duty towards his family and their salvation (verse 6). In this Chapter we also read about the exemplar women of God (Mary and wife of the Pharaoh) and their opposites (the wives of Noah and Lot) (verses 10-11).

### takaathur (suurat at-- )

### سورة التكاثر

Chapter of Rivalry in Worldly Gains

This is Chapter 102 of the Qur'an, taking its title from the word in the first verse, meaning competing with each other in amounts of worldly gains, including number of relations and followers. People are warned, "But nay, ye soon shall know [the reality]. Again, ye soon shall know!" What is this Reality? It is Hell-fire prepared for those totally engrossed in worldly gains, to the neglect of preparation for the Hereafter.

### takwiir (suurat at-- )

### سورة التكوير

Chapter of the Rolling Up

This is Chapter 81 of the Qur'an, taking its title from verb "kuwwirat" ('rolled up') in the first verse. Twelve events that accompany the arrival of the Day of Judgment are mentioned in the first 14 verses. This is followed by assertions that start with, "So, surely, I call to witness the Planets that recede..." and the declaration that "this is the word of a most honourable Messenger...Nor is it the word of Satan accursed ... Surely, this is no less a Message to the Worlds [With benefit] to whoever among you is seeking the Straight Path". Interspersed between these verses we read some characterization of Gabriel and the prophet Muhammad (verses 15-29).

## Talaaq (suurat aT-- )

## سورة الطلاق

Chapter of Divorce

This is Chapter 65 of the Qur'an, taking its title from the divorce related rules, starting with verse 1 and continuing through verse 7. (The other set of detailed rules are found in Chapter 2, verses 228-241.) The rest of the Chapter includes a warning to those who insolently disobey the commands of their Lord and an invitation to the men of understanding to fear God Who has sent them a Messenger that leads believers and doers of righteous acts from darkness to Light and Who is the Creator of the heavens and the earth and "comprehends all things in [His] knowledge." (verses 8-12)

## tawbah (suurat at- )

## سورة التوبة

Chapter of Repentance

This is Chapter 9 of the Qur'an, and it is the only chapter that does not begin with "basmalah". Sometimes, it is called "suurat baraa'ah" (the first word in the Chapter. The openings of the Chapter declare "baraa'ah" ('disavowal or dissolution of treaty obligations') towards hostile polytheists (verses 1-4), justifying this with their treacherous behaviour towards the followers of Islam (See, e.g., verses 7-10 and 13). In this Chapter the ruling of prohibition of disbelievers' entry into Mecca is also declared (28). Many verses deal with relations between Muslims and non-Muslims and hypocrites. Reference to the Prophet's hiding in the cave, along with his friend Abu Bakr, in their "hijrah" ('migration') to Medina is made (verse 40). Verse 60 specifies the eight categories of people who deserve "Sadaqah" ('charity), including "zakaah" (alms giving).

## tiin (suurat at-- )

## سورة التين

Chapter of the Fig

This is Chapter 95 of the Qur'an, taking its name from the word in the first verse. The Chapter asserts that God "has created man in the best of forms or moulds. Then do We abase him [to be] the lowest of the low, except such as believe and do righteous deeds, for they shall have a reward unfailing". This is a sure matter, because God is the wisest of Judges.

## Tuur (suurat aT-- )

**سورة الطور**

Chapter of the Mount

This is Chapter 52 of the Qur'an, taking its title from the word in the opening verse. This Chapter has been summarized in the following, "All Signs of God, including previous Revelations, point to the inevitable consequences of ill-deeds and good deeds: how can people deny or ignore the Message of Revelation?"

# Ww

## waaqi'ah (suurat al-- )

**سورة الواقعة**

Chapter of the Inevitable Event

This is Chapter 56 of the Qur'an, taking its title from the word mentioned in the first verse of the Chapter and refers to the Hour of Judgment. In this Chapter people are classified into three categories, with regards to their future life in the Hereafter, Companions of the Right Hand, Companions of the Left Hand and those Foremost in the Hereafter. The fate of each category is described: (1) the Foremost or the nearest to God (verses 10-26 and 88-9), (2) the Companions of the Right Hand (verses 27-38 and 90-1) and (3) the Companions of the Left Hand (41-56 and 92-94). Among the verses frequently cited are verses 77- 79, " Indeed is a noble Qur'an . In a Register well protected.Which [the Qur'an] none shall touch but those who are (ritually) clean." According to this rule, non-Muslims and even Muslims who are not in a state of ritual purity and cleanliness ("muTahharuun") are not allowed to touch the Qur'an in its original, Arabic text. The recitation of this Chapter every evening is recommended for protection from poverty.

# Yy

## yaasiin (suurat --)

**سورة يس**

Chapter of Yaasiin

This is Chapter 36 of the Qur'an, taking its title from the first verse, which a combination of two letters. Some exegetists claim that the word refers to Prophet Muhammad, being a combination of the vocative 'yaa' and 'siin' or the combination itself is a title of the Prophet (PBUH). It has been reported that the Prophet (PBUH) called this Chapter "the heart of the Qur'an". If fact, many people in the Muslim World memorize it and recite it frequently on certain occasions. In the Hadeeth Muslims are recommended to recite this Chapter over the deceased person.

In this Chapter we find the verse that was recited by Prophet Muhammad (PBUH) on the way out of his home to emigrate to Medina walking in between the ranks of young pagans who were waiting to strike him with their drawn swords, and he put dust on their heads, since they were miraculously put to sleep in their standing position. This is the verse which translates, "And We have put before them a barrier and behind them a barrier and covered them, so they do not see." (verse 9)

## yuunus (suurat ---)

## سـورة يونس

Chapter of Jonah

This is the 10th chapter of the Qur'an. It takes its title from the name of Prophet "yuunus" (Jonah) (verse 98). In this Chapter we find many verses that remind people of God's favours and their duty to obey Him. Stories of some prophets of God, including Noah, Moses and Aaron's encounters with Pharaoh, the exodus of the Israelites from Egypt, by safely crossing the sea, and the drowning of the Pharaoh (75-92), are mentioned in this chapter.

In this Chapter we find the third reference to freedom of belief, which translates, "And had your Lord willed, those on earth would have believed - all of them entirely. Then, [O Muhammad] , would you compel the people in order they become believers?!" (verse 99) We also read one of the verses that challenge people to produce the like of the Qur'an (verse 38).

## yuusuf (suurat --)

## سـورة يوسـف

Chapter of Joseph

This is Chapter 12 of the Qur'an. Most of this Chapter revolves around the story of Prophet

Joseph. We read about his father (Jacob) and his jealous brothers, and his life in Egypt: his brothers abandoning him in a well, unjustly sold as a slave, imprisonment for resisting carnal temptation and his becoming a ruler, a Divine reward and favour bestowed upon him, and his family joining him to stay in Egypt. An exemplar model of chastity is found in Joseph's story.

# Zz

## zalzalah (suurat az-- )

### سورة الزلزلة

Chapter of the Earthquake

This is Chapter 99 of the Qur'an, taking its title from the word that comes in both verbal and nominal forms in the first verse. Some translators prefer the word 'convulsion' instead of earthquake. Both words seem to be correct, especially since the second verse points out to the Earth throwing up or out her burdens (from within), referring to the Resurrection, when "people proceed in groups sorted out, to be shown the deeds they (had done)." (verse 6) Everyone will see whatever he had done of good or evil, however insignificant it might be (7-8).

## zukhruf (suurat az- )

### سورة الزخرف

Chapter of Gold Ornaments

This is Chapter 43 of the Qur'an, taking its title from the word which occurs in verse 35. In that verse and the preceding one we are told that having silver roofs and silver stairways and gold ornaments are not proofs of God's being pleased with the owners. For "all this is nothing but enjoyment of the present life. The Hereafter, in the sight of your Lord, is for the righteous." (35). As in many other chapters, we read many instances of the contrast between the lives and lots of believers versus unbelievers clearly illustrated.

## zumar (suurat az- )

### سورة الزّمَر

Chapter of the Groups

This is Chapter 39 of the Qur'an, taking its title from the word that uniquely occurs in this Chapter in verses 71 and 73. Contrasting believers with unbelievers and the lot of each is a running theme of the Chapter (See, e.g., verses 70-75, the last three of which are frequently recited). Among the verses often quoted are the following: (1) "Say: 'O my servants who have transgressed against their souls! Despair not of the Mercy of God: for God forgives all sins. He is Oft-Forgiving, Most Merciful." (verse 53) This is being cited as evidence of the unlimited Divine Mercy and Forgiveness of sinners who return and repent to Him. (2) "No just estimate have they made of God, such as due to Him..." (verse 67), which warns people of underestimating the Powers of God.

Bearman, P J and T. Bianquis (2005) Encyclopaedia of Islam: Index of Subjects. Leiden: Brill.

Bewley, Aisha. (1998) Glossary of Islamic Terms. London: Ta Ha Publishers. (English comments)

Hughes, Thomas P. (1977) Dictionary of Islam: A Cyclopaedia of the Doctrines, Rites, Ceremonies etc. of the Islamic Religion. New Delhi: Cosmo Publications. (English comments)

Kamali, Mohammad Hashim (2003) "Glossary" in his Principles of Islamic Jurisprudence. Cambridge: The Islamic Texts Society.

Khodir, Omar. (1998) A Dictionary of Islamic Terms. Newark, N.J.: Islamic Book Service. (English comments).

Maqsood, Ruqayyah Waris (1998). A Basic Dictionary of Islam. New Delhi: Al-Risala (The Islamic Centre). (Arabic & English words with .English comments)

McAuliffe, Jane (Editor) Encyclopaedia of the Qur'an. 5 volumes. Leiden: Brill.

Mir, Mustansir. (1987) Dictionary of Qu'anic Terms and Concepts. New York & London: Gari and Publishing, Inc.

Nettton, Ian Richard (1997) A Popular Dictionary of Islam, Rvd Ed. London: Curzon. (Arabic and English terms explained in English).

Penrice, John (1983) A Dictionary and Glossary of the Kor-an. Beirut: Librairie du Liban. (English comments).

Qazi, M.A. (1979) A Concise Dictionary of Islamic Terms. Revised by M.S. El-Dabbas. Chicago: Kazi Publications. (English comments).

Saleh, Mahmoud I. (2002). Dictionary of Islamic Words and Expressions: Arabic-English. Riyadh: Al-Muntada al-Islami.

الندوي ، عبدالله عباس (1983) قاموس ألفاظ القرآن الكريم (عربي-إنجليزي). جدة : دار الشروق. (شرح إنجليزي)

هارون، نبيل عبدالسلام هارون . المعجم الوجيز لألفاظ القرآن الكريم . القاهرة: دار النشر للجامعات، 1997م.

هلال ، هيثم (2003) معجم مصطلح الأصول : تعريفات لغوية -شروحات لكتب لأصول- نبذات تاريخية. بيروت : دار الجيل .

وزارة الأوقاف والشؤون الإسلامية (1404هـ / 1984م) معجم الفقه الحنبلي (مستخلص من كتاب المغني لابن قدامة) ، راجع الطبعة د. عبدالستار أبوغدة ود. محمد سليمان الأشقر. الكويت : الوزارة .

وزارة الأوقاف والشؤون الإسلامية (من -1966 ) موسوعة الفقه الإسلامي . الكويت : الوزارة.

## ب- مراجع إنجليزية:

Abughosh, Bassam and Shaqra, Wafa Zaki. (?) A Glossary of Islamic Terminology. London: Taha Publishers, Ltd.

Al-Faruqi, Isma-il Raji (1986) Toward Islamic English. Hernden, VA.: International Institute of Islamic Thought. (Arabic with English explanations)

Azmi, Aurang Zeb. (2002) The Handy Concordance of the Quran (English-Arabic). New Delhi: Goodword Books PVT Ltd. (English comments).

Bearman, P J, Th. Bianquis, CE Bosworth, E van Donzel and WP Heinrichs (--2006) Encyclopaedia of Islam, New Edition. 12 volumes. Leiden: Brill.

القليبي ، موسى بن محمد موسى (ق 11هـ) معجم الألفاظ القرآنية ومعانيها (المسمى : التحفة القلبية في حل الألفاظ القرآنية) تحقيق محمد محمد داود ز القاهرة : مكتبة الآداب ، 2002م.

كامل ، فؤاد (1993) قاموس المصطلحات الصوفية (عربي-إنجليزي-فرنسي). بيروت : دار الجيل.

كنعان ، أحمد محمد . (2006) الموسوعة الطبية الفقهية . بيروت : دار النفائس .

المالكي ، د عبدالله أبوعشي وعبداللطيف الشيخ إبراهيم (1415هـ / 1995م) معجم المصطلحات الدينية (عربي-إنجليزي و إنجليزي-عربي) . الرياض : مكتبة العبيكان .

المجلس الأعلى للشئون الإسلامية ، وزارة الأوقاف المصرية . موسوعة الفقه الإسلامي . القاهرة: المجلس. (على الشبكة العنكبوتية)

المجلس الأعلى للشئون الإسلامية ، وزارة الأوقاف المصرية . موسوعة المفاهيم . القاهرة: المجلس. (على الشبكة العنكبوتية)

مجمع اللغة العربية (1401هـ / 1981م) معجم ألفاظ القرآن الكريم . القاهرة : دار الشروق .

مجمع اللغة العربية (1424هـ / 2003م) معجم مصطلحات أصول الفقه . القاهرة : المجمع.

(مرتب عربيا مع الشرح ، والمقابلات الإنجليزية).

المنشاوي ، محمد صديق (1996م) قاموس مصطلحات الحديث النبوي : قاموس بجميع مصطلحات المحدثين مرتبة أبجديا . القاهرة : دار الفضيلة .

المنير، محمود (1424هـ / 2004م) معجم التبيان في أعلام القرآن. المنصورة . ج م ع: دار الوفاء للطباعة والنشر والتوزيع.

نجيب . د عزالدين محمد (2006) قاموس المصطلحات الدينية وبه معاني جميع ألفاظ القرآن الكريم (عربي-إنجليزي) . القاهرة: مكتبة ابن سينا . (شرح باللغتين)

لبنان ناشرون .

العجم ، د. رفيق . موسوعة مصطلحات أصول الفقه عند المسلمين . بيروت : مكتبة لبنان ناشرون .

عطية الله ، أحمد (1980) القاموس الإسلامي . القاهرة : مكتبة النهضة . (صدرت الأجزاء الأولى فقط)

علوب ، د. عبدالوهاب (1996) معجم الأمين للآثار والأديان : معجم لألفاظ الحضارة والعمارة والآثار والأديان مع التركيز على ألفاظ الحضارة الإسلامية (إنجليزي-عربي وفارسي-عربي) القاهرة: الأمين للنشر والتوزيع. (شرح عربي)

فاخوري ، محمود و صلاح الدين خوام (2003) موسوعة وحدات القياس العربية والإسلامية وما يقابلها من المقاديرالحديثة . بيروت : مكتبة لبنان ناشرون

الفاروقي ، حارث سليمان (1983) المعجم القانوني (عربي-إنجليزي) ، ط2. بيروت: مكتبة لبنان ناشرون .

فالح ، أبو عبدالله عامرعبدالله (1417هـ /1997م) معجم ألفاظ العقيدة . الرياض : مكتبة العبيكان.

الفيشاوي ، سعد (2007) المعجم العلمي للمعتقدات الدينية . القاهرة: الهيئة المصرية العامة للكتاب. (مرتب حسب المصطلحات الإنجليزية ، مع مقابلاتها العربية وشرح باللغة العربية).

قلعة جي ، د محمد رواس. (2005) الموسوعة الفقهية الميسرة ، مجلدان .بيروت : دار النفائس

قلعة جي ، د محمد رواس ود. حامد صادق قنيبي (1417هـ/ 1988م) معجم لغة الفقهاء (عربي-إنكليزي) مع كشاف إنكليزي-عربي بالمصطلحات الواردة في المعجم ، ط 2 . بيروت : دار النفائس . (شرح عربي)

قلعة جي ، د محمد رواس ود. حامد صادق قنيبي وقطب مصطفى سانو(2007) معجم لغة الفقهاء (عربي-إنكليزي- فرنسي) . بيروت : دار النفائس . (شرح عربي)

دغيم ، د. سميح (2004) موسوعة مصطلحات الإمام فخر الدين الرازي. بيروت : مكتبة لبنان ناشرون .

دغيم ، د. سميح (2003) موسوعة مصطلحات ابن تيمية. بيروت : مكتبة لبنان ناشرون .

دغيم ، د. سميح . موسوعة مصطلحات علم الكلام الإسلامي. بيروت : مكتبة لبنان ناشرون .

الراسخ ، عبدالمنان . معجم اصطلاحات الأحاديث النبوية . بيروت : دار ابن حزم، 2004م.

سانو، د قطب مصطفى . معجم مصطلحات أصول الفقه (عربي-إنجليزي) . بيروت ودمشق: دار الفكر، 2000م . (شرح عربي)

سعدي أبو حبيب (1402هـ / 1982م) القاموس الفقهي لغة واصطلاحا . دمشق : دار الفكر .

الشرباصي ، د. أحمد (1981) المعجم الاقتصادي الإسلامي . بيروت: دار الجيل .

الشنقيطي ، الشيخ المختار أحمد محمود (1993) الترجمان والدليل لآيات التنزيل ، جزءان. الرياض : دار روضة الصغير .

صالح ، د محمود إسماعيل (2001م) معجم الألفاظ والتعابير الإسلامية (عربي-إنجليزي) مع مسرد باللغة العربية . الرياض : المنتدى الإسلامي . (شرح إنجليزي)

عبد المعطي ، محمد (1423هـ/2002م) الوجيز في علوم القرآن ، مصطلح الحديث ، أصول الفقه . القاهرة: دار التوزيع والنشر الإسلامية .

عبدالمنعم ، د. محمود عبدالرحمن (1999) معجم المصطلحات والألفاظ الفقهية ، 3 أجزاء . القاهرة : دار الفضيلة .

عبيد ، حمدي . القاموس الإسلامي (عربي-إنجليزي وإنجليزي-عربي)، ط2 . القاهرة: شركة الصفوة للنشر والتوزيع والطباعة ، 1998م .

العجم ، د. رفيق (2001) موسوعة مصطلحات الإمام الغزالي . بيروت : مكتبة

بيان رسالة اصطلاحات الصوفية الواردة في "الفتوحات المكية" . بيروت : دار إحياء التراث العربي.

الجوهري ، علي . قاموس المصطلحات الدينية (انجليزي-عربي ) القاهرة : دار الفضيلة، 2001م.

الحرش ، سليمان مسلم و حسين إسماعيل الجمل (1417هـ/ 1996م) معجم مصطلحات الحديث . الرياض : مكتبة العبيكان .

حرف لتقنية المعلومات (د ت) القاموس الإسلامي (عربي-إنجليزي-فرنسي-ماليزي-إندونيسي) – قرص مدمج حاسوبي. الرياض : شركة حرف.

حفني ، عبدالمنعم . (1987). معجم مصطلحات الصوفية ، ط 2. بيروت : دار المسيرة.

حماد ، د نزيه (1414هـ/ 1993م) معجم المصطلحات الاقتصادية في لغة الفقهاء . الرياض : شركة الراجحي المصرفية للاستثمار .

الحمد ، محمد بن إبراهيم (1427هـ/ 2006م) مصطلحات في كتب العقائد: دراسة وتحليل. الرياض: دار خزيمة .

الحنفي ، قاسم بن عبدالله القونوي (توفي 978هـ) أنيس الفقهاء في تعريفات الألفاظ المتداولة بين الفقهاء. بيروت: دارالكتب العلمية ، 2004.

الخضراوي ، ديب (1416هـ/ 1995م) قاموس الألفاظ الإسلامية (عربي-إنجليزي) . دمشق : اليمامة للطباعة والنشر والتوزيع . (شرح عربي)

الخوارزمي ، أبوعبدالله محمد بن أحمد بن يوسف (1401هـ / 1981م) مفاتيح العلوم ، ط 2 . القاهرة : مكتبة الكليات الأزهرية .

دار النفائس . (2007) موسوعة الأديان الميسرة ، طبعة منقحة ومزيدة . بيروت : دار النفائس.

الدرش ، سليمان و حسين الجمل (1417هـ/ 1996) معجم مصطلحات الحديث . الرياض : مكتبة العبيكان.

## منشورات عربية :

أبوالدهب ، أشرف طه (2002) المعجم الإسلامي: الجوانب الدينية والاجتماعية والاقتصادية. القاهرة: دار الشروق.

أبوالفتوح ، محمد حسين . معجم ألفاظ الحديث النبوي في صحيح البخاري ، المجلد الأول. بيروت : مكتبة لبنان ناشرون

أبي خزام ، د. أنور. معجم المصطلحات الصوفية . بيروت : مكتبة لبنان ناشرون.

الأًصبهاني ، أبو القاسم الحسين بن محمد المعروف بالراغب الأصبهاني (ت 503هـ) المفردات في غريب القرآن تحقيق وضبط محمد سيد كيلاني . بيروت : دار المعرفة للطباعة والنشر والتوزيع .

الأندلسي ، الشيخ أثيرالدين أبو حيان (1409هـ/ 1989م) ترتيب تحفة الأريب بمافي القرآن من الغريب . . تحقيق وترتيب وتقديم د. داود سلوم ود/ نوري حمودي القيسي . القاهرة : عالم الكتب ومكتبة النهضة العربية .

الأنصاري ، زكريا بن محمد (ت 926هـ) الحدود الأنيقة والتعريفات الدقيقة ، تحقيق مازن المبارك. بيروت : دار الفكر المعاصر، 1991.

بن نجم ، علاء الدين . معجم مصطلحات أصول الفقه. بيروت : مكتبة الرشد ناشرون ، 2004م.

جب، هـ .ا. ر. و ج. هـ. ك كالمرز (تحرير،1985) الموسوعة الإسلامية الميسرة ، مجلدان . ترجمة دكتور راشد البراوي . القاهرة : مكتبة الأنجلو المصرية .

الجبوري، د نظلة . نصوص المصطلح الصوفي في الإسلام. بغداد : بيت الحكمة ، 1999م.

الجرجاني ، الشريف علي بين محمد (1424هـ/ 2003 م) كتاب التعريفات ويليه

# مراجع معجمية في المصطلحات الإسلامية

# الكشاف العربي

المعجم) والشيء نفسه ينطبق على الخلط بين الهمزة والعين والحروف المفخمة وغير المفخمة ، كما أسلفنا من قبل.

حيث إن الألفاظ تكتب كما تنطق ، فقد وردت مشكولة (أي شاملة لحروف العلة الدالة على الحركات في اللغة العربية) ، من ثم نجد أن الحرف المفتوح يسبق المكسورثم يأتي المضموم ، أي a, i, u ، فكلمة كَتَبَ kataba تأتي قبل كُتِبَ kutiba ، والكلمة مَثَل mathal تأتي قبل مِثل mithl .

جدير بالذكر أيضا أنه مراعاة للقارىء متوسط الثقافة تجنبنا استخدام رموز غير مألوفة كتلك التي يستعملها المستشرقون في كتابة بعض الحروف العربية ، بما ذلك الحركات الطويلة والتي أشرنا إليها بتكرار الحركة (مثلا kataba, kaataba) مقابل كَتَبَ وكاتَبَأخيرا ، تيسيرا على الباحث العربي عن الألفاظ والتعابير العربية ، وضعنا كشافا بها مرتبا حسب نطقها (وليس جذرها) بالحرف العربي ، متبوعا برقم الصفحة التي ترد فيها الكلمة أو العبارة في صلب المعجم.

والله أسأل أن يسد هذا العمل ولو جزءا يسيرا من الفراغ الكبير في مجال المعاجم الإسلامية ، وأن ينفع به الإسلام والمسلمين.

المؤلف

الرياض ، ربيع الأول 1432هـ

# ترتيب المداخل في المعجم:

كما أسلفت أعلاه ، تم ترتيب مداخل المعجم على أساس نطق الكلمات العربية مكتوبا بالحرف اللاتيني ، متبوعا بالصورة العربية للكلمة ، ثم الترجمة ، ثم الشرح أو التعليق باللغة الإنجليزية ، مع الإحالة إلى المداخل ذات العلاقة وكذلك إلى الآيات في القرآن الكريم المتعلقة بالمصطلح . لذلك كل ما على الباحث أن يفعله هو أن يبحث عن الكلمة أو العبارة في موضعها حسب الترتيب الهجائي الإنجليزي ، علما بأنه لعدم وجود حروف لاتينية خاصة ببعض الأصوات العربية فقد كتبت بأقرب حرف لاتيني (مع التمييز بين الحروف باستخدام الحرف اللاتيني الكبير للأصوات العربية المفخمة كالصاد والطاء). (انظر transliteration table في المقدمة الإنجليزية ، حيث نورد جدولا بالحروف العربية وما يقابلها بالحرف اللاتيني.)

# تأمل ملاحظة مايلي:

لغياب حرف لاتيني للهمزة والعين فقد تم اللجوء إلى الرمز الذي يستخدمه المستشرقون لهذا الغرض ، وهو استخدام رمز( ʼ ) للهمزة والعين (حسب الاتجاه). لكن نظرا لأن هذا الرمز ليس حرفا ، فهذا يعني أن الكلمات التي تبدأ بحرفي الهمزة والعين ، سترد في باب الحركة التي تتبعها ، مثل "أب" التي ترد تحت abb) a) و"أم" تحت umm) u) و"علّة" تحت ʻillah) i) .

نظرا لأن الترتيب الألفبائي الإنجليزي لايميز بين الحروف الكبيرة capital والصغيرة small ، فسيجد الباحث أن الكلمات العربية التي تبدأ بالحرف المفخم (ص ، ض ، ط ) ترد مع مقابلاتها غير المفخمة (س ، د ، ت أي S, D, T) باستثناء الظاء التي غالبا ما ينطق بها غير العرب زايا مفخمة . لذلك ترد مع حرف الزاي (زكاة ، ظلم مثلا في باب ال z) ، حيث كتبت الزاء z صغيرة والظاء Z كبيرة (zakaah, Zulm).

راعينا النطق التقريبي الذي يتلفظ به الأعاجم الحروف العربية عند كتابتنا للألفاظ العربية بالحرف اللاتيني ، وذلك كما في خلطهم بين الحاء والهاء )كتبتا H, h في

المصطلحات الإسلامية التي يصعب معرفة معانيها عن طريق المعاجم اللغوية التقليدية ، حيث إن هذه تعنى عادة بالمعاني اللغوية العامة للألفاظ ، وليس بالمعاني الاصطلاحية الخاصة . كذلك نجد أن معظم المسلمين من غير العرب لايجيدون قراءة الحرف العربي ، بله الترتيب الألفبائي وجذور الكلمات العربية. فكان لابد من اللجوء إلى ترتيب المداخل وفق نطق الكلمات والعبارات العربية مكتوبة بالحرف اللاتيني ، متبوعة بالكلمة في صورتها العربية ، ثم بالترجمة المقابلة مع شيء من الإيضاح والتعليق لكل مصطلح وتعبيرباللغة الإنجليزية ، مع الإحالة كثيرا إلى مواضع المصطلح في النص القرآني (حيث نذكر رقم السورة والآية أوالآيات ذات العلاقة ، بدلا من إيراده مما يضاعف حجم المعجم) .

## المحتوى اللغوي للمعجم:

حاولت جاهداً أن يكون المعجم مما خف وزنه وغني محتواه ، فكان لابد من التركيز على الألفاظ والتعابير الشائعة قدر الإمكان ، مثل: "توحيد ، ألوهية ، قدر، إيمان، اليوم الآخر، القيامة ... " (من علم التوحيد) و"صلاة، صدقة ، تقوى ، حرام ، حلال ، مندوب ، نافلة ،تهجد ... " (من فقه العبادات) و"بيع السلم ، المضاربة ، المرابحة... " (من فقه المعاملات) و"استصلاح ، استحسان ، إجماع ، قياس ... " (من علم أصول الفقه) و"حديث قدسي ، راوي الحديث ، حسن ، صحيح ، ضعيف ، مسند ، مرفوع ، متواتر... " (من علم أصول الحديث) و "إدغام، غنة ، إخفاء ، إبدال ، مد لازم ، مخرج الحرف ... " (من علم التجويد) و "صدق ، أمانة ، رياء ، كبرياء ، غيبة ، نميمة " (من علم الأخلاق) ، إضافة إلى التعبيرات الشائعة على ألسنة المسلمين ، مثل : "السلام عليكم ، الحمد لله ، سبحان الله ، لاحول ولاقوة إلا بالله ( وألفاظ الإشارة إليها مثل: تسليم ، حمدلة ، تسبيح ، تهليل ، حوقلة...).

إكمالا للفائدة رأيت أن أضيف بعض أسماء الأعلام المهمة ، مثل أسماء الأنبياء والملائكة، الخلفاء الراشدين، بعض أئمة الحديث والفقه ، الغزوات ، أسماء السور القرآنية – التي أفرد لها ملحق خاص بها).

## بسم الله الرحمن الرحيم

# مقدمة الطبعة الثالثة للمعجم

الحمد لله الذي من أياته اختلاف الألسنة والألوان والصلاة والسلام على من تكلم بأشرف لسان ، لسان عربي مبين . أما بعد:

فإبان عملي في المركز الإسلامي بواشنطن منذ ما يقرب من الأربعين عاما وخلال السنوات التالية وجدت أثناء اتصالي بالمسلمين من غير العرب وبالدعاة والمترجمين العرب سواء أكان ذلك في سان فرانسسكو أم ديترويت أم لندن أم غيرها من البلدان لاحظت وجود مشكلة يواجهها هؤلاء وأولئك: ألا وهي فهم معاني المصطلحات والتعابير الإسلامية أوترجمتها إلى اللغة الإنجليزية بطريقة صحيحة ومفهومة للمتلقي الناطق بالإنجليزية ، مما استوجب وضع معاجم لهذا الغرض . فكانت هناك جهود هنا وهناك ، كما كانت هناك اتجاهات مختلفة للتعامل مع المصطلح الإسلامي العربي (أيبقى عليها كما هي ، وتكتب بالحرف اللاتيني، أم تترجم إلى أقرب كلمة أو تعبير إنجليزي . ولكل فريق حججه ، كما أشرت إلى ذلك في دراسة لي حول هذا الموضوع).

في ضوء نظرة فاحصة إلى الغاية من مثل هذا المعجم وجمهوره المستهدف ، وجدت أنه قد يكون من الأجدى وضع معجم يأخذ بعين الاعتبار القارىء غير الناطق بالعربية في المقام الأول سواء أكان مسلما أم من غير المسلمين. وقد أدى هذا إلى النظرفي

بسم الله الرحمن الرحيم

# معجم الألفاظ
## والتعابير الإسلامية

### عربي بالحرف
### اللاتيني - إنجليزي

(مع شرح باللغة الإنجليزية وكشاف بالحرف العربي)


د/ محمود إسماعيل صالح
أستاذ اللسانيات التطبيقية



الطبعة الثالثة
1432هـ / 1120م

DARUSSALAM
دار السلام للنشر والتوزيع

معجم الألفاظ
والتعابير الإسلامية

# DARUSSALAM

GLOBAL LEADER IN ISLAMIC PUBLICATION

## • U.A.E

**Darussalam, Sharjah U.A.E**
Tel: 00971-6-5632623 Fax: 5632624
Sharjah@dar-us-salam.com.

## • PAKISTAN

**Head Office:**
**Darussalam,** 36 Lower Mall, Lahore
Tel: 0092-42-724 0024 Fax: 7354072
**Rahman Market,** Ghazni Street
**Urdu Bazar**, Lahore
Tel: 0092-42-7120054 Fax: 7320703
**Karachi,** Tel: 0092-21- 4393936
Fax: 0092-21- 4393937
**Islamabad,** Tel: 0092-51-2500237
Fax: 0092-51-2281513

## • U.S.A

**Darussalam, New York,**
486 Atlantic Ave, Brooklyn
New York-11217, Tel: 001-718-625 5925
Fax: 718-625 1511
E-mail: darussalamny@hotmail.com.
**Darussalam, Houston**
P.O Box: 79194 Tx 77279
Tel: 001-713-722 0419
Fax: 001-713-722 0431
E-mail: houston@dar-us-salam.com

## • CANADA

**Nasiruddin Al-Khattab**
2-3415 Dixie Rd. Unit # 505
Mississauga, Ontario L4Y 4J6, Canada
Tel: 001-416-4186619

## • FRANCE

**Distribution : Sana**
116 Rue Jean Pierre Timbaud
75011 , Paris ,France
Tel: 0033 01 480 52928
Fax 0033 01 480 52997

## • U.K

**Darussalam,**
**International Pablications Ltd.**
Leyton Business Centre
Unit-17, Etloe Road, Leyton,
London, E10 7BT
Tel: 0044 20 8539 4885
Fax:0044020 8539 4889
Website:www.darussalam.com
Email:info@darussalam.com
**Darussalam,**
**International Pablications Ltd.**
Regents Park Mosque 146 Park Road,
London NW8 7GR Tel: 0044-207725
2246
Fax: 0044 20 8539 4889
**Dar Makkah International**
23-25 Parliament Street
Off Jenkins st., off Coventry rd.
Small Heah - Birmingham B10-OQJ
Tel: 0044 0121-7739309-
07815806517- 07533177345
Fax: 0044 1217723600

## • AUSTRALIA

**Darussalam,**
153, Haldon St. Lakemba (Sydney)
NSW 2195, Australia
Tel: 0061-2-97407188
Fax: 0061-297407199
Mobile: 0061-414580813
Res: 0091-297580190
Email: abumuaaz@hotmail.com
**The Islamic Bookstore**
Ground Floor-165 Haldon Street
Lakemba, NSW 2195, Australia
Tel: 0061-2-97584040
Fax: 0061-2-97584030
Email: info@islamicbookstore.com.au
Web site:www.islmicbookstore.com.au

## • SRI LANKA

**Darul Kitab**
6, Nimal Road, Colombo-4
Tel: 0094 115 358712
Fax: 115-358713
E-mail:info@darulkitabonline.com
**Darul Iman Trust**
Importers, Exporters
77 , Vajiragnana Mawatha,
Colombo-09,
Siri Lanka
Tel: 009411 2669197
Fax: 009411 2688102
E-mail: ibhmaradana@yahoo.com

## • INDIA

**Darussalam india**
58 & 59, Mir Bakshi Ali Street,
Royapettah, Chennai - 600014.
Tamil Nadu, India.
Tel: 0091 44 45566249
Mob: 0091 98841 12041
**Islamic Books International**
54, Tandel Street (North)
Dongri, Mumbai 4000 09, India
Tel: 0091-22-2373 4180
E-mail:ibi@irf.net
**Huda Book Distributors**
# 455, Purani Haveli
Hyderabad - 500002.
Tel: 0091 40 2451 4892
Mob: 0091 98493 30850
**M/S Buraqh Enterprises**
# 176 Peter's Road,
Indira Garden, Royalpettah,
Chennai - 600014. India
Tel: 0091 44 42157847
Mob: 0091 98841 77831
E-mail:
buraqhenterprises@gmail.com